PARADOX

AND

PERCEPTION

PARADOX AND PERCEPTION

Measuring Quality of Life in Latin America

Carol Graham
Eduardo Lora
editors

INTER-AMERICAN DEVELOPMENT BANK

BROOKINGS INSTITUTION PRESS
Washington, D.C.

Copyright © 2009
THE BROOKINGS INSTITUTION
1775 Massachusetts Avenue, N.W., Washington, DC 20036.
www.brookings.edu

Library of Congress Cataloging-in-Publication data
Paradox and perception : measuring quality of life in Latin America / Carol Graham and Eduardo Lora, editors.
    p.   cm.
Includes bibliographical references and index.
Summary: "Improves our understanding of the determinants of well-being in Latin America using a broad 'quality-of-life' concept that challenges standard assumptions in economics, including those about the relationship between happiness and income. Builds upon new economic approaches related to the study of happiness, finding some paradoxes as respondents evaluate their well-being"—Provided by publisher.
ISBN 978-0-8157-0326-6 (pbk. : alk. paper)
1. Income distribution—Latin America. 2. Equality—Latin America. 3. Latin America—Social conditions—21st century. I. Graham, Carol, 1962– II. Lora, Eduardo. III. Inter-American Development Bank.

HC130.I5P37 2009
339.2098—dc22   2009030945

9 8 7 6 5 4 3 2 1

Printed on acid-free paper

Typeset in Adobe Garamond

Composition by Circle Graphics, Inc.
Columbia, Maryland

Printed by R. R. Donnelley
Harrisonburg, Virginia

Contents

List of Figures, Tables, and Boxes

FIGURES

TABLES

BOXES

Foreword

The 2008–09 economic crisis—with its implications for the living standards of citizens in countries around the world—has heightened the debate on how to best measure human welfare. While income measures are fundamental to that exercise, economists are increasingly adopting new approaches and broader tools to answer questions about the effects of different environmental and institutional arrangements on well-being. There has been a burgeoning interest in the study of happiness in particular, based on surveys of reported well-being. These surveys provide new tools for measuring the effects of phenomena such as economic crisis, macroeconomic volatility, crime and corruption, and rapid urbanization—all of which are features of Latin America's development trajectory—on individual welfare.

In *Paradox and Perception,* the authors take the study of happiness as a point of departure and use a broader "quality of life" approach to studying well-being in the region. The approach incorporates basic needs but also extends beyond them to include capabilities, the "livability" of the environment, and life appreciation and happiness. Latin America's diversity in culture and levels of development provide a laboratory for studying how quality of life varies with a number of objective and subjective measures. These measures range from income levels to job insecurity and satisfaction, to schooling attainment and satisfaction, to measured and self-assessed health, among others.

The authors' analysis finds a number of paradoxes as the region's respondents evaluate their well-being. These include the paradox of "unhappy growth" at the macroeconomic level, "happy peasants and frustrated achievers" at the microlevel, and surprisingly high levels of satisfaction with public services among the region's poorest respondents, despite the poor performance of those services as measured in objective terms and relative to those that wealthier citizens have access to. The findings have important substantive links with several of the region's realities, such as high levels of income inequality, volatile macroeconomic performance, and low expectations of public institutions and faith in the capacity of the state to deliver. Identifying these perceptions, paradoxes, and their causes will contribute to the crafting of better public policies, as well as to our understanding of the ways politics conditions and shapes economic and social policies in the region. *Paradox and Perception* provides a timely analysis of these issues at a time that economic and political challenges are exposing stark differences between market-friendly, stable democracies with living standards approximating those of the OECD, and with the institutional capacity to mitigate the effects of the current crisis, and more fragile economies already struggling with issues of deep poverty and political polarization before the global downturn began.

STROBE TALBOTT   LUIS ALBERTO MORENO
President   *President*
The Brookings Institution   *Inter-American Development Bank*

Acknowledgments

The contributions in this book stem from research conducted in research institutions throughout Latin America under the auspices of the Network of Research Centers of the Inter-American Development Bank, as well as at Brookings and U.S. universities.

The editors of the volume would like to thank Jere Behrman and Ravi Kanbur, who, as advisors of the network project, provided continuous intellectual support to both the editors and the authors, and contributed with helpful comments on various drafts.

Valuable insights and suggestions from Suzanne Duryea, Rita Funaro, Leonardo Gasparini, Fidel Jaramillo, Santiago Levy, Philip Musgrove, Juan Carlos Navarro, Hugo Ñopo, Carmen Pagés, Carlos Pascual, William Savedoff, Ernesto Stain, Bernard van Praag and Carlos Eduardo Velez are acknowledged by the authors.

At Brookings, Soumya Chattopadhay and Mario Picon provided valuable research assistance, and Janet Walker was pivotal from the perspective of the press. At the Inter-American Development Bank, research assistance by Juan Camilo Chaparro, Lucas Higuera and María Victoria Rodríguez was instrumental to the project, while Myriam Escobar-Genes, Carlos Andres Gómez-Peña and Eduardo Montero Monge provided invaluable logistic and editorial assistance.

Graham acknowledges generous financial support from the Tinker Foundation for this project, and from Liberty Mutual Group for the Brookings Latin America initiative.

1

How Latin Americans Assess Their Quality of Life: Insights and Puzzles from Novel Metrics of Well-Being

CAROL GRAHAM AND JERE R. BEHRMAN

This book is an attempt to better our understanding of the determinants of welfare in Latin America and the Caribbean,[1] a region that is diverse in terms of culture and levels of development. Some countries in the region are approaching developed country standards of living, while others approximate the per capita income levels of sub-Saharan Africa. Further, as is well-known, the region has relatively high intra-country variations in per capita income—indeed with the highest inequalities of any of the major world regions. These per capita income differences, in addition to the region's cultural diversity, provide a laboratory for studying how quality of life varies with a number of important objective and subjective measures, including per capita income but also including others such as job insecurity, job satisfaction, schooling attainment, educational quality, nutritional insecurity, personal insecurity, mortality, and self-assessed health.

The concept of quality of life is a broad one, which incorporates basic needs but extends beyond them to include capabilities, as typically measured by the United Nations Development Program's human development index (UNDP's HDI); the "livability" of the environment, as measured by income per capita and growth; and life appreciation and happiness, as measured by well-being surveys. In this book we focus on reported or subjective well-being ("happiness"

---

1. Throughout this chapter, for brevity and ease of reading, the terms "Latin America" and "Latin Americans" are used inclusively to embrace the countries and people of the Caribbean.

or "satisfaction"), a concept that differs from but complements other indicators of the quality of life. Our analysis builds upon a number of new approaches in economics, particularly those related to the economics of happiness.

In addition to standard "objective" data such as on income, consumption, schooling attainment, mortality and job insecurity, our study relies heavily on surveys of reported well-being, both at a general level and in specific domains. This is a fundamental departure from traditional economics. Most economists historically have shied away from the use of survey data on expressed well-being and instead relied on revealed preferences—via consumption and investment choices—as a basis for analysis. The rationale is that answers to questions about well-being are not good signals of the preferences and constraints underlying actual behavior; there is no consequence to answering surveys, thus they do not clearly identify underlying preferences and/or constraints. In contrast, consumption and investment choices usually reflect a conscious choice about expenditure trade-offs. If the constraints are known, then preferences can be identified more accurately. In addition, unobserved heterogeneities in factors such as personality traits can bias the manner in which people answer surveys.

Yet in recent years the use of survey data on well-being has become more accepted. The increase in the number of economists working with such survey data over the past decade has been nothing short of remarkable.[2] In part this is because econometric techniques have been developed that allow control for some of the unobserved error/personality traits that might significantly bias the interpretation of responses on well-being as reflecting underlying preferences. And the increasing coverage of large samples across countries and regions with varying levels of development and other conditions gives survey data on well-being tremendous analytical potential. Research by psychologists, meanwhile, demonstrates that answers to surveys are in large part validated by psychological and neurological measures of happiness and well-being.

While the traditional reliance on revealed preferences has informed a number of important questions, there are some limitations. One is that there is increasing evidence that factors other than rational choice may drive important consumption and investment choices, including addiction or self control problems on the one hand and low expectations norms on the other. These factors may help explain a number of consumption choices that would otherwise appear perverse from a welfare perspective. A second is that there are a number of choices that revealed preferences approaches cannot answer, precisely because individuals are constrained in their abilities to make those choices, due to lack of agency, lack of information, and other factors related to poverty or discrimination, among other reasons.

2. Clark, Frijters, and Shields (2008).

The use of survey data on well-being is not without its problems, however, some of which are relevant to all kinds of data and some of which are more important for survey questions on well-being. A particularly important question in terms of well-being data is that of question framing. How questions are asked, and where they are placed in the survey can make a big difference in the responses. Subjective well-being has both cognitive and affective components, and different questions capture more or fewer of these elements. Open-ended happiness questions, for example, capture more of the affective components than do more framed questions, such as the best possible life question or domain satisfaction questions. Which questions are used can have significant effects on the relationship that is found between happiness and critical correlates.

An important example is the relationship between happiness and income. There is a major debate in the literature on the relationship between happiness and income across countries and over time. This began with Richard Easterlin's (1974) seminal work demonstrating that there was not a relationship between happiness and income over time as countries got wealthier—the so-called Easterlin paradox. While Easterlin found that countries that were desperately poor were less happy than those above a minimum per capita income threshold, his work also showed that above that threshold happiness does not seem to increase with additional income, at least not in a linear manner. There is still a great deal of debate about whether there is an Easterlin paradox or not.

Some recent work based on a new and broader cross-country dataset from the Gallup World Poll has challenged the Easterlin paradox and highlights a strong and consistent relationship between per capita income levels and average country-level happiness.[3] The findings are surely provocative, but it is not clear that they are fully comparable to Easterlin's, for two reasons. The first is question framing. The "life satisfaction" variable they rely on in the Gallup Poll is based on Cantril's 1965 ladder of life question, which asks respondents to compare their lives to the best possible life they can imagine. That frames the question much more than does an open-ended life satisfaction question (as Easterlin used). Surely when asked to compare, respondents in very poor countries are aware that life is likely better in wealthier ones, not least because of widespread access to the media and the Internet.

Affect questions typically (and not surprisingly) have less of a relationship with income than do more framed questions, such as the best possible life. Graham, Chattopadhyay, and Picon (2008), using the Gallup World Poll, find that the income and happiness relationship holds across countries for the best possible life, economic satisfaction, and the economic ladder questions, but not for life purpose and freedom to choose in life questions. Howell and Howell (2008), using a meta-analysis of 111 samples from 54 developing countries, find

---

3. See Deaton (2008) and Stevenson and Wolfers (2008).

Figure 1-1. *Happiness and Income per Capita, 1990s*

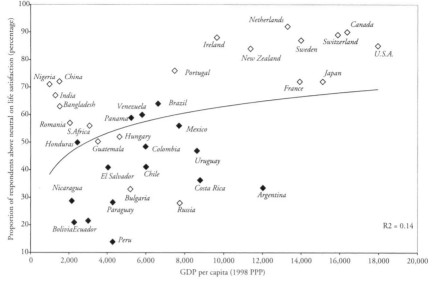

Source: Graham and Pettinato (2002).

that the income-subjective well-being relationship is stronger when subjective well-being is measured as life satisfaction—a cognitive assessment (instead of happiness, an emotional assessment).

Secondly, there were far fewer developing countries in the sample when Easterlin did his original work. Since then, the Gallup Poll has included a large number of new countries: small, poor countries in sub-Saharan Africa and the transition economies, which have seen the dismantling of existing social welfare systems and dramatic falls in happiness. So the more linear relationship between income and happiness may not be driven by rising incomes and happiness in the rich countries, but by low or falling incomes and happiness in a large number of small countries at the bottom of the distribution.

Yet even the opposite extremes of the debate recognize that there is some relationship, albeit a modest one, between income and happiness across countries, with wealthier countries showing higher levels of happiness than much poorer ones.[4] Graham and Pettinato (2002), based on a large sample of Latin American (and OECD) countries and an open-ended life satisfaction question, also demonstrate this trend, although within each of the poor and rich country sets there is not a clear income-happiness relationship (see figure 1-1). Howell and Howell find that

4. One issue underlying the debate is what kind of "happiness" question is used. More open-ended happiness or life satisfaction questions (generally speaking how satisfied are you with your life, for example) are typically less correlated with per capita GDP than are more framed questions, such as Cantril's best possible life ladder.

the income-subjective well-being relationship is weakest among the wealthiest developing countries in their 54-country sample, and strongest among the poorest and least educated samples. They also find that the effect is strongest when economic status is defined as a stock variable (wealth or assets) rather than as a flow variable (income).[5] Thus conclusions about the critical relationship between happiness and income are very much affected by the questions that are used and by the sample of countries that is available.

Another issue is where in the survey well-being questions are placed. Best practice suggests that open-ended life satisfaction or happiness questions should be placed first in the survey so that they are not biased or framed by other questions, such as about the nature of employment, financial situation, or marital status. Yet not all surveys employ this practice, and scholars have no choice but to compare happiness questions across countries or regions that are in different places in surveys, adjusting to the extent possible the expected bias caused by question placement.

Like all data, working with survey data on well-being requires accepting such limitations and potential biases. Regardless, the progress that economists and psychologists have made in recent years in the collection and analysis of survey data on well-being is providing new insights for assigning relative weights to income and non-income variables in determining human well-being or welfare.

The variables used in this study to measure well-being and quality of life are by definition multi-faceted. We use individual and national level variables, as well as objective and subjective indicators. For objective indicators at the individual level, we use the standard socioeconomic and demographic variables, such as age, gender, employment status, housing characteristics, income, and schooling levels. We also include assessments of interpersonal conditions, such as friendships and community engagement, and relative measures of economic status, such as reference group income. These objective indicators are matched with respondents' assessments of their happiness, life satisfaction, satisfaction with domains such as security, health, education, and jobs, as well as assessments of the general situation of the country and the state of public services.[6]

At the national level, our variables include economic indicators such as GDP, inflation, and levels of poverty and inequality, as well as political and institutional variables, such as rule of law and the quality of public institutions. These are then benchmarked against national averages of individual responses to happiness and life satisfaction questions, as well as those about the general situation of the country, economy, and public services.

We rely primarily on the Gallup World Poll for our measures of well-being. The world poll has been conducted annually for years, but since 2006 has expanded

5. Howell and Howell (2008).

6. Luttmer (2005), Inter-American Development Bank (IDB) (2008), and Graham and Felton (2006).

its coverage to over 130 countries, of which 23 to 25 are from Latin America, depending on the year, and also includes several questions about life satisfaction. Approximately 1,000 individuals are interviewed in each country, and the surveys are nationally representative. There are over 100 quality-of-life-related questions in the Gallup World Poll, and 25 of them are asked in Latin America only. We complement the Gallup World Poll data with various other data sources, such as standard household surveys on income and employment. We also make some use of the Latinobarometro public opinion survey, which has been polling approximately 18,000 respondents across 18 countries in the region for over a decade. The survey also covers approximately 1,000 respondents per country and achieves national representation in most.[7]

In departing from a strict reliance on traditional income indicators, we accept their importance, but also allow for the possibility that they are deficient along a number of dimensions. Gross Domestic Product (GDP), for example, excludes non-market activities that may affect welfare (for example, leisure time, social interactions) and includes market activities that have negative externalities for quality of life (such as pollution-increasing economic activity). We attempt to complement these traditional data with various indicators of quality of life. Happiness is meant to be a comprehensive evaluation of people's lives, and therefore an essential part of our analysis of quality of life. But aggregate measures of happiness are also deficient, as they are influenced by psychological and cultural biases, as well as inter-temporal problems: what makes people happy in the short run (say lower taxes) may not make them better off in the long run.

Because any one measure of well-being alone is likely to be insufficient to accurately and fully assess welfare or quality of life, we rely on a variety of measures and comparison of the results that they yield to get deeper insights into quality of life in the region than any one measure alone would yield. Indeed, we believe that some of the most important information is in the gaps or inconsistencies in the results based on different measures.

In the studies presented in this book, as well as earlier ones, we find a number of paradoxes in which positive results as assessed by one indicator are negative as assessed by another. While the authors discuss each of these in detail in chapter 3, they are worth noting in this chapter for two reasons. Firstly, they challenge some of the standard assumptions in traditional economics, such as the relationship between income and happiness, and provide a conceptual frame for our analysis. Secondly, they have important substantive links with several of the region's real-

7. The samples are nationally representative except for Brazil and Paraguay. The survey is produced by the Latinobarometro, a non-governmental organization (NGO) based in Santiago de Chile and directed by Marta Lagos (www.Latinobarometro.org). The first survey was carried out in 1995 and covered eight countries. Funding began with a grant from the European Community and is now from multiple sources. Access to the data is by purchase, with a four-year lag in public release. This paper includes data collected in 2007, the latest available year.

ities, such as high levels of income inequality, volatile macroeconomic performance and high levels of insecurity, and generally low expectations of public institutions and faith in the capacity of the state to deliver.

Main Findings

Happiness in Latin America

The simplest and perhaps most fundamental exercise in the book is to assess the
determinants of happiness across the region and over time. Building from earlier
work on happiness in the region by Graham and Pettinato (2002), based on the
Latinobarometro, we ran similar happiness equations for the 18 countries in the
region based on more recent Gallup data. While there are some modest differences,
including in the phrasing of the happiness question (an open-ended happiness question in the Latinobarometro and the best possible life question in Gallup), the baseline results are very similar. This serves, among other things, as a robustness check.[8]

As in virtually every context where happiness has been studied, there is a positive relationship between income and happiness *within* countries in Latin
America, although it is not necessarily a linear one. Also as in other contexts, the
relationship between age and happiness has a *U-shape*, with the low point being
somewhere between 50 years (in the Latinobarometro) and 61 years of age
(based on Gallup and the best possible life question). Employment, health, and
marriage are all positively and significantly correlated with happiness, while
being unemployed is negatively correlated. Women are happier than men in the
Gallup dataset, while there is no gender difference in the Latinobarometro. Again,
question phrasing may make a difference here, as the Gallup question is the best
possible life ladder, while the Latinobarometro is an open-ended happiness question, and men and women may respond differently to the frames.

The Gallup Poll has some additional variables that correlate with happiness,
some of them to a surprising degree. Friendships matter to the well-being of the
average Latin American more than health, employment or personal assets, and
only slightly less than food security. This varies according to income levels, meanwhile, with the rich valuing work and health more, and the poor valuing friendships (see figure 4-3 in chapter 4). These friendships most likely provide important
coping mechanisms for the poor in the absence of publicly provided safety nets.
Whether they serve as strong or weak ties in the Granovetter (1973) sense, with
weak ties being more important for upward mobility and for acquisition of information, is an open question. Reporting religion to be important and having access
to a telephone are also positively correlated with happiness in Latin America.

---

8. In a second order exercise, this time based on ten years of pooled Latinobarometro data for
1997–2007, Graham and Chattopadhyay (2008) ran the same equations and again confirm the basic
results.

The life domains that are most relevant to happiness in the region are economic satisfaction, the importance of friends, work, health, and housing satisfaction (in that order of importance). Trust in education and satisfaction with one's city, meanwhile, are negatively correlated with happiness. Having a high optimism score, defined as higher levels of happiness than socio-demographic traits would predict (based on principal components analysis across domains), a variable that proxies for innate character traits, is strongly and positively correlated with life satisfaction. We use this residual or optimism score as a proxy or control for inherent character traits in many of our regressions.

When individual perceptions are compared to national ones, individuals in the region are typically more positive about their own individual situation than they are about their country's situation. This holds for both general satisfaction and satisfaction with one's economic situation. These findings reflect a general optimism bias among individuals in the region. In both cases, there are gaps between perceived and objective indicators, with a downward bias in the perceived indicators that is much stronger for richer than for poorer countries. This likely reflects rising aspirations in the wealthier countries, among other factors.

Perceptions Paradoxes

Public perceptions are not always informed by objective trends; indeed, some of the most important information may be found in the gaps between perceptions and objective trends. One reason for these gaps is imperfect information. The public typically relies on anecdotes in the media for its information, such as accounts of a recent corruption scandal or a botched privatization. In contrast, economists make assessments of the welfare gains or losses of particular policies based on aggregate and often complex datasets that are not easily understood by the average citizen. And, for example, the "success" of privatization—measured by its marginal welfare benefits that result in broader public access to services at similar tariff rates—is hardly the makings of a news story that captures public attention.

At the individual level, it is typically not the poorest people that are most frustrated or unhappy with their conditions or the services that they have access to. Graham and Pettinato (2002) identified a phenomenon that is now termed the "happy peasant and frustrated achiever" paradox. Very poor and destitute respondents may report high or relatively high levels of well-being, while much wealthier ones with greater available opportunities report much lower ones. This may be because the poor respondents either have a higher natural level of cheerfulness or have lower expectations, while the wealthier ones have higher and possibly rising expectations (or are naturally more curmudgeon-like). Regardless of the balance between objective conditions and individual character traits driving the paradox, it presents challenges when inferring policy-relevant information from opinion surveys.

At the country level is found a related paradox that we have called the "paradox of unhappy growth." As noted above, there is much debate in the literature about the extent to which per capita GDP levels and average happiness across countries are correlated. Based on the Gallup World Poll in 122 countries around the world, Lora and Chaparro, in chapter 3, find that countries with higher levels of per capita GDP have, on average, higher levels of happiness, as found by most scholars, as noted above. Yet controlling for levels of per capita GDP, they find that individuals in countries with positive growth rates have lower happiness levels—the paradox of unhappy growth (see table 3-2 in chapter 3).[9]

The paradox is stronger for countries above mean per capita GDP in the sample (which is above the middle income developing country level). For the richer countries, higher growth rates are associated with lower happiness levels, as well as with lower economic, health, job, and housing satisfaction. The only variable that is significant and negative on growth for poor countries is health satisfaction (and one could posit many reasons why the change in work habits that often accompanies growth booms might be negative for health). When the sample is split according to growth rates, the negative effects of growth on well-being only hold for countries with above-average rates.[10] In a separate study, Graham and Chattopadhyay, using Latinobarometro data, also find evidence of an unhappy growth effect, albeit a modest one. When they include the current GDP growth rate in the equation, as well as the lagged growth rate from the previous year (controlling for levels), they find that the effects of growth rates—and lagged growth rates—are, for the most part, negative.[11]

It may well be that this unhappy growth is driven by its nature in rapidly changing economies, where growth is often accompanied by changes in rewards to different skill sets and increased job insecurity for some groups, and by increases in vertical or horizontal inequality or both. Latin America in recent decades certainly fits this pattern, which may help explain unexpected pockets of frustration in relatively prosperous countries like Chile.

A third, related paradox is the "aspirations paradox." Lora and Chaparro in chapter 3, and Graham and Chattopadhyay (using different datasets) find that there is no clear relationship between average per capita income levels and satisfaction with education and health systems across countries in the region. Within countries, wealthier respondents are more likely to be satisfied with their health

9. Deaton (2008), and Stevenson and Wolfers (2008) also find evidence of an unhappy growth effect in the Gallup World Poll.

10. Stevenson and Wolfers (2008), also based on a worldwide Gallup sample as well as on earlier data from the World Values survey going back several decades, and again controlling for levels, find insignificant effects of growth in general, but negative effects of rapid growth, as in the case of the Irish miracle and the Korean growth boom.

11. The results are significant or just short of significant depending on the specification. Results are available from the authors in Graham and Chattopadhyay (2008).

than are poor ones. Still, there is clearly an "optimism bias" in the responses of the poorest. Those in the highest quintile in the region hold 57 percent of the income (on average), while those in the poorest quintile hold 4 percent. But the differences in their perceptions are much smaller. Seventy-nine percent of individuals in the highest quintile declare themselves satisfied with their material or economic quality of life, while 57 percent of those in the lowest quintile say they are satisfied. There is a similar "optimism bias" in the responses of the poor as they assess their living conditions and public policies in their countries. Informal sector workers, for example, report less job insecurity than do formal sector workers, even though their objective conditions are far more precarious than their formal sector counterparts.[12]

This paradox is likely due to lower expectations and poorer available information among those living in poorer contexts, as well as lower expectations. For wealthier individuals and respondents in wealthier countries, aspirations and awareness may go up as much if not more rapidly than improvements in service provision (and/or economic growth). At the same time, there is also inconsistent usage of available information such as test scores among slightly wealthier respondents. A surprisingly small amount of school choice, for example, is informed by test score results.[13] This, among other things, may contribute to increased public frustration in the face of improvements in service quality, to the extent that improvements in quality also heighten awareness among previously less informed (and more satisfied) users.

The paradoxes stand out in our analysis and frame our findings. They are of varying levels of importance, depending on the quality of life domain that is studied. Not surprisingly, economic domains are more affected by aspirations related paradoxes than other domains, such as health assessments or life purpose assessments (which are by definition more personal and subjective). The gaps between perceptions and objective measures, meanwhile, seem to be greater at the individual level rather than at the average country level (perhaps not a surprise as there is more variance); for richer rather than poorer countries (as relative deprivation effects seem to increase as average wealth increases); and for poorer rather than richer individuals (perhaps because they have less good information to make assessments, as well as lower expectations).[14] And while there are paradoxes and puzzles, it is precisely in identifying these gaps between subjective and objective measures of welfare, and seeking an explanation for them, that this book provides a contribution to our understanding of quality of life in Latin America and beyond.

When one compares the responses of individuals within countries, there is clearly the optimism bias that we refer to above among the poor. While the indi-

---

12. IDB (2008), chapter 7, and Graham and Chattopadhyay (2008).
13. IDB (2008), chapter 7.
14. IDB (2008) and Graham and Felton (2006).

vidual subjective rankings of quality of services and satisfaction with personal economic situations of those in the wealthiest quintile are slightly higher than those in much poorer quintiles, the difference in the scores is an order of magnitude smaller than is the difference in their income levels or access to and quality of services.

As in many other contexts where happiness has been studied, the incomes of others have effects on individual happiness. While wealthier people are happier than less wealthy ones on average, people of similar income levels are less happy when the incomes of those in a relevant reference group, ranging from neighbors to professional cohorts, to towns and cities, are higher.[15] The same effect holds for Latin America, based on analysis from the Gallup Poll, as well as from the Latinobarometro.

For the Gallup Poll for Latin America, reference group income is positively correlated with life satisfaction (in a ladder of life question) but negatively correlated with satisfaction with one's standard of living, job, and housing, as shown in chapter 3. In earlier work based on Latinobarometro, Graham and Felton (2006) find that average country-level incomes do not matter to individual happiness, but relative income differences—measured as distance from the mean for the average income in one's country—does matter. Thus even though a poor peasant in Honduras is half as wealthy as a poor Chilean, the former is happier because his/her distance from mean income is smaller. This effect holds across cities of different sizes, but is stronger for large cities, where there is more income variance, and smaller for small cities, where average income levels are positively correlated with happiness (even though relative incomes are still negatively correlated).[16]

When the Gallup sample is split into above and below median income groups, the comparison effect holds for both groups, with the difference being that health satisfaction is significant and negative for the below-average group, but insignificant for the rich, while job satisfaction is significant and negative for the rich but not for the poor, implying that the poor and the rich value different domains as they make comparisons. When the sample is split into urban and rural, the effects largely hold for the urban cohorts but not for the rural ones (analogous, in a way, to the city size findings discussed above).

The early chapters of the book provide greater detail on what we know about the determinants of happiness in the region, as well as on the relationship between happiness and income, as discussed above. Subsequent chapters cover the determinants of satisfaction in various domains—nutrition, health, education, and jobs—in greater detail, as well as the effects of crime on well-being.

15. Graham and Felton (2006), Luttmer (2005) and Kingdon and Knight (2007).
16. Because there is not a good income variable in the Latinobarometro, the authors use an index of assets to proxy for wealth/income. See Graham and Felton (2006).

Cárdenas, Di Maro and Mejía in chapter 5 consider different types of insecurity that can affect perceived well-being: nutritional, personal, and job insecurity. One major finding is that nutritional insecurity seems to be playing the main role in explaining perceived well-being. Job insecurity has a significant and negative, but smaller, effect on perceived well-being. Personal insecurity seems to have an effect only on some measures of life satisfaction. There is also evidence of adaptation to crime; as crime increases, the well-being effects diminished. His benchmark results show that for the same increase in life satisfaction a 1-percentage point decrease in the incidence of nutritional insecurity is equivalent to a 3.9-percentage-point decrease in job insecurity and a 4.8-percentage-point decrease in the measure of personal insecurity. He also finds that responses of life satisfaction to insecurity are not dramatically different along income distribution and schooling levels, although there are some modest ones. Individuals near the top of the income distribution manage to partly offset the negative consequences of nutritional insecurity in terms of life satisfaction and being illiterate seems to lead to a more negative response of life satisfaction to nutritional insecurity.

Graham and Lora in chapter 6 analyze health perceptions. They first report the absence of a clear association between reported health satisfaction and objective health measures such as infant mortality or life expectancy. In part this may reflect the paradox noted above: some of those who are relatively poor in this domain, such as respondents from Guatemala, report being relatively satisfied in comparison with those who by objective measures have much better health, such as respondents from Chile. They also report significant gender-age interactions, with a decline in reported health satisfaction that is fairly continuous for aging men but with much sharper declines for women after age 50. They further report strong differences by socioeconomic strata, but which are not as strong as the gaps between objective indicators.

Graham and Lora also look at health status as assessed by the European Quality of Life-5 Dimensions Index (EQ-5D), a widely used health assessment based on individual responses to questions about difficulties along five dimensions: mobility, self care, usual acts, pain, and anxiety. Their dataset is unique in having both the EQ-5D index scores and health and life satisfaction responses for a large cross-country sample. EQ-5D scores correlate closely with health and life satisfaction, with the association being much stronger for health than life satisfaction. They also find variance across demographic cohorts. The elderly, for example, suffer lower (negative) health satisfaction effects from problems with mobility but higher than average effects from pain and anxiety. Their analysis highlights the extent to which individuals have more difficulty adapting to conditions that are associated with uncertainty, such as pain and anxiety, than to physical shocks, which may be negative but are one-time events.

Cárdenas, Mejía and Di Maro in chapter 7 analyze the way in which perceptions on the quality of education affect well-being and explore if educational quality perceptions are determined by objective educational outputs, such as international standardized tests scores (for example, PISA scores) and individual educational attainment. Their results indicate that educational quality perceptions are positively correlated with standardized test scores but negatively correlated with individual educational attainment. They also find that favorable perceptions on the quality of education are positively associated with higher individual well-being, even after controlling for individual educational attainment and other traditional determinants of well-being.

Menezes-Filho, Corbi and Curi in chapter 8 investigate the determinants of job insecurity and social security participation. They find that, on average, 20 percent of Latin American workers feel insecure about their jobs, with the numbers varying from about 10 percent in Paraguay to 27 percent in Mexico. About 40 percent of Latin American workers contribute to a retirement plan, with the lowest rates occurring in Bolivia, Honduras and Paraguay (20 percent) and the highest reaching 70 percent in Chile and Uruguay. Moreover, having a regular job has a positive and significant association with life satisfaction, even conditional on health, wealth and other subjective measures that may capture respondents' frame of mind at the time of the interviews. Job satisfaction is also strongly related to life satisfaction and job insecurity is strongly inversely related with life satisfaction. Rather surprisingly, formal labor market status (measured by the contribution to a retirement plan) has no association with life satisfaction.

Indeed, there is some evidence that formal sector workers feel the negative effects of job insecurity more strongly. This could be explained by the low aspirations paradox: informal sector workers have already come to expect insecurity and are therefore less bothered by it, and/or by a selection bias: more risk-averse workers select into more secure formal sector jobs, trading off flexibility and independence for security, and remain anxious about it. A bad-quality, low-ranking formal-sector job with long and rigid working hours could easily be worse than a relatively decent informal sector job. Individuals working in countries with more regulated social security systems seem to feel more confident about their jobs, while the opposite occurs in countries where firing costs are high relative to normal wages. In general, there is a similar optimism bias in the assessments of the poor in the domain satisfactions (and among informal workers, who tend to be poorer than the average) as there is in the income domain. These results are discussed in detail in the respective chapters in the volume.

Promises and Pitfalls for Public Policy

Can our study of quality of life in the region contribute to better policy? There are a number of reasons why it can. Surely novel insights into the determinants of individual well-being have important implications for policy. They can also help explain why there are, at times, seemingly perverse public responses to particular policy measures. Factors such as optimism bias, the negative effects of reference group incomes, or the paradox of unhappy growth are rarely taken into account in the design of policy, yet they can surely influence the public's reactions.

At the same time, there are many reasons why that same information cannot be directly applied to policy recommendations. Growth, for example, may be unsettling in the short term, but is necessary for poverty reduction and for sustainable welfare policies in the long term. And the satisfaction of the very poor with mediocre services because of low expectations may make their lives more tolerable in the short term, but does not justify less expenditure on them from a welfare perspective. The extent to which concerns for relative income differences—which affect life satisfaction—should drive policy is a normative question; the answer will likely vary a great deal across societies.

There is wide debate about how relevant well-being research results are to policy. Layard (2005) makes perhaps the boldest statement about the potential of happiness research to improve people's lives directly via changes in public policy. He highlights the extent to which people's happiness is affected by status—resulting in a rat race approach to work and to income gains, which in the end may reduce well-being. He also notes the strong positive role of security in the workplace and in the home, and of the quality of social relationships and trust. He identifies direct implications for fiscal and labor market policy—in the form of taxation on excessive income gains and via re-evaluating the merits of performance-based pay.

While many economists would not agree with Layard's specific recommendations, there is nascent consensus that happiness surveys and quality of life approaches more generally can serve as an important complementary tool for public policy. A number of scholars—such as Ed Diener and Martin Seligman; and Danny Kahneman and Alan Krueger—advocate the creation of national well-being accounts to complement national income accounts.[17] The idea behind these accounts is that well-being in a number of areas, from happiness and health to education and job satisfaction, could be tracked and assessed, in the same way that Gross National Product (GNP) tracks income trends over time, and serve as a complement to GNP data.

Our findings on life, health, and job satisfaction, as well as satisfaction in other domains, can serve as a first step in the development of quality of life or well-being accounts for the region, if they are deemed useful. They provide a means of comparing satisfaction in these domains across individuals in different socioeconomic cohorts within and across countries. A plausible second step would be to generate data that could be compared across time as well. The advantage of having these data for Latin America, a region that encompasses countries at very

---

17. Diener and Seligman (2004) and Kahneman and others (2004).

different levels of development and some of which are still changing rapidly, is the opportunity to study how these indicators of quality of life vary with the development cycle.

Despite the potential contributions that quality of life research can make to policy, a sound note of caution is necessary in directly applying the findings, both because of the potential biases in survey data on well-being and because of the difficulties associated with analyzing these kind of data in the absence of controls for unobservable personality traits and other factors and endogenous choices. Happiness surveys at times yield anomalous results that provide novel insights into human psychology—such as adaptation and coping during economic crises—but do not necessarily translate into viable policy recommendations.

One example, which is analogous to that of lower job insecurity among informal sector workers (because their expectations are lower) is the more generalized finding that unemployed people are typically happier in regions or areas with higher unemployment rates. The positive effect that reduced stigma has on the well-being of the unemployed seems to outweigh the negative effects of a lower probability of future employment.[18] One possible interpretation of the implications of these results for policy—raising unemployment rates—would obviously be a mistake. At the same time, the research suggests a new focus on the effects of stigma on the welfare of the unemployed, which is relevant information. A parallel example is provided by the differentials between health satisfaction that is relatively high in Guatemala in comparison with Chile. The interpretation that welfare would be increased by reducing objective health status in Chile to Guatemalan levels would again be misguided.

These promises and pitfalls apply to Latin America. Certainly, there is great promise in understanding a variety of phenomena, many of them poverty related, that revealed preferences cannot tell us much about. As noted above, two sets of questions come to the fore. The first of these is the welfare effects of macro and institutional arrangements that individuals are powerless to change, such as macroeconomic volatility, inequality, or weak governance structures. The poor in a region where access to political as well as economic opportunities is unequally shared are obviously least able to express their preferences (as they are the least able to circumvent the system, or vote with their feet and emigrate, or put their assets abroad). Yet they may suffer the negative welfare effects from inequality.

The other set of questions are those in which behaviors are not the result of preferences, but of norms, addiction, or self control problems. Any number of public health–related questions, such as obesity, cigarette smoking, and other phenomena, can and have been addressed by happiness surveys, and could be usefully analyzed in the region, as it suffers from many of these. Equally important,

---

18. Clark and Oswald (1994), Stutzer and Lalive (2004), and Eggers, Gaddy and Graham (2006).

though, are those behaviors that are driven by low expectations resulting from social norms such as discrimination based on race or caste. If the poor have low expectations for their own and their children's futures—and if that is exacerbated by high and persistent levels of inequality as in Latin America—their behavior on any number of fronts, ranging from investing in their children's education, to saving, to public health attitude could be compromised. If those behaviors are merely analyzed as a result of revealed preferences, then the policy implications will be very different than if they are analyzed in the context of the well-being costs associated with those behaviors.[19]

A second area of much promise for applying well-being surveys to policy is in the understanding of the importance of non-income variables, such as health, education, employment status, gender rights, environment, and any number of other variables to well-being and quality of life. Standard approaches, which rely on income-based measures of well-being, tend to underweight the importance of these variables. Happiness and other well-being surveys not only highlight their importance but also allow us to attach relative weights to them. Along those lines, the recent move to develop national well-being indicators in both the United States and the United Kingdom is based on the assumption that happiness surveys can help us better gauge the relative weights of these variables, as well as track how those relative weights change over time across large samples. Our study of quality of life is a first step toward creating these kinds of data for Latin America.

While there are certainly many promises for applying the results of well-being surveys to policy, there are also many caveats. Three in particular stand out in the context of quality of life in the region.

The first is the extent to which individuals adapt to many situations, both upward and downwards.[20] This has clear implications for a region with very volatile growth. A number of studies suggest that people's expectations rise with rapid income growth and/or income gains and then drop with recessions and/or income losses. This will obviously affect trends in well-being indicators—and at minimum introduce instability or inconsistencies—as economies change throughout the region. Our paradox of unhappy growth is a good example of this.

A related issue, which we discussed above, is the so-called happy peasant and frustrated achiever paradox. In this instance, there are many cases where very poor and uninformed respondents, who either have a high set point (cheery nature) or low expectations, report they are very happy, even though they live in destitute

---

19. Graham (2008), Graham and Ladkawalla (2006) and Gruber and Mullainathan (2002).

20. Herrera and others (2006), for example, using panel data for Peru and Madagascar, finds that people's expectations adapt upwards during periods of high growth and downwards during recessions, and that this adaptation is reflected in their assessments of their life satisfaction. People are less likely to be satisfied with the status quo when expectations are adapting upwards. Graham and Pettinato (2002) have similar findings for Peru; more recent work on China by Whyte and Hun (2006) confirms the direction of these findings.

poverty. The implications of this information for policy are very unclear. Should policy raise the peasant's awareness of how bad his or her situation is in order to raise expectations, although risking making her miserable? Should policy leave the peasant ignorant?

This raises the difficult normative question of how policy factors in set point/ character differences. Should policy listen to the naturally unhappy respondents who have a tendency to complain more than to others? How much is expectations and how much is character, for example? And if the expectations of the rich are so much higher than those of the poor, what does that imply for the allocation of public service resources?

A third issue is cardinality versus ordinality. Happiness surveys are ordinal in nature and do not attach cardinal weights to the answers. Thus no distinction is made by either interviewers or respondents between the value of raising a respondent from happy to very happy versus from unhappy to happy. The Gallup World Poll, meanwhile, has both a zero to one life satisfaction question and a 10 point best possible life ladder. Again, these scores are ordinal rather than cardinal. Yet if these measures are really used to guide policy, does it become necessary to attach such weights? Does unhappiness matter more than happiness, for example? How does one choose between a policy that raises a happy person to very happy versus one that raises an unhappy person to just happy status? Many of these choices require normative judgments that are difficult for policymakers to make.

Perhaps a more fundamental question is whether happiness should be a policy objective. Are happy people successful or complacent, for example? There is some evidence that happier people, on average, perform better in the labor market and are healthier.[21] In other words, being happy *may* have positive causal effects on behavior (the causality could run in both directions). And certainly very unhappy or depressed people have all sorts of related negative externalities. But the evidence also suggests that there is a top limit to this. Psychologists find that those that answer happiness questions near the top end of a 10 point scale are indeed more successful, but the effects are stronger around the 7 to 9 range rather than at the very top of the scale.[22] And there are certainly examples of very successful and creative people who are miserable for most of their lives. On average, though, it seems that happiness is correlated with better outcomes than is unhappiness or misery, and eliminating the latter seems a worthwhile objective for policy.

The definition of happiness is fundamental to resolving these questions. Attempting such a definition is clearly beyond the scope of this book. Philosophers have provided a range of definitions over centuries. A more recent attempt to define happiness, by Kenny and Kenny (2006), seems particularly well suited to thinking about happiness and policy. Kenny and Kenny define happiness as

---

21. Graham, Eggers and Sukhtankar (2004).
22. See Diener and others (2006) and Diener and others (1999).

having three separate components: contentment, welfare, and dignity. Happiness defined simply as contentment seems an inappropriate objective for public policy. Yet when it is defined as a combination of these three factors, it seems more relevant, particularly for a region such as Latin America and the Caribbean where the major policy challenge is not extreme poverty but relative poverty, vulnerability, and inequality of income and opportunity.

Imposing a definition of happiness and/or quality of life does not answer the question of how much weight policymakers should put on happiness as an objective versus others such as growth, policy reforms, and fiscal stability. There are inter-temporal considerations as well. Reforms may and often do make people unhappy in the short term, but in the long run may guarantee them more prosperity and well-being. There is a significant body of evidence, from both the behavioral economics and the happiness literatures, that individuals are loss averse and value losses disproportionately to gains. The happiness literature shows that individuals adapt very quickly to income gains but much less quickly to losses, and more to changes in income than to changes in status.[23] These behaviors will mediate the average citizen's tolerance for the inter-temporal choices most reforms entail.

There is also significant evidence of hyperbolic discounting: individuals will trade off much larger future benefits for much smaller short-term ones; it is not a coincidence that most developed economies have forced savings schemes. Some work by Graham and collaborators, meanwhile, which is in the initial stages, suggests that high levels of inequality or low levels of social mobility, and related low expectations, can result in higher discount rates (and therefore more hyperbolic discounting) for those in the lower income ranks. This discounting can apply to areas such as public health as well as in the income realms, and may help explain why phenomena such as obesity are concentrated among lower-income cohorts, at least in the developed economies.[24]

Certainly, understanding these behaviors is potentially important for policymakers. But can we use short-term well-being questions and surveys as a gauge for policy? The information may be more useful for explaining lack of public support for what would seem to be promising policies than it is as a guide to policy choice. Structural policy reforms, for example, can result in major changes in income and status and related unhappiness for particular cohorts, at least in the short term, while producing gains in the aggregate in the long term.

Latin America has for years suffered from the threat and the reality of populist politics and policies, which have primarily manifested themselves in fiscal profligacy for short-term political gain at the expense of longer-term investments in the

---

23. The classic work on income losses and gains is Kahneman and Tversky (1991). For status changes, see di Tella and MacCulloch (2006).
24. Graham and Felton (2006), Felton and Graham (2005), and Graham (2008).

structural changes in the macroeconomic and social policy realms that could generate sustainable growth and poverty reduction.[25] With the widespread turn to the market and acceptance of democratic institutions throughout most of the region in the 1990s, voting behavior seems to have matured and begun to resemble patterns in developed countries in some countries. There have been several rounds of leadership change—including with significant shifts on the ideological spectrum—without fundamental changes in economic policy in countries ranging from Brazil to Chile, El Salvador and Peru. There have also been cases of countries undergoing significant economic crisis and still retaining democratic institutions and some continuity in economic management, as in Argentina. Voters are, for the most part, also making the important distinction that characterizes mature democracy: that between support for systems of government and economic arrangements as opposed to specific governments in power.[26]

At the same time, there are also significant pockets of political instability and increasing support for populist politicians and policies, such as Venezuela, Ecuador, and Bolivia, where popular backlash against market reforms has also resulted in an erosion of democratic institutions. In these countries, the future of constitutional democracy as well as of market economies is at risk.

How can surveys of happiness and other quality of life domains be relevant in such a context? If the results of happiness surveys were directly applied to policy, they could, at least in theory, lend support to populist politicians. If the results of a national happiness or quality of life study show that the majority of citizens prefer inflation to unemployment (as happiness surveys in most contexts, including Latin America, suggest), those results could fuel irresponsible fiscal policies in countries that are very vulnerable to hyper-inflation (which indeed makes people very unhappy). The kinds of structural reforms that are necessary for long-term growth, meanwhile, are unlikely to be supported by a population that has a high tendency for hyperbolic discounting. How many voters will report that they are happier than before in the throes of a controversial privatization or tax reform, the benefits of which are not immediately clear, for example?

Latin America is a region where there is reform fatigue, risk and loss aversion due to past experience with macroeconomic volatility and other crises, and a large proportion of the population that is, at least in theory, vulnerable to hyperbolic discounting, due to high levels of persistent inequality. Perhaps the most useful role for happiness surveys and quality of life approaches in this context is in helping us understand and better navigate the political outcomes that can result. Is it really irrational if one is poor and unemployed in Ecuador to support an anti-system politician in the hope of change and a possible short-term improvement?

25. See, for example, Dornbusch and Edwards (1991).
26. Stokes (2006), Weyland (2002), Lora and Olivera (2005), and Graham and Sukhtankar (2004).

And understanding what makes people most unhappy with the policy context, via well-being surveys, might also help reformists avert the kind of policy mistakes—such as an over-emphasis on rapid growth at the expense of other objectives such as investments in social welfare systems—that lead to populist or "hyperbolic" politics as a backlash.

A complementary role for well-being and quality of life research is to provide a tool that allows tracking public attitudes across a range of quality of life domains across countries and over time. The learning that will accompany that exercise, meanwhile, will shed light on the most appropriate role for happiness and quality of life indicators in the formulation of policy in the future.

The remainder of this volume addresses a number of these themes in greater detail, as well as provides the detailed empirical evidence for the results—and the paradoxes—that we have highlighted in this introductory chapter.

References

Cantril, H. 1965. *The Pattern of Human Concerns.* Rutgers University Press.

Clark, A., and Oswald, A. 1994. "Unhappiness and Unemployment." *The Economic Journal* 104 (424): 648–59.

Clark, A., Frijters, P., and Shields, M. 2008. "Relative Income, Happiness, and Utility: An Explanation for the Easterlin Paradox and Other Puzzles." *Journal of Economic Literature* 46 (1): 95–144.

Deaton, A. 2008. "Income, Health, and Well-Being around the World: Evidence from the Gallup World Poll." *Journal of Economic Perspectives* 22 (2): 53–72.

Di Tella, R., and MacCulloch, R. 2006. "Happiness and Adaptation to Income and to Status." Mimeo, Harvard University.

Diener, E., Suh, E. M., Lucas, R. E., and Smith, H. 1999. "Subjective Well-Being: Three Decades of Progress." *Psychological Bulletin* 125: 276–302.

Diener, E., and Seligman, M. 2004. "Beyond Money: Toward an Economy of Well-Being." *Psychological Science in the Public Interest* 5 (1): 1–31.

Diener, E., Lucas, R. E., and Scollon, C. N. 2006. "Beyond the Hedonic Treadmill: Revisions to the Adaptation Theory of Well-Being." *American Psychologist* 61: 305–14.

Dornbusch, R., and Edwards, S. 1991. *The Macroeconomics of Populism in Latin America.* University of Chicago Press.

Easterlin, R. A. 1974. "Does Economic Growth Enhance the Human Lot? Some Empirical Evidence." In P. A. David and M. Reder, eds. *Nations and Households in Economic Growth: Essays in Honor of Moses Abramovitz.* Stanford University Press.

Eggers, A., Gaddy, C., and Graham, C. 2006. "Well Being and Unemployment in Russia in the 1990's: Can Society's Suffering Be Individual's Solace?" *Journal of Socio-Economics* 35.

Felton, A., and Graham, C. 2005. "Variance in Obesity across Countries and Cohorts: Some Evidence from Happiness Surveys." CSED Working Paper No. 48. Brookings.

Graham, C., and Pettinato, S. 2002. *Happiness and Hardship: Opportunity and Insecurity in New Market Economies.* Brookings.

Graham, C., and Sukhtankar, S. 2004. "Does Economic Crisis Reduce Support for Markets and Democracy in Latin America? Some Evidence from Surveys of Public Opinion and Well-Being." *Journal of Latin American Studies* 36: 349–77.

Graham, C., Eggers, A., and Sukhtankar, S. 2004. "Does Happiness Pay? An Initial Exploration Based on Panel Data from Russia." *Journal of Economic Behavior and Organization* 55: 319–42.

Graham, C., and Felton, A. 2006. "Inequality and Happiness: Insights from Latin America." *Journal of Economic Inequality* 4 (1): 107–22.

Graham, C., and Ladkawalla, D. 2006. "Cheap Food, Societal Norms, and the Economics of Obesity." *Wall Street Journal Econoblog,* August 25, 2006.

Graham, C. 2008. "Happiness and Health: Lessons—and Questions—for Public Policy." *Health Affairs* 27 (1): 72–87.

Graham, C., and Chattopadhyay, S. 2008. "Public Opinion Trends in Latin America (and the U.S.): How Strong Is Support for Markets, Democracy, and Regional Integration?" Paper prepared for the Brookings Partnership for the Americas Commission, Washington, D.C.

Graham, C., Chattopadhyay, S., and Picon, M. 2008. "The Easterlin and Other Paradoxes: Why Both Sides of the Debate May Be Correct." Paper presented to Princeton University Conference on International Differences in Well Being, Princeton, N.J.

Granovetter, M. 1973. "The Strength of Weak Ties." *American Journal of Sociology* 78 (May): 1360–79.

Gruber, J., and Mullainathan, S. 2002. "Do Cigarette Taxes Make Smokers Happier?" Working Paper No. 8872. Cambridge, MA: National Bureau of Economic Research.

Herrera, J., Razafindrakoto, M., and Roubaud, F. 2006. "Governance, Democracy and Poverty Reduction: Lessons Drawn from Household Surveys in Sub-Saharan Africa and Latin America." Mimeo, Inter-American Development Bank, Washington, D.C.

Howell, R., and Howell, C. 2008. "The Relation of Economic Status to Subjective Well-Being in Developing Countries: A Meta-Analysis." *Psychological Bulletin* 134 (4): 536–60.

Inter-American Development Bank (IDB). 2008. *Beyond Facts: Understanding Quality of Life in Latin America.* Harvard University Press.

Kahneman, D., and Tversky, A. 2000. "Choices, Values, and Frames." In *Choices, Values, and Frames,* edited by D. Kahneman and A. Tversky, pp. 1–17. New York: Russell Sage and Cambridge University Press.

Kahneman, D., Krueger, A., Schkade, D., Schwarz, N., and Stone, A. 2004. "Toward national well-being accounts." *AEA Papers and Proceedings* 94 (2): 429–34.

Kenny, A., and Kenny, C. 2006. *Life, Liberty, and the Pursuit of Utility.* Cambridge: St. Andrews' Press.

Kingdon, G., and Knight, J. 2007. "Communities, Comparisons, and Subjective Well Being in a Divided Society." *Journal of Economic Behavior and Organization* 64 (1).

Layard, R. 2005. *Happiness: Lessons from a New Science.* New York: Penguin Press.

Lora, E., and Olivera, M. 2005. "The Electoral Consequences of the Washington Consensus." *Economia* 5 (2): 1–61.

Luttmer, E. 2005. "Neighbors as Negatives: Relative Earnings and Well-Being." *Quarterly Journal of Economics* 120 (3): 963–1002.

Stevenson, B., and Wolfers, J. 2008. "Economic Growth and Subjective Well-Being: Re-Assessing the Easterlin Paradox." Paper presented to the Brookings Panel on Economic Activity.

Stokes, S. 2006. "Public Opinion and Market Reforms: The Limits of Economic Voting." *Comparative Political Studies* 29: 499–519.

Stutzer, A., and Lalive, R. 2004. "The Role of Social Work Norms in Job Searching and Subjective Well Being." *Journal of the European Economic Association* 2 (4): 696–719.

Weyland, K. 2002. *The Politics of Market Reform in Fragile Democracies: Argentina, Brazil, Peru, and Venezuela.* Princeton University Press.

Whyte, M., and Hun, C. 2006. "Subjective Well Being and Mobility Attitudes in China." Mimeo, Harvard University.

2

Objective and Subjective Deprivation

LEONARDO GASPARINI, WALTER SOSA ESCUDERO,
MARIANA MARCHIONNI, AND SERGIO OLIVIERI

Deprivation is arguably the main social concern in the world. Just to mention one example, the first Millennium Development Goal (MDG) of the United Nations is halving poverty from 1990 to 2015. Although usually associated with income poverty, it has long been recognized that the concept of deprivation has multiple dimensions, including the lack of assets and opportunities and the own perception of low standard of living and social exclusion.

Research on multidimensional deprivation in Latin America and the Caribbean (LAC) has been less systematic than in the developed world, in part due to lack of relevant data. Although all national household surveys in the region include questions on income, and many also on assets, it is difficult to provide a consistent picture for the region due to substantial differences in the questionnaires. In addition, questions on perceptions and self-assessment of living standards are not common in the LAC national household surveys.

This chapter makes extensive use of the Gallup World Poll, which may help to overcome those difficulties. This survey provides rich data on a wide range of issues in over 130 countries, 23 of them from LAC. The Gallup Poll has two main advantages over national household surveys: it includes a larger and much richer set of questions on quality of life and perceptions, and the survey design and questionnaires are similar across countries.

This chapter is aimed at providing evidence on the multiple dimensions of deprivation in LAC by exploiting the Gallup World Poll combined with the national household surveys. In particular, we estimate levels and patterns of income, multi-dimensional non-monetary, and subjective deprivation for all countries in the region based on Gallup data, and compare the results with those from household surveys.

Income in the Gallup World Poll

The main source of information for this chapter is the 2006 wave of the Gallup World Poll, an ambitious survey conducted in more than 130 countries worldwide since that year, which provides the widest coverage to date on reported well-being. The country samples are nationally representative. The interviews are conducted by telephone in countries with land line coverage of 80 percent or more of the population, and in person in the rest of countries. The LAC countries fall into the latter category. Household members were selected randomly (from those 15 years or older) to avoid bias coming from interviewing only the first available household member.

Because the survey has the same questionnaire in all the countries, it provides a unique opportunity to perform cross-country comparisons.[1] The Gallup World Poll is particularly rich in self-reported measures of quality of life, opinions and perceptions. It also includes basic questions on demographics, education, and employment, and a question on household income.

The 2006 wave of the Gallup World Poll surveyed 141,739 persons, 21,200 of them from the 23 LAC countries included in the survey (all the 17 Latin countries plus the main nations in the Caribbean according to their population: Cuba, Dominican Republic, Haiti, Jamaica, Puerto Rico and Trinidad and Tobago). The country samples have around 1,000 observations, except in Haiti, Jamaica, Puerto Rico and Trinidad and Tobago, where around 500 observations were collected.

The basic socio-demographic statistics (age, gender composition, number of children and rural-urban composition) from the Gallup Poll seem to be consistent with those from the household surveys collected by the National Statistical Offices (NSO) of the LAC countries.[2] However, in a few countries, there are important discrepancies, which cast some doubts on the national representativeness of the poll, as it will be discussed later in this chapter.

In spite of its drawbacks and limitations, income adjusted by demographics is widely used as a proxy for individual well-being.[3] In most countries poverty and

---

1. Deaton (2007) is one of the first studies using the 2006 Gallup Poll.

2. For this purpose the datasets processed at the *Centro de Estudios Distributivos Laborales y Sociales* (CEDLAS 2007) were used. These datasets are part of the Socio-Economic Database for Latin America and the Caribbean project (SEDLAC project) carried out by CEDLAS and the World Bank's LAC Poverty Group (LCSPP), with the help of the Program for the Improvement of Surveys and the Measurement of Living Conditions in Latin America and the Caribbean (MECOVI). For more information see www.cedlas.org.

3. See Deaton (1997) and Sen (2000), among many others.

inequality are officially measured over the distribution of income. This is certainly the case in LAC, where consumption data are seldom available in household surveys.

The reason to include an income question in the Gallup survey is certainly not to collect independent estimates of income and poverty, but rather to enable comparisons of different variables (for example, perceptions and opinions) among income groups. This type of analysis would be reliable provided that income estimates using the Gallup Poll are roughly consistent with those derived from in principle more rigorous sources, like the national household surveys.

The Gallup Poll includes a single question on monthly total household income before taxes. The question is clear, but it is too simple and reported in value brackets, leading to just a rough measure of income. The question is placed almost at the end of the questionnaire, which may imply a higher rate of non-response and a lower quality of information. The value brackets are expressed in local currency units, and hence they differ across countries, even when expressed in U.S. dollars adjusted for purchasing power parity differentials. One source of difficulty is that the number of brackets is different in each country (from 4 in Colombia to 20 in Bolivia).

To at least partially overcome these difficulties, a homogeneous monthly household income variable in U.S. dollars was computed for each respondent by (i) randomly assigning a value in the corresponding bracket of the original question in local currency units; and (ii) translating this value to U.S. dollars using country exchange rates adjusted for purchasing power parity.[4]

As mentioned, the rate of non-response for the income question is high (13 percent on average, with maximum values in Trinidad and Tobago, 38 percent, and Honduras, 33 percent).[5] Although the non-response seems to be concentrated in many countries in the well-off category, the magnitude of the non-response and the bias resulting from it do not appear to be very different from what is observed in household surveys.

Most welfare analyses are carried out in terms of household income adjusted for the demographic composition of the household. The Gallup Poll includes questions for the number of adults and children. Unfortunately, the 2006 dataset includes the answers to the number of adults in only three LAC countries.[6] In addition, the number of children is not recorded in Honduras and Nicaragua, and valid answers are less than 70 percent in Argentina and Mexico.

The number of members in each household was estimated by adding the number of children under 15 reported in the Gallup Poll to the average number of adults (above 15) computed from the national household surveys. For each coun-

4. Gallup carries out a simpler standardization process for all countries, taking just the midpoints in each bracket, and provides in the user dataset a categorical income variable with 29 brackets (variable *wp4898*).

5. The income non-response is substantially higher in the Gallup 2007 (24 percent).

6. In 2007 only six LAC countries have valid answers to this question.

try the average for four groups is taken according to the area of residence (urban or rural) and the type of household (with or without children) and these means applied to the corresponding households in the Gallup survey. In addition, the number of children in households with missing information in Honduras, Nicaragua, Argentina and Mexico was estimated using data for the 2007 round.

After these computations it is possible to compare incomes from the Gallup World Poll with those from the official national household surveys, which are the main sources of information on household incomes in the LAC countries. These surveys usually include a relatively large number of questions aimed at capturing all sources of income. However, while household surveys are surely a better source for national income data than the Gallup Poll, the latter has the big advantage of a similar questionnaire across countries, and hence it might compete with national surveys as a data source for international comparisons.

While the Gallup Poll was carried out in 2006, not all national surveys from the CEDLAS project correspond to that year (10 out of 21). To make the two information sources more comparable, all incomes are taken from the national household surveys to year 2006 by adjusting for the nominal growth rate of each country (and thus implicitly assuming no distributional changes between the year of the survey and 2006). Comparisons between the two sources are summarized in table 2-1.[7] On average mean (median) income in Gallup is 66 percent (77 percent) of the value in national household surveys. Only in Jamaica and Venezuela are incomes in Gallup higher than in the household surveys. In most countries the shares of both the poorest and the richest quintiles are somewhat smaller than in household surveys. In contrast, the share of the fourth quintile, for instance, is larger in the Gallup surveys of all LAC countries, except in Venezuela.[8]

The linear correlation across countries between per capita income in Gallup and the national household surveys is positive, significant but not too high (0.64), even when deleting the main deviants—Honduras and Venezuela. When taking the medians the correlation coefficient rises to 0.76, and to 0.93 when deleting Honduras and Venezuela. The ranking across countries between the two information sources is similar. The Spearman rank correlation is 0.73 when considering the means and 0.67 when taking the medians of the household per capita income distributions.[9]

Some comparisons with per capita incomes from National Accounts may also be relevant, although there are a host of reasons why mean income may differ

7. Cuba and Puerto Rico were ignored due to data limitations of the household surveys.

8. A more detailed comparison of the distributions shows that, when adjusting incomes for the difference in means, the distributions are reasonable close in several countries. However, the distributions in Chile, Uruguay, and Venezuela look clearly more unequal with the Gallup data. Instead, the Gallup income distributions in Argentina, Honduras, and Nicaragua seem more egalitarian than with official data.

9. The correlations are lower when using the 2007 Gallup data.

Table 2-1. *Per Capita Incomes, 2006*
US$ purchasing power parity

				Share by quintiles				
		Mean	*Median*	*1*	*2*	*3*	*4*	*5*
Latin America								
Argentina	Gallup	222	184	4.6	10.1	16.1	22.2	45.6
	HH survey	481	327	3.5	8.2	13.6	21.9	52.8
Bolivia	Gallup	95	59	2.7	7.3	12.3	21.0	56.7
	HH survey	161	95	2.9	7.4	12.0	19.5	58.2
Brazil	Gallup	243	156	2.3	7.6	13.0	21.9	55.3
	HH survey	411	223	2.6	6.4	11.0	18.6	61.5
Chile	Gallup	357	189	2.0	6.3	10.7	19.4	61.6
	HH survey	562	311	3.8	7.3	11.1	17.8	60.0
Colombia	Gallup	101	78	10.1	13.3	15.5	22.0	38.4
	HH survey	443	220	1.4	5.5	10.0	18.1	65.0
Costa Rica	Gallup	262	202	2.3	8.4	15.5	23.6	50.2
	HH survey	485	316	3.8	8.4	13.2	20.9	53.7
Ecuador	Gallup	127	87	3.7	8.7	13.6	21.6	52.3
	HH survey	243	142	3.5	7.5	11.8	18.9	58.3
El Salvador	Gallup	135	94	1.7	7.4	13.9	22.9	54.2
	HH survey	222	148	3.2	8.6	13.6	21.8	52.9
Guatemala	Gallup	90	69	1.7	7.9	15.0	23.1	52.3
	HH survey	152	100	3.7	8.2	13.1	20.7	54.3
Honduras	Gallup	219	204	1.6	11.8	18.6	27.8	40.3
	HH survey	264	156	2.3	6.7	12.0	20.0	59.0
Mexico	Gallup	133	98	2.9	9.1	15.1	22.7	50.2
	HH survey	319	198	3.4	8.0	12.5	19.7	56.3
Nicaragua	Gallup	112	104	0.3	8.4	18.5	28.4	44.5
	HH survey	252	154	3.8	7.7	12.3	19.2	57.1
Panama	Gallup	156	102	1.2	6.3	13.1	22.3	57.1
	HH survey	285	164	2.6	6.7	11.7	20.1	59.0
Paraguay	Gallup	165	97	1.8	5.7	11.7	21.6	59.2
	HH survey	345	193	2.9	7.0	11.4	19.1	59.5
Peru	Gallup	115	78	2.5	7.5	13.6	22.2	54.2
	HH survey	265	171	4.0	8.0	13.0	20.7	54.3
Uruguay	Gallup	330	216	3.2	7.9	13.3	22.4	53.2
	HH survey	517	344	3.2	8.1	13.4	21.6	53.7
Venezuela	Gallup	201	111	2.4	6.6	11.4	20.2	59.4
	HH survey	144	100	2.8	8.6	13.9	21.8	52.9

Table 2-1. *Per Capita Incomes, 2006 (continued)*
US$ purchasing power parity

		Mean	*Median*	Share by quintiles				
				1	*2*	*3*	*4*	*5*
The Caribbean								
Dominican	Gallup	163	96	2.1	6.8	11.8	21.4	57.9
Republic	HH survey	444	264	4.0	7.7	12.0	19.4	56.9
Haiti	Gallup	69	52	2.2	8.4	15.1	22.7	51.6
	HH survey	99	51	2.4	6.2	10.4	17.6	63.4
Jamaica	Gallup	365	268	3.1	7.7	14.0	23.5	51.7
	HH survey	220	111	0.1	3.2	10.1	20.1	66.5

Source: Authors' calculations based on Gallup World Poll (2006) and national household surveys.
HH survey = Household Survey.

Note: While the Gallup Poll was carried out in 2006, not all national surveys available correspond to that year (10 out of 21). To make the two information sources more comparable, all incomes from the national household surveys were taken to year 2006 by adjusting for the nominal growth rate of each country (and thus implicitly assuming no distributional changes between the year of the survey and 2006).

between National Accounts and household or opinion surveys, the most important being that while surveys record disposable incomes mostly from labor sources and transfers, National Accounts take into account all sources of income derived not just from labor, but also from all other factors of production. There is a reasonable degree of matching between mean income in Gallup and per capita GDP from National Accounts for the LAC countries. The linear correlation is 0.59 for the full sample, but rises to 0.75 when deleting the main outlier (Jamaica). However, Argentina and Mexico have mean incomes in the Gallup survey too low compared to their National Account figures. Nonetheless, the ranking of countries from the two sources is very similar (the Spearman rank correlation coefficient is 0.85).

Income Deprivation

While the previous section dealt with the whole income distribution, this section focuses on measures of income poverty or deprivation, as defined by certain income threshold. There is a long-standing literature on the measurement of poverty. Even restricting the analysis to income poverty, the literature remains huge. The most widespread way of measuring poverty in an international context is by using the poverty lines set at one or two dollars a day adjusted for purchasing power parity differentials.[10] Although these lines have been criticized, their simplicity and the lack of reasonable and easy-to-implement alternatives have made them the standard for international poverty comparisons.

10. Ravallion and others (1991).

The standard practice to get the international poverty lines in local currency values is taking the equivalent to US$1.0763 in domestic currency using a large international study on prices carried out in 1993, and taking that value to the date of a given survey using the national Consumer Price Index (CPI).[11] This one-dollar poverty line is multiplied by two to get the two-dollar line. Table 2-2 shows several poverty measures obtained by applying the one-dollar and two-dollar lines to the distribution of household per capita income from the Gallup Poll. Poverty statistics are shown for all countries for which computation of poverty lines was possible. According to these estimates the headcount poverty ratio[12] in the region is 37.2 percent when using the two-dollar line, and 17.2 percent when using the one-dollar line. Poverty is higher in the Caribbean due to the presence of Haiti. Poverty ranges from 9.4 percent in Puerto Rico to 82.9 percent in Haiti (poverty line of two dollars). In Latin America poverty ranges from 22 percent in Chile to 60.5 percent in El Salvador. Puerto Rico, Cuba, Jamaica, the Southern Cone and Costa Rica also present relatively low income poverty levels, while some Andean and Central American countries are in the other extreme of the ranking. The main results do not change when considering alternatively the one-dollar or the two-dollar lines, or when three alternative poverty indicators are used: the headcount ratio, the poverty gap and the Foster-Greer-Thorbecke—FGT(2).[13] In fact, all the linear and rank correlation coefficients between the indicators mentioned are statistically significant and high (higher than 0.95 in most cases).

The main sources for poverty estimates in LAC are the national household surveys. This chapter takes the estimates of income deprivation using the two-dollar poverty line from a database produced by CEDLAS.[14] Since there are no poverty estimates for 2006 available for all countries, a similar procedure to the one described above is followed: it is assumed a neutral growth in per capita income (at the same rate as per capita GDP growth) from the year of the latest household survey available until 2006.

On average, poverty in the Gallup Poll is 16 points higher than in national household surveys when using the two-dollar line. This gap is naturally linked to the differences in incomes between the two sources discussed in the previous section. More than being concerned about the specific poverty levels that arise from the Gallup Poll, this chapter cares about the rankings and comparisons across countries, and across population groups within countries. There is a positive significant correlation between poverty estimates using the Gallup Poll and those computed at CEDLAS with national household survey microdata (the correlation

11. Deaton (2003) and World Bank (2004).
12. Headcount poverty ratio is the proportion of the national population with incomes below a given threshold (or thresholds).
13. The FGT(2) is a poverty index that, in contrast to the headcount ratio and the poverty gap, takes into account the income distribution within the poor. See Deaton (1997) for details.
14. CEDLAS (2007). See www.cedlas.org for results and methodological details.

Table 2-2. *Poverty in Latin America and the Caribbean, 2006*

	Gallup data						Household survey data
	Headcount ratio[a]		Poverty gap		Foster-Greer-Thorbecke, FGT (2)[b]		Headcount ratio[a]
	Poverty line		Poverty line		Poverty line		Poverty line
	US$ 1	US$ 2	US$ 1	US$ 2	US$ 1	US$ 2	US$ 2
Latin America	**16.5**	**36.5**	**8.6**	**17.5**	**6.0**	**11.6**	n.a.
Argentina	7.8	22.9	3.8	8.8	2.4	5.3	8.5
Bolivia	32.3	58.8	14.9	31.0	9.5	20.5	41.6
Brazil	14.0	25.7	7.5	13.7	5.3	9.6	13.3
Chile	12.1	22.0	6.1	11.6	4.0	7.9	3.5
Costa Rica	13.7	25.4	7.8	13.9	6.2	10.0	7.0
Ecuador	16.7	45.8	7.8	19.6	5.1	11.8	29.0
El Salvador	33.4	60.5	19.8	33.5	14.9	24.4	34.4
Guatemala	28.9	50.3	17.2	29.0	13.2	21.2	32.7
Honduras	16.9	23.0	13.0	16.5	11.8	14.1	34.5
Mexico	22.7	43.3	11.5	22.1	7.6	15.0	16.4
Nicaragua	35.2	59.5	24.9	35.9	22.0	28.7	41.3
Panama	18.4	32.6	12.9	19.3	10.7	15.0	13.8
Paraguay	33.9	54.9	17.7	30.7	11.8	21.9	23.2
Peru	33.1	57.8	16.5	31.1	11.0	21.4	25.9
Uruguay	9.6	25.6	3.8	11.0	2.1	6.3	3.7
Venezuela	12.8	28.8	6.3	13.3	4.2	8.6	27.7

(continued)

Table 2-2. *Poverty in Latin America and the Caribbean, 2006 (continued)*

	Gallup data						Household survey data
	Headcount ratio[a]		Poverty gap		Foster-Greer-Thorbecke, FGT (2)[b]		Headcount ratio[a]
	Poverty line		Poverty line		Poverty line		Poverty line
	US$ 1	US$ 2	US$ 1	US$ 2	US$ 1	US$ 2	US$ 2
The Caribbean	**32.1**	**54.9**	**17.2**	**31.1**	**12.2**	**21.9**	n.a.
Cuba	10.9	22.4	6.9	11.6	5.5	8.4	n.a.
Dominican Republic	23.3	45.4	12.1	23.4	8.5	15.9	11.6
Haiti	52.7	82.9	28.4	49.9	20.1	35.7	78.0
Jamaica	5.5	17.8	2.9	6.8	2.0	4.1	32.9
Puerto Rico	4.4	9.4	3.3	5.2	2.9	3.9	n.a.
Latin America and The Caribbean	**17.2**	**37.2**	**9.0**	**18.0**	**6.3**	**12.0**	

Source: Authors' calculations based on microdata from Gallup World Poll (2006) and national household surveys.

n.a. = not available.

a. The unit of the headcount ratio is the percent of total population under the given poverty lines.

b. The FGT(2) is a poverty index that takes into account the income distribution within the poor. See Deaton (1997) for details.

coefficient is 0.59 for LAC and 0.86 for Latin America, or 0.92 for Latin America without Venezuela).

The poverty ranking that arises from the two alternative data sources turns out to be similar (the Spearman rank correlation coefficient is 0.90). Chile, Argentina, Costa Rica and Uruguay are the countries where income deprivation is less serious, while Bolivia, Nicaragua and El Salvador are located in the other extreme. Haiti ranks as the country with the highest income deprivation level in the region.

A statistical analysis based on microsimulations was performed to assess the extent to which the differences in the poverty ratios from both information sources come from differences in the distribution of observable characteristics ("characteristics effect"), the return to these characteristics ("parameters effect") or a scalar factor.[15] The main conclusion of the analyses is that the characteristics effect is a negligible source of the differences between the two sources. In Uruguay the difference is basically due to a scale effect, while in Chile, El Salvador and Peru it is due to the parameters effect.

Even if income is not well measured in the Gallup Poll, and poverty figures drawn from that survey substantially differ from household surveys, the income information in Gallup may still be useful for some purposes, if the correlation with real incomes is high. One such purpose is comparing variables between the poor and the non-poor. For instance, suppose one is interested in assessing whether the income poor feel significantly less happy than the non-poor. The Gallup survey will be helpful to identify the income poor and the non-poor. If income levels in the Gallup Poll are weakly estimated but the rank is fine, it is possible to impose a figure for the proportion of poor people taken from other source (for example, household surveys) and carry out the exercise of comparing non-income variables across income poverty groups.

In summary, despite a much rougher approximation to per capita income, the picture of poverty in Latin America and the Caribbean viewed through the Gallup lens is not very different from the one obtained with household survey microdata. Poverty levels are highly correlated across both information sources, the poverty rankings are comparable, and in general the poverty profiles are roughly consistent.[16]

---

15. See Bourguignon and others (2004). The methodology implies two basic steps: (i) running similar income models for each country in both information sources; and (ii) estimating a counterfactual income distribution in source one if some parameters or characteristics were those of source two. Further details are explained in Gasparini and others (2008).

16. Further details can be seen in Gasparini and others (2008). However, there seem to be problems with some variables in some countries, and also likely with the national representativeness of the Gallup survey in a few countries that should be revised and corrected in the next rounds of the Poll to increase the reliability and usefulness of the data.

Objective Non-monetary Deprivation

It has long been argued that deprivation goes beyond the income dimension. Amartya Sen has extensively argued in favor of extending the measurement of deprivation to the dimension of functionings and capabilities.[17] Brandolini and D'Alessio (1998), among others, have assessed the operational content of this approach. The United Nations Human Development Index (UNDP-HDI) is perhaps the most well-known measure that follows the spirit of Sen's approach. More recently, Osberg and Sharpe (2005) proposed an Index of Economic Well-Being that takes into account assessments of consumption, accumulation, distribution, and security.

There is also a growing literature in LAC on the measurement of poverty beyond the income paradigm.[18] In fact, several Latin American countries routinely compute indicators of multidimensional poverty usually based on the access to housing, water, sanitation and education (*NBI* indicators, as per its initials in Spanish).

This section deepens on the measurement of well-being with the Gallup data to other variables beyond income. In particular, it focuses the analysis to household consumption of some services. The Gallup Poll 2006 has information on access to a set of basic services—water and electricity—and to a set of communication and information goods and services: phone (fixed and cellular), TV, computer and Internet.[19]

On average, 92.5 percent of Latin Americans report having access to water in their dwellings or lots.[20] There are differences across income poverty groups: 84.7 percent of the income poor report having access to water.[21] The differences are smaller in the case of electricity: the share of respondents with access is 94.8 percent among the poor and 98.1 percent among the non-poor. The access to water in LAC is higher, on average and for the poor, than in the rest of the developing world. The access to electricity is also relatively high. On average 30 percent of the income poor in LAC have access to a fixed phone. The share of those with a cell phone is similar. There are substantial differences across countries: while about 68 percent of the income poor in Chile have a cell phone, that proportion drops to just 2 percent among the income poor in

---

17. Sen (1984).

18. See Attanasio and Székely (2001).

19. The 2006 wave of the Gallup Poll also contains information on housing ownership and access to sanitation, but only for Honduras and Nicaragua. The 2007 wave contains information on ownership of an automobile, access to cable TV, washing machine, freezer and DVD player. For an extension of the analysis of this section to this set of durables see Gasparini and others (2008).

20. For the full set of statistics on the access to basic services and information goods and services see Gasparini and others (2008).

21. Naturally, propositions like this one are conditional on the methodology adopted to define the income poor.

Honduras. In LAC while 21.4 percent of the non-poor have a personal computer, the proportion drops to 5.4 percent for the poor. Almost 10 percent of respondents have access to Internet in their homes; the share falls to 1 percent in the case of the income poor.

Indices of Non-monetary Multidimensional Deprivation

The key steps in the measurement of multidimensional deprivation are (i) to define the set of variables to be included in the indicator; (ii) to define a structure of weights; and (iii) to set a poverty line.

Regarding the first point, we follow a restricted approach and include the set of goods and services available in the 2006 wave of the Gallup Poll: water, electricity, phone, television, personal computer and Internet. To deal with the second step a conventional factor analysis method is used. This method takes the correlation structure of the chosen variables into account, and, in a way, makes the structure of the weights endogenous.[22] The *factors* that summarize the information contained in the data are obtained by principal component analysis. This method reduces the dimensionality of the problem to a single indicator that allows dividing the population unambiguously into two groups provided a threshold value is set.

This is precisely the third stage. Unfortunately, as in any poverty analysis, the choice of a threshold is highly arbitrary. For comparison with the income poverty approach of the previous section, a poverty line is set in the space of the linear indicator discussed above that implies a share of the LAC population below that threshold equal to the income poverty headcount ratio with the two-dollar line, which is 37.2 percent. Naturally, imposing this threshold implies losing the possibility of comparing aggregate LAC poverty figures across methodologies (which is anyway a debatable goal), but allows to gain in comparability at the country level.

It is important to briefly discuss conceptually the approach outlined above. It is debatable whether this approach really identifies *deprivation* in a meaningful way. After all, the list in step (i) includes some goods that are not really basic needs (for example, computer), and leaves out others that arguably are (for example, food). Moreover, as explained above, the *deprivation line* has nothing to do with any real threshold in needs or capacities. What the approach does is identify relative deprivation in terms of an index based on the consumption and access to some services available in the Gallup Poll. That index could be interpreted as a non-monetary proxy for the individual well-being. People with less access to water, electricity, phone, television, computer and Internet presumably have command over a smaller set of all goods and services available in the economy than the rest of the population, and hence they would have higher chances of attaining lower levels of well-being. They are *deprived,* at least in a relative sense. This limited asset-based

---

22. For an explanation of the methods see Hardle and Simar (2007).

approach is an alternative to the income-based approach implemented in the previous section, where individual well-being is proxied by just the household per capita income.[23]

Now it is possible to compute a one-dimensional index based on the access to water, electricity, telephone, cell phone, personal computer, and Internet in the 2006 Gallup Poll.[24] Table 2-3 shows the headcount ratios based on the index when setting the threshold to generate an aggregate poverty level of 37.2 percent (the LAC income poverty rate). The headcount ratio based on this criterion ranges from 11.7 percent in Chile to 67 percent in Nicaragua. Southern Cone countries, Costa Rica, Jamaica and Colombia have relatively low levels of multidimensional poverty. In the other extreme Nicaragua, Haiti, Paraguay and Honduras rank high in that poverty ladder.[25]

The national household surveys also have information on services and durable goods. That information enables to estimate a one-dimensional index with both the Gallup and the national surveys based on the same set of variables: water, electricity, telephone and personal computer. As in the analysis above, a threshold is chosen to get the same LAC headcount ratio (37.2 percent). Table 2-3 shows the headcount ratios for each country. Multidimensional deprivation ranges from 9.2 percent in Chile to 82 percent in Haiti, using data from household surveys. The correlation across countries with the Gallup data is high, but far from perfect. Paraguay and Mexico, for instance, look too poor according to Gallup. In Paraguay this result is driven by the report of a substantially lower access to water (compared to the household survey), while in Mexico it is due to a lower reported access to telephone and personal computer. In both sources Haiti and Nicaragua rank at the top of the multidimensional deprivation ladder, while Chile and Uruguay rank at the bottom.

Subjective Welfare and Deprivation

As mentioned previously, current income is the most widely used welfare proxy in distributive analysis, mostly due to its wide availability and ease of quantitative cross-country comparisons. Nevertheless, a recent stream of literature has empha-

23. This multidimensional approach will be extended below to consider other variables. Unfortunately, a basic needs approach (NBI) similar to that carried out by some LAC statistical offices cannot be implemented with the Gallup 2006, since information is lacking on almost all relevant variables: housing, sanitation and education.

24. Ownership of a television set was ignored in the index because it is not recorded in the surveys of Brazil, Mexico, and Venezuela. The addition of this variable yields a small and not significant marginal contribution to the index.

25. Since the 2007 wave of the Gallup Poll has information on additional variables (automobile, cable TV, DVD player, washing machine, and freezer) it is possible to extend the analysis to include these assets. The country headcount ratios computed from the new index (forcing again the LAC headcount ratio to be 37.2 percent) are correlated in a positive and significant way with the previous ones, but the correlation is not very high.

Table 2-3. *Multidimensional Deprivation*

	Headcount ratios (percentage of total population)		
	Gallup (i)	Gallup (ii)	Household (iii)
Latin America			
Argentina	19.4	30.7	16.5
Bolivia	52.6	60.1	62.6
Brazil	38.7	36.7	17.2
Chile	11.7	22.6	9.2
Colombia	17.7	24.8	20.1
Costa Rica	19.8	21.5	17.9
Ecuador	27.2	34.4	29.3
El Salvador	37.6	37.3	54.9
Honduras	63.4	65.5	65.2
Mexico	46.0	41.8	14.9
Nicaragua	67.0	59.8	71.0
Panama	31.7	43.0	27.6
Paraguay	63.8	71.7	35.5
Peru	56.9	52.0	44.0
Uruguay	14.6	16.5	12.9
Venezuela	30.0	n.a.	n.a.
The Caribbean			
Dominican Republic	47.0	58.2	38.7
Haiti	64.2	73.1	82.0
Jamaica	15.8	35.7	31.8

Source: Authors' calculations based on microdata from Gallup World Poll (2006) and national household surveys.

n.a. = not available.

Note: Poverty line set to generate a Latin America and the Caribbean (LAC) headcount ratio similar to the LAC income poverty ratio with US$ 2 a day (37.2%).

Column (i) based on access to water, electricity, telephone, cell phone, TV, computer, and Internet at home.

Columns (ii) and (iii) based on access to water, electricity, telephone, and personal computer.

sized the use of alternative and hopefully more realistic measures of welfare, in particular those arising from questions targeted directly at self perceived notions of well-being.

Following Arias and Sosa Escudero (2004), ASE (2004) henceforth, and Ravallion and Lokshin (2002), *objective* assessments of deprivation are any reproducible quantification of this assessment. On the other hand, *subjective* assessments are self-produced classifications where the individual assigns herself into the deprived/non-deprived status based on her own "subjective" perceptions. As an example, take the case of poverty as studied by ASE (2004). Their objective measure of poverty is obtained by comparing current income to a standard official poverty line. Their subjective measure comes directly from a survey question that asks individuals "Do you consider yourself poor/non-poor?" Interviewers are instructed about the subjectivity of the response, and not to interfere with the person interviewed asking for explanations or giving directions on how to answer this question. Individuals are instructed to classify themselves in only one of the groups.

A recurrent finding of this literature is that there exist significant differences between self-rated and objective measures of poverty, which have implications not only on the "true" quantification or characterization of aggregate poverty, but also on the analysis of their determinants.[26] This may have important consequences to the design of programs aimed at poverty alleviation. For example, for the Bolivian case ASE (2004) find that quechua speaking people tend to classify themselves as poor even when income discrepancies within this ethnic group are large. Hence policy measures targeted to low-income individuals may not be supported by this group of people, who perceive that the target should be based on ethnicity. Consequently, one purpose of this section is to study the patterns of similarities and discrepancies between *objective* and *subjective* measures of deprivation using the Gallup Survey.

Besides these discrepancies, there are other interesting results that deserve further empirical clarification. First, an interesting result of this literature is that many indicators like education, ethnic characteristics or place of residence are relevant determinants of subjective poverty. Second, these socioeconomic factors remain significant as determinants of self rated poverty even after controlling for current income, which reflects the fact that the multidimensional nature of deprivation is not appropriately captured by income. Third, even after controlling for a large vector of socioeconomic characteristics available in household surveys (including also income, consumption and assets), unobserved factors play an important role in determining poverty and, in turn, welfare. This speaks about the inherent complexity of characterizing deprivation. Finally, keeping other factors constant, it requires a substantial effort in terms of income compensation to alter significantly the probability of being poor: the effect of income is very mild if other more permanent factors (like family education or ethnicity) remain unmodified.

Subjective Welfare in the Gallup World Poll

Data availability on subjective perceptions of welfare has been a major limitation for the empirical analysis of this topic. Household surveys seldom include such questions and, if so, they appear in supplements for certain periods. Additionally, for political reasons, governmental statistical offices are sometimes reluctant to include subjective questions in official surveys. Consequently, the availability

26. See Ravallion and Lokshin (2002) and ASE (2004).

Table 2-4. *Specific Questions on Subjective Welfare from Gallup World Poll*

Variable code	Question
WP16	Please imagine a ladder/mountain with steps numbered from zero at the bottom to ten at the top. Suppose we say that the top of the ladder/mountain represents the best possible life for you and the bottom of the ladder/mountain represents the worst possible life for you. If the top step is 10 and the bottom step is 0, on which step of the ladder/mountain do you feel you personally stand at the present time?
WP17	Please imagine a ladder/mountain with steps numbered from zero at the bottom to ten at the top. Suppose we say that the top of the ladder/mountain represents the best possible life for you and the bottom of the ladder/mountain represents the worst possible life for you. On which step of the ladder/mountain would you say you stood 5 years ago?
WP18	Please imagine a ladder/mountain with steps numbered from zero at the bottom to ten at the top. Suppose we say that the top of the ladder/mountain represents the best possible life for you and the bottom of the ladder/mountain represents the worst possible life for you. Just your best guess, on which step do you think you will stand on in the future, say 5 years from now?
WP30	Are you satisfied or dissatisfied with your standard of living, all the things you can buy and do?
WP40	Have there been times in the past twelve months when you did not have enough money to buy food that you or your family needed?
WP43	Have there been times in the past twelve months when you did not have enough money to provide adequate shelter or housing for you and your family?
WP44	Have there been times in the past twelve months when you or your family have gone hungry?

Source: Authors' compilation from Gallup World Poll (2006).

of the Gallup survey data opens a much relevant possibility to explore these issues in detail.

Table 2-4 presents a list of some sample questions available in the 2006 Gallup data set that are used in this chapter for self-assessed welfare analysis. Questions WP16, WP17 and WP18 ask individuals to rank themselves ("subjectively") in a 0 to 10 scale, 0 being the worst and 10 the best present (WP16), past (WP17) and future (WP18) level of welfare. Question WP30 asks individuals to state whether they are satisfied or not with their living standard, and questions WP40 and WP43 ask persons whether or not in the last year they felt they lacked enough money to satisfy their food (WP40) or shelter (WP43) needs. Question WP44 asks directly whether or not in the last year they felt hungry. The subjective nature of the answers of these questions is not straightforward, but in all cases questions refer to individuals' perceptions on how they felt or how much they needed (food or shelter, for example). Overall, there is a high rate of response: in most cases above 95 percent.

A summary of the responses to these questions is presented in table 2-5.[27] Consider first question WP16: "*Please imagine a ladder/mountain with steps numbered from zero at the bottom to ten at the top. Suppose we say that the top of the ladder/mountain represents the best possible life for you and the bottom of the ladder/mountain represents the worst possible life for you. If the top step is 10 and the bottom step is 0, on which step of the ladder/mountain do you feel you personally stand at the present time?* The outcome of questions of this sort has been studied extensively in the subjective welfare literature.[28] The average response for LAC is 5.88, with 5.97 for Latin America and 5.50 for the Caribbean. This compares to 7.10 for high-income OECD countries. Interestingly, the average result for LAC is higher than the similar figure for East Asia and Pacific, Europe and Central Asia, Middle East and North Africa, South Asia, and sub-Saharan Africa, the latter with the lowest score (see also figure 2-1).

Question WP17 asks the same as WP16 but with respect to the *past* five years and WP18 with respect to the *future*. Overall, responses are lower when individuals look into the past and higher when they look forward, that is, in comparable scales people feel now better than in the past, and perceive that they will be even better in the future (see figure 2-1 above). In general, most countries obey this pattern, except for the cases of El Salvador and Paraguay, where the ranking is reversed.

Concerning overall satisfaction (question WP30) in Latin America, 67 percent of individuals classify themselves as "satisfied," and the same figure for the Caribbean is 56 percent, with 65 percent the relevant figure for the aggregate LAC region. This compares to 83 percent in high-income OECD countries and 39 percent in sub-Saharan countries, to mention two extreme cases. Compared to other regions of the world, LAC runs behind East Asia and Pacific, Middle East and North Africa, and South Asia, in contrast to the previous case (as measured by question WP16) in which LAC ranks better.

According to question WP40, 66 percent of the individuals in the LAC region declare to have had enough money to purchase food in the last year, a figure to be compared to 91 percent for high-income OECD countries and to 46 percent in the sub-Saharan countries, again the two extreme cases. Once again, LAC runs behind East Asia and Pacific, Middle East and North Africa, South Asia, and now Europe and Central Asia.

Regarding housing needs, differences are milder: 81 percent of the individuals in the LAC region declare to be satisfied in terms of their housing needs, the

27. In the analysis that follows questions WP30, WP40, WP43 and WP44 have been recoded slightly in order to facilitate interpretation and comparison with other questions. All these questions are binary and are recoded so that "1" means satisfied and "0" not-satisfied. For example, question WP30 is left unaltered (1 is satisfied, 0, not satisfied). Question WP40 has been recoded so that 1 actually means "had enough money to buy food" and 0 "had not enough money." Questions WP43 and WP44 were treated similarly.

28. See, for example, Ravallion and Lokshin (2002) for Russia.

Table 2-5. *Basic Descriptive Statistics on Subjective Welfare*[a]

Country	Life satisfaction ladder (WP16)	Life satisfaction ladder (in the past) (WP17)	Life satisfaction ladder (in the future) (WP18)	Living standard satisfaction (WP30)	Enough money to purchase food (WP40)	Enough money for housing (WP43)	Gone hungry (WP44)
	0–10 scale			*Percent of individuals*			
Latin America	**5.97**	**5.64**	**7.19**	**67**	**67**	**81**	**81**
Argentina	6.34	5.70	7.60	66	76	91	89
Bolivia	5.40	4.85	7.05	70	59	73	73
Brazil	6.53	5.66	8.61	67	75	74	n.a.
Chile	6.28	5.89	7.45	70	78	90	87
Colombia	6.06	5.65	7.91	72	68	80	84
Costa Rica	7.09	6.79	7.72	78	73	87	93
Ecuador	5.15	5.29	6.23	67	65	81	76
El Salvador	5.65	5.83	5.49	61	60	85	77
Guatemala	6.07	5.94	6.87	73	77	90	83
Honduras	5.52	4.94	7.11	69	59	76	70
Mexico	6.73	6.27	7.69	72	67	81	n.a.
Nicaragua	5.07	5.00	6.25	63	56	76	71
Panama	6.24	5.61	8.12	64	69	83	85
Paraguay	4.84	5.64	5.17	46	64	86	85
Peru	5.07	4.62	6.75	53	53	77	71
Uruguay	5.66	5.60	6.83	60	72	88	89
Venezuela	7.32	6.23	8.47	81	59	64	n.a.
The Caribbean	**5.50**	**5.13**	**7.23**	**56**	**62**	**78**	**70**
Cuba	5.46	4.73	7.09	n.a.	n.a.	n.a.	n.a.
Dominican Republic	5.21	4.71	7.76	57	53	79	66
Haiti	3.81	4.10	5.09	40	37	41	25
Jamaica	6.31	5.23	8.29	53	75	93	79
Puerto Rico	6.62	7.02	7.41	79	74	83	94
Trinidad and Tobago	5.76	5.68	7.32	51	75	91	87

(continued)

Table 2-5. *Basic Descriptive Statistics on Subjective Welfare*[a] *(continued)*

Country	Life satisfaction ladder (WP16)	Life satisfaction ladder (in the past) (WP17)	Life satisfaction ladder (in the future) (WP18)	Living standard satisfaction (WP30)	Enough money to purchase food (WP40)	Enough money for housing (WP43)	Gone hungry (WP44)
	0–10 scale			*Percent of individuals*			
Latin America and the Caribbean	**5.88**	**5.54**	**7.19**	**65**	**66**	**81**	**79**
High income: OECD	7.10	6.56	7.60	83	91	92	98
High income: non-OECD	6.36	6.06	7.19	76	89	91	95
Low income	4.45	3.91	6.52	48	54	72	58
Lower middle income	4.97	4.51	6.47	58	69	77	83
Upper middle income	5.69	5.37	6.81	55	74	82	89
Other							
East Asia and Pacific	5.62	5.06	6.84	74	78	82	92
Europe and Central Asia	5.11	4.79	6.22	48	76	79	93
Middle East and North Africa	5.29	4.92	6.69	71	82	84	93
North America	7.36	6.55	8.12	82	90	94	n.a.
South Asia	5.03	4.26	6.68	73	75	77	75
Sub-Saharan Africa	4.24	3.75	6.50	39	46	73	51
Western Europe	7.18	6.66	7.63	86	91	91	99

Source: Authors' calculations based on data from Gallup World Poll (2006).

n.a. = not available.

a. WP refers to question number in the Gallup World Poll 2006 questionnaire. OECD = Organization for Economic Cooperation and Development.

Note: After dropping the "Don't know" and "Refused" responses, there are no observations left for Cuba in questions WP30, WP40, WP43, WP44, and for Brazil, North America, and Venezuela in question WP44. There are no income data for Africa, Asia, and OECD countries.

Figure 2-1. *Current, Past and Future Life Satisfaction*

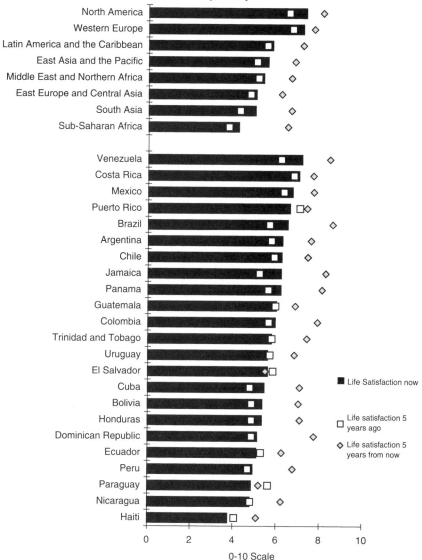

0-10 Scale

Source: Authors' calculations based on Gallup World Poll (2006).

extreme cases being now 92 percent in the rich OECD countries and 73 percent in the sub-Saharan countries. Now LAC performs better along this dimension than Europe and Central Asia, South Asia, and sub-Saharan Africa.

To summarize, in overall terms LAC performs like a country in the upper middle income group in terms of aggregate satisfaction, and a similar result holds in terms of satisfaction with housing needs. In line with most regions, individuals perceive an improvement and are optimistic, in the sense that they perceive to be better off in the future compared to the present and the past. It is in terms of food needs that LAC countries decline in this overall ranking and now compare to a low middle income country. This is an important result, since it suggests that LAC inhabitants either value basic needs other than food high or are more satisfied in other dimensions (housing, for example), in order to compensate for its low performance in terms of food needs, so that they end up placed in an intermediate position in the aggregate.

Cross-country comparisons within the LAC region are revealing (see figure 2-1 again). In terms of present and past welfare (questions WP16 and WP17) Venezuela, Costa Rica, Mexico and Puerto Rico rank the highest. Haiti, Peru and the Dominican Republic rank in the bottom. Regarding the future, Brazil now ranks clearly in the top of the distribution, a considerable change compared to its intermediate position when individuals are asked about their situation five years ago. Another extreme case is Paraguay: its inhabitants rank themselves in an intermediate situation when asked about the past and place themselves in the extreme bottom of the distribution when asked about the present and the future. The rankings induced by the overall satisfaction question (WP30) are consistent with the previous results.

Results regarding question WP40 (food) are striking. Now Chile, Guatemala and Argentina rank in the top, with Haiti, Peru and the Dominican Republic with the worst performance. That is, the bottom of the distribution remains comparable to that induced by overall welfare notions, but the top of the distribution changes, so the first positions are now occupied by countries previously in an intermediate position. The most interesting case is that of Venezuela, which is systematically ranked in the top when overall welfare is studied, while in terms of food needs it ranks in the bottom.

In terms of housing, Jamaica performs the best followed by Argentina, Trinidad and Tobago and Chile, that is, the same group ranked in the top in terms of food needs, so similar remarks as in the previous paragraph hold. The cases of Brazil and Venezuela are of considerable attention. Both countries rank extremely high in terms of overall satisfaction and are placed in the bottom when housing needs are considered.

Subjective Welfare and Deprivation

The next natural step is to construct deprivation measures based on subjective assessments of welfare. The methodological concerns that arise when translating income into poverty hold when trying to classify individuals into "deprived/non-deprived" status, in the sense that the transition between these two situations occurs in a discontinuous fashion when using an underlying continuous welfare measure. In the case of income-based poverty, this is usually performed by comparing income to a "poverty line" that separates the poor from the non-poor.

In order to produce similar classifications based on a welfare index, it is important to keep in mind some features of the distribution of responses to welfare questions. Table 2-6 presents the cumulative proportion of responses to the question that referred to present welfare on a 0 to 10 scale. A striking feature is that, with the exception of Haiti, step 5 seems to be a "modal" response: step 5 concentrates a rather large proportion of respondents, and this proportion is substantially higher than responses in adjacent steps (4 or 6). For LAC as a whole, 24.5 percent of the interviewed individuals position themselves in step 5, with 9 percent and 11.4 percent in immediately adjacent steps. Even when faced with an ordinal scale, individuals tend to converge to a "focal" midpoint. This feature complicates separating the "deprived" from the "non-deprived" since certain values induce large jumps in the cumulative distribution of welfare and hence the discrimination between these two groups is expected to be sensitive to the choice of the appropriate welfare threshold.

In order to compare objective with subjective deprivation it is convenient to use the *cumulative* responses up to each step. The overall poverty rate based on the two-dollar line is 37.2 percent. The steps that more closely accumulate this proportion of individuals in the subjective scale are the 4th and the 5th, that is, 25 percent of the individuals self rate in steps 4 or below, and 49.9 percent in steps 5 or below (see table 2-6). Therefore, step 4 (or 5) can be taken as an approximate subjective poverty line for the region.

Based on this threshold, the proportion of individuals that rank themselves in steps 4 (or 5) or below could be considered the subjective-based poverty rate of each country. The last three columns of the table present the position of each country in the rankings induced by the objective (two-dollar line) and subjective poverty measurements (steps 4 and 5). For example, Costa Rica is ranked 4th and 1st in the objective and subjective ranking, respectively. Bolivia ranks 15th in objective terms and 12th when the subjective ranking is used (step 4).

Another more straightforward alternative to define the deprived is to rely directly on binary variables in the Gallup Poll. Consequently, from this point of view we consider as "deprived" those individuals that declare to be dissatisfied with their living standard (WP30), food purchases (WP40) and housing (WP43). Question WP44, which asks individuals whether they went hungry in the recent past, is surely interesting and very relevant, but is plagued with non-responses: in fact, it is not available for countries like Brazil, Mexico and Venezuela. Nevertheless, we also incorporate this question into the analysis. Results are summarized in table 2-7.

Income-based poverty in the LAC region is 37.2 percent. Answers related to self-perceived welfare as measured by question WP16 leave 23.4 percent (using step 4 as the threshold) and 49.5 percent (using step 5) of respondents below the threshold, the average between these two figures being 36.5 percent. The propor-

Table 2-6. *Cumulative Distribution of Subjective Welfare*

Country	Headcount income[a]	Answers to Question WP16											Ranking by poverty income[b]	Ranking by 4th step[b]	Ranking by 5th step[b]
		0	1	2	3	4	5	6	7	8	9	10			
Latin America	0.4	2.8	5.0	8.5	15.1	23.9	49.5	60.9	73.4	86.2	91.0	100	n.a.	n.a.	n.a.
Argentina	0.2	1.1	2.2	4.5	7.9	13.6	35.1	48.7	70.2	89.9	95.6	100	3	2	5
Bolivia	0.6	1.5	2.7	5.5	11.7	23.0	60.8	77.7	86.9	95.6	97.3	100	15	12	15
Brazil	0.3	2.0	3.4	6.6	10.3	15.4	34.3	43.8	58.3	77.9	84.2	100	6	3	2
Chile	0.2	1.1	3.6	6.0	10.0	18.6	45.0	58.3	73.9	86.6	90.7	100	2	8	8
Colombia	n.a.	2.1	4.7	7.7	14.2	22.0	45.4	55.0	70.5	85.6	90.4	100	n.a.	10	9
Costa Rica	0.3	0.8	1.8	2.0	4.7	8.8	24.8	36.5	51.6	74.7	85.7	100	4	1	1
Ecuador	0.5	3.5	8.6	14.5	23.6	35.4	65.7	75.3	84.1	92.2	94.6	100	11	16	16
El Salvador	0.6	1.5	3.4	6.9	13.8	24.4	52.4	66.1	78.1	89.6	93.7	100	16	13	13
Guatemala	0.5	1.5	2.3	4.3	9.9	19.3	50.5	63.5	76.4	89.0	93.1	100	12	9	11
Mexico	0.4	0.7	1.9	4.3	9.7	16.7	34.5	45.1	58.9	79.1	91.1	100	9	4	3
Panama	0.3	2.7	3.6	5.9	10.4	18.1	44.6	57.8	71.6	83.4	89.2	100	8	6	7
Paraguay	0.5	3.2	6.1	12.5	22.5	35.2	76.9	84.7	92.4	96.1	97.4	100	13	15	18
Peru	0.6	4.9	8.3	15.1	26.1	39.9	68.0	79.0	87.7	94.2	95.8	100	14	18	17
Uruguay	0.3	2.8	4.9	7.0	13.7	22.0	47.5	60.4	77.3	91.3	94.5	100	5	14	12
Venezuela	0.3	2.9	3.8	4.8	7.9	11.5	27.3	36.9	49.5	65.6	73.0	100	7	11	10
The Caribbean	0.5	4.1	7.7	12.9	21.5	31.9	53.5	66.0	77.7	87.6	92.0	100	n.a.	n.a.	n.a.
Dominican Republic	0.5	10.4	15.3	21.0	29.7	37.3	58.2	67.5	74.8	84.1	88.3	100	10	17	14
Haiti	0.8	2.0	8.4	26.9	48.3	67.9	83.8	91.4	96.2	99.0	100.0	100	17	19	19
Jamaica	n.a.	0.4	0.9	2.1	8.8	18.3	34.5	53.7	76.3	88.2	95.5	100	n.a.	7	4
Puerto Rico	0.1	3.8	6.8	8.6	11.8	17.0	36.3	43.9	57.1	72.7	80.2	100	1	5	6
Latin America and the Caribbean	0.4	3.0	5.4	9.2	16.0	25.0	49.9	61.7	73.8	86.4	91.1	100			

Source: Authors' calculations based on data from Gallup World Poll (2006).

n.a. = not available.

a. Headcount income units are the percentage of the toal population that falls below the US$2 per day (purchasing power parity) poverty line.

b. Ranking among the countries on the country column for which data is available.

Table 2-7. *Subjective and Income-Based Poverty*[a]

Country	Headcount ratio based on income (percentage of people out of total population)	Best possible life (WP16)	Living standard satisfaction (WP30)	Money to buy food (WP40)	Money to provide housing (WP43)	Have not gone hungry (WP44)	Poverty by 5th step of WP16
Latin America	**36.5**	**21.7**	**33.2**	**33.0**	**18.6**	**18.8**	**49.5**
Argentina	22.9	14.1	34.3	24.4	8.9	11.3	35.1
Bolivia	58.8	22.3	29.6	40.7	27.3	27.1	60.8
Brazil	25.7	17.2	33.3	25.5	26.2	n.a.	34.3
Chile	22.0	15.8	30.1	22.0	9.6	13.4	45.0
Colombia	n.a.	21.3	27.9	32.4	20.4	15.9	45.4
Costa Rica	25.4	8.8	22.4	26.5	12.6	7.4	24.8
Ecuador	45.8	33.1	32.7	34.7	18.7	23.8	65.7
El Salvador	60.5	25.4	39.1	39.6	14.7	23.4	52.4
Guatemala	50.3	16.4	27.0	23.3	10.0	17.3	50.5
Mexico	43.3	14.3	27.8	33.1	19.1	n.a.	34.5
Panama	32.6	16.9	35.8	30.8	16.7	14.6	44.6
Paraguay	54.9	33.9	53.9	35.8	13.9	15.1	76.9
Peru	57.8	34.2	46.7	46.8	22.7	29.0	68.0
Uruguay	25.6	24.3	40.2	27.7	11.9	11.2	47.5
Venezuela	28.8	10.1	19.2	41.0	36.3	n.a.	27.3

(continued)

Table 2-7. *Subjective and Income-Based Poverty*[a] *(continued)*

Country	Headcount ratio based on income (percentage of people out of total population)	Best possible life (WP16)	Living standard satisfaction (WP30)	Money to buy food (WP40)	Money to provide housing (WP43)	Have not gone hungry (WP44)	Poverty by 5th step of WP16
The Caribbean	**54.9**	**30.7**	**43.8**	**38.4**	**22.1**	**30.1**	**53.6**
Dominican Republic	45.4	36.0	43.0	46.6	20.6	33.7	58.2
Haiti	82.9	67.2	60.1	63.2	59.0	75.5	83.8
Jamaica	17.8	16.2	46.7	25.1	7.2	20.8	34.5
Puerto Rico	9.4	17.0	21.3	25.9	16.7	5.5	36.3
Latin America and the Caribbean	**37.2**	**23.4**	**34.8**	**33.8**	**19.1**	**20.8**	**49.9**

Source: Authors' calculations based on microdata from Gallup World Poll (2006).

n.a. = not available.

a. WP refers to the variable number in the Gallup World Poll 2006 dataset.

Note: Cuba and Trinidad and Tobago were not included because after dropping the "Don't know" and "Refused" responses there were no observations left for Cuba in questions WP30, WP40, WP43, WP44, and there is not an income poverty line available for Trinidad and Tobago. After dropping the "Don't know" and "Refused" responses, there are no observations left for Brazil, Mexico, and Venezuela in question WP44.

tions of individuals dissatisfied with their general living standard (WP30) and with food (WP40) are, respectively, 34.8 percent and 33.8 percent.

These are aggregate measures, and within regions they may induce different classifications. For example, in Latin America the headcount-based poverty rate is 36.5 percent, higher than that induced by the proportion of dissatisfied individuals according to question WP30 (average of 33.2 percent). At the country level, the greatest positive disparities appear in the cases of Bolivia and Haiti for Latin America and the Caribbean, respectively. In each of these countries, the income poverty headcount ratio is much larger than the proportion of unsatisfied individuals.

Finally, it is worth mentioning some basic socio-demographic characteristics of the poor. Table 2-8 presents an (unconditional) profile of the poor for the aggregate LAC region, for all the alternative poverty classifications used in this section. We start by splitting the population in age groups and count the proportion of poor in each sub-group. A first relevant result is that the age profile for income-based poverty is clearly decreasing, that is, as we move into older groups poverty decreases, with figures ranging from 39 percent in the youngest partition (16 to 25 years old) to 36 percent in the older group. When we consider poverty as it arises from answers to question WP16 (overall present satisfaction, below step 4), the pattern is clearly *increasing*: the youngest group has a poverty rate of 19 percent and the oldest group 31 percent. The remaining dimensions present an increasing pattern except for the oldest group, where poverty decreases. The next line computes the mean age of the poor and non-poor. Now differences are smaller. In income-based poverty the poor are 38 years old on average while the non-poor are 40, slightly older. This pattern gets reversed for all other dimensions, the poor being slightly older than the non-poor. The largest difference in age appears in the case of poverty as measured by question WP16, where the difference in age is significant: 42.1 years old for the non-poor and 37.9 for the poor.

This reversion in the poverty-age profile when taking the subjective dimension of deprivation into consideration is an important result for the long-standing debate on the measurement of old-age poverty, which bears relevant implications on the targeting of social policies.[29]

Considering the income poverty measure, 42 percent of the poor are male, compared to 47 percent of the non-poor. This poverty bias against females is in part due to a higher share of female-headed households among the poor. If the mother lives with her children, and the father lives alone, it is more likely for the mother to be income poor, at least when measuring poverty with per capita income. It is interesting to notice that this bias against women also holds in terms of some subjective variables related to food consumption (money to buy food, and hunger), but not in terms of general satisfaction.

---

29. See Deaton and Paxson (1998) and Gasparini and others (2007) for the LAC case.

Table 2-8. *Subjective-Based Poverty Profiles in Latin America and the Caribbean*[a]

	Headcount ratio based on income		Best possible life (WP16)		Living standard satisfaction (WP30)		Money to buy food (WP40)		Money to provide housing (WP43)		Have not gone hungry (WP44)	
	Poor	Non-poor	Poor	Non-poor	Poor	Non-poor	Poor	Non-poor	Poor	Non-poor	Poor	Non-poor
Population share by age												
16–25	39	61	19	81	30	70	30	70	16	84	19	81
26–40	41	59	25	75	39	61	36	64	19	81	23	77
41–64	35	65	29	71	41	59	37	63	18	82	21	79
65+	36	64	31	69	34	66	32	68	15	85	19	81
Age (mean)	38.2	39.9	42.1	37.9	40.1	38.3	39.6	38.6	39.0	39.0	39.2	38.9
Share males	42	47	46	45	46	45	43	46	44	45	44	46
Family size	5.0	3.9	4.5	4.2	4.4	4.2	4.6	4.1	4.6	4.2	4.6	4.2
Children under 12 years old	2.1	1.1	1.6	1.4	1.6	1.4	1.7	1.3	1.7	1.4	1.7	1.4
Water	0.79	0.94	0.81	0.91	0.84	0.91	0.82	0.92	0.80	0.91	0.77	0.92
Employed	0.36	0.48	0.38	0.44	0.42	0.42	0.39	0.44	0.40	0.43	0.37	0.43

Source: Authors' calculations based on microdata from Gallup World Poll (2006).
a. WP refers to the variable number in the Gallup World Poll 2006 dataset.

As expected, family sizes are larger among the poor, but differences are small, the largest case being the one associated to income-based poverty: the poor with a family size of five members as compared with less than four in the case of the non-poor. This difference becomes much smaller when all other poverty dimensions are considered. Regarding children under 12, the poor differ significantly from the non-poor, based on income poverty: the poor have on average 2.1 children, which is almost *twice* the average of the non-poor (1.1). Similar differences, once again, are milder when comparing poor vs. non-poor along other dimensions. For example, figures are 1.7 and 1.3 for the classification based on food purchases.

This result is again important for the poverty and social policy debate. In particular, it implies that means-tested targeting schemes based on household per capita income, or directly the number of children, may imply significant biases when other dimensions of deprivation are considered.

In summary, income poverty seems to be more clearly related to socioeconomic characteristics, that is, the poor and non-poor differ more significantly than when compared along other "subjective" notions of deprivation. Nevertheless, poverty profiles have several elements in common along the different deprivation dimensions. This is compatible with two facts. First, as previous literature has suggested, subjective and objective (income based) notions obey systematic patterns and hence are predictable from its basic determinants.[30] Second, both objective and subjective welfare, though systematic, are difficult concepts that bear a similar significant relation to some basic determinants (age profiles, socioeconomic structure, etc.), in spite of the fact that a large proportion of the variability still depends on difficult-to-measure variables, like social capital or other idiosyncratic individual and country-specific factors. The fact that these notions coincide along some dimensions is surely encouraging and suggests that the study of subjective welfare may add relevant systematic information not captured by income. This line of reasoning is explored in more detail in the following section.

The Dimensionality of Deprivation

The underlying method up to now has been the following: first a relevant welfare notion is identified, variables in the survey are associated to a particular notion, and then a statistical method is used to produce an aggregate index that is later used to classify individuals into the "poor/non-poor" status.

A natural question to ask at this point is which is the "dimensionality" of welfare and hence of deprivation? In an extreme case there is a single underlying notion of welfare, and from this point of view all questions related to welfare are

---

30. Ravallion and Lokshin (2002) and Arias and Sosa Escudero (2004).

seen as proxies that differ among themselves due to measurement errors and to their degree of accuracy with respect to the unobserved, single-dimensional welfare concept. In the opposite extreme case, welfare is a truly multidimensional concept that cannot be appropriately captured by any single notion. Hence, from this point of view, questions related to welfare may be summarizing a particular dimension or several of them.

In this section, a more agnostic approach is taken that explores directly the problem of dimensionality of welfare. This approach starts by looking at most variables involved in the previous sections, but without clustering them into groups, with the goal of asking how many relevant underlying dimensions of welfare they represent. Most of the variables are indeed highly correlated. For example, question WP16, which asks about present welfare, is obviously correlated with the same question but refers to the past (WP17) and the future (WP18). Having a personal computer or Internet access at home is also highly correlated with income. However, in spite of these relevant correlations, with this information it is hard to find obvious patterns among so many variables.

An alternative is to focus on the correlations among the summary welfare indicators constructed in the previous sections. This is achieved by looking at household per capita income, the standardized index of non-monetary welfare, and a similar index of subjective welfare constructed from the variables used in the previous section.[31] Correlations are, again, significant, but far from perfect. The correlation between income and the index of non-monetary welfare is 0.46, while that between subjective welfare and non-monetary welfare is 0.35. The lowest correlation is between subjective welfare and income (0.28). These results are consistent with previous literature, in the sense that subjective notions of welfare are statistically correlated with income, even though this correlation is low. The significant correlation discards the (sometimes) claimed idea that subjective welfare measures highly idiosyncratic factors that do not obey systematic patterns. But the low correlation suggests that income accounts for a considerable part of the variation in welfare.[32]

A final exercise to explore the dimensionality of welfare is to rely on a factor analytic model, using all the variables considered separately in the three approaches.[33] To that end, principal component analysis is used, taking all variables, for all the countries in the Latin American and Caribbean region. Results

---

31. The first principal component of variables WP16, WP17, WP18, WP30, and WP40 is used.

32. As a robustness check, similar correlations were computed for low- and high-income individuals. Overall, correlations are smaller when the sample is split, but results remain qualitatively unchanged: correlations, though smaller, are significantly different from zero. The pairwise correlations between subjective welfare and non-monetary or income measures are virtually identical in both groups. Interestingly, the correlation between non-monetary welfare and income is higher for richer individuals.

33. The technical details are explained in Gasparini and others (2008).

Table 2-9. *Factor Analysis Results*

Variable	Factor 1	Factor 2	Factor 3	Uniqueness
Best possible life (WP16)	0.12	0.86	0.09	0.25
Life satisfaction ladder (in the past) (WP17)	0.07	0.53	0.10	0.71
Life satisfaction ladder (in the future) (WP18)	0.08	0.77	0.00	0.39
Living standard satisfaction (WP30)	−0.08	−0.48	−0.13	0.74
Money to buy food (WP40)	0.22	0.32	0.29	0.76
Income in $US purchasing power parity	0.65	0.16	0.11	0.54
Access to water	0.06	0.11	0.72	0.47
Access to electricity	0.01	0.01	0.76	0.42
Access to phone(s)	0.40	0.12	0.49	0.58
Access to personal computer	0.82	0.08	0.09	0.32
Access to Internet	0.84	0.06	−0.01	0.28
Access to cell phone	0.40	0.20	0.14	0.78

Source: Authors' calculations based on data from Gallup World Poll (2006).

are shown in table 2-9.[34] Each coefficient represents how each variable is weighted in each factor, and hence higher values represent variables relatively more important in the factor.

Factor interpretation is usually idiosyncratic, but the results obtained suggest very clear patterns. The first factor relies on income and assets that bear a strong relation with income, like having a cellular or regular phone or a personal computer. This is the factor that best represents all the variables. The second factor focuses on the subjective questions; variables weakly correlated with income that still retain relevant information regarding welfare that cannot be accounted for by income. Finally, the last factor seems to capture very basic needs, related to having access to water or electricity.

Therefore, a simple factor analytic model suggests that welfare can be appropriately summarized by three orthogonal dimensions. Strikingly, the first one is precisely captured by income. This is an interesting result since it speaks about the importance of income-based assessments of welfare status. Nevertheless, the relevance of the two other factors also shows that welfare is a truly multidimensional phenomenon that cannot be fully captured by income. The second factor can be labeled as the "subjective factor." The fact that all subjective variables are strongly related among themselves and that they load similarly on the same factor suggests

34. Using the standard rule of retaining factors associated to Eigen values greater than one, the method indicates that the 12 variables considered can be appropriately summarized by three orthogonal factors, the three factors accounting for 0.48 of the total variability. It is well known that factor estimates ("loadings") are unique up to orthogonal transformations (Johnson and Wichern, 1998), and hence it is standard practice to use particular rotations that help interpret the obtained factors. A varimax rotation of the three retained factors is used in this study, the results of which are shown in the table.

that some average of them may well represent this dimension of welfare. Finally, the third factor, which can be labeled as "basic needs," suggests that notions of welfare arising from standard "unsatisfied basic needs" methods, that include the access to basic services like water or electricity, may add relevant information not necessarily captured by income.

Assessing the Adequacy of Income-based Poverty Lines with Subjective Information

Income-based poverty lines are usually constructed by "inverting" expenditure patterns, that is, a consumption basket is exogenously determined and individuals who cannot afford this basket are rendered as poor. If the relationship between expenditures and income is tight enough, then poverty classifications based on income and expenditures should not differ considerably.

In order to quantify the adequacy of income-based poverty lines, a simple exercise is inverting subjective welfare levels in order to find income thresholds that can be used to separate the poor from the non-poor. To be precise, consider a simple example, given by question WP30 in the 2006 Gallup Poll, which asks individuals whether they are "*satisfied or dissatisfied with your standard of living, all the things you can buy and do.*" The goal of the exercise is to find the income level that best separates the "not-satisfied" from the "satisfied": this will be our implicit poverty line.

More concretely, let p be the probability that an individual classifies herself as "satisfied" given her level of income y, and assume that these magnitudes are linked through a simple possibly non-linear relation $p = G(y)$, where $G(\ )$ is an unknown function.

The implicit poverty line is the income level that makes an individual indifferent between classifying herself as "satisfied" and "non-satisfied." Suppose that individuals classify themselves as satisfied if given their income, $p > p^*$, where p^* is a probability threshold that distinguishes the satisfied from the non-satisfied. Then, the implicit poverty line y^p is the level of income that solves $y^p = G^{-1}(p^*)$.

In order to implement this exercise, an observable binary variable s has to be specified that classifies individuals into "satisfied" and "unsatisfied," and their incomes. Since s is a Bernoulli variable, $E(s) = p = G(y)$. Then, the unknown $G(y)$ function can be estimated through a non-parametric regression estimator without assuming a possibly unrealistic functional form.[35]

---

35. A lowess estimator is used, which is a robustified local polynomial regression. Basically, an initial local polynomial non-parametric regression is fit using standard k-nearest neighborhood methods, and then it is iteratively robustified (in the sense of making it resistant to outliers) by reweighing observations. See Cleveland (1993) for an intuitive expositions, or Hardle (1990, pp. 192–93) for a description of the algorithm.

To implement this, framework questions WP30 (satisfaction with living standard) and WP40 (having enough money to buy food) are used, while y is household per capita income (in dollars adjusted by purchasing power differentials). Based on this information, the corresponding $G(y)$ functions are estimated non-parametrically.

The choice of the cutoff point is surely arbitrary. A natural choice is to adopt the standard practice of fixing it to the proportion of cases for which the binary indicator is equal to 1 (proportion of satisfied individuals), labeled in the literature as the "base rate." This is a common practice in probit-logit analysis and has been suggested by several authors as a "fair" choice.[36] It is also common to use 0.5 as a cutoff, that is to predict that an individual is "satisfied" if the predicted probability of satisfied is greater than that of not being satisfied. A problem with this second choice is that in the case of question WP30 it implies an out-of-range prediction. More precisely, in the case of food satisfaction (WP40) the proportion of satisfied individuals among those with zero income is 0.41, while the proportion corresponding to those satisfied in general terms (WP30) among the zero income group is 0.59. These figures can be taken as raw estimates of the intercepts of the probability functions G( ), and then 0.41 and 0.59 are the minimum values of probabilities of satisfaction where each model implicitly operates.

The implicit income poverty line for food satisfaction is US$37 when the probability cutoff is 0.5, and US$163 when the cutoff is set at 0.659 (the unconditional proportion of satisfied individuals). A comparable figure for overall satisfaction (WP30) is US$177.

It is interesting to notice that the widely used one-dollar-a-day line is equivalent to a monthly income of US$32.7.[37] That figure is very close to our estimate of the implicit poverty line associated to the question on food satisfaction with $p^* = 0.5$ (that is, monthly US$37). From this analysis the one-dollar-a-day threshold would be a reasonable poverty line to measure and analyze food deprivation. Instead, the other two implicit lines of the table are close to five dollars a day, that is, values much higher than the typical two-dollar line used to analyze moderate poverty.

Concluding Remarks

This chapter has provided evidence on the multiple dimensions of deprivation in Latin America and the Caribbean by exploiting a new dataset, the Gallup World Poll. In particular, levels and patterns of income, multidimensional nonmonetary, and subjective deprivation were estimated for all countries in the

---

36. See Menard (2000) for a detailed discussion on prediction and classification in binary choice models.

37. That is, 1.0763 a day times 30.42 days. See Chen and Ravallion (2007) for details.

region based on Gallup data, and the results compared with those from household surveys.

Since the Gallup Poll has the same questionnaire in all the countries in the world, it provides a unique opportunity to carry out a truly international analysis of social issues. However, some inconsistencies arise when comparing statistics drawn from the Gallup Poll to those obtained from national household surveys. The cross-country correlations of variables between Gallup and other information sources are almost always positive and significant, but some linear and rank correlations are too low from an economic point of view, often due to the presence of dubious estimates for some countries in the Gallup Poll. However, the Gallup Poll is a worthwhile source for international comparisons, promising future improvements in the quality of the survey in some countries. Some of the Gallup Poll's questions could turn it into an essential source for international research.

The Gallup World Poll includes a question on monthly total household income before taxes. Based on that, a measure of household per capita income was constructed and an income-poverty analysis was carried out. According to Gallup data, Puerto Rico and Cuba, the Southern Cone, and Costa Rica have economies with relatively low income-poverty levels, while some Andean and Central American countries are in the other extreme of the ranking. Haiti stands up as the economy with the highest incidence of income poverty in the region.

On average, poverty in the Gallup Poll is 16 points higher than in national household surveys when using the two-dollar poverty line. However, the poverty ranking that arises from the two alternative data sources turns out to be similar.

The measurement of well-being with the Gallup data was extended to other variables beyond income. In particular, this chapter focused the analysis in household consumption of some services. To reduce the dimensionality of the problem to a single indicator, we relied on conventional factor analysis. Southern Cone countries, Costa Rica and Venezuela have relatively low levels of multidimensional deprivation. In the other Central American countries, Paraguay, Haiti and Cuba ranked high on that poverty ladder.

The Gallup World Poll provides an opportunity to explore the issues of subjective welfare and deprivation in detail. We find that the rank correlation between income and subjective poverty is positive and significant, suggesting that subjective-based poverty is significantly related to its objective counterpart. On the other hand, the correlation is far from high, suggesting that income represents only part of a more complex, multidimensional structure behind welfare.

In several countries income poverty is lower among the elderly. However, in some dimensions older people feel more deprived than younger people. Also, family size is larger among the income poor, but the gap becomes substantially narrower when other poverty dimensions are considered. These results are important for the poverty and social policy debate. In particular, they imply that means-tested targeting schemes based on household per capita income or the number of children may imply significant biases when other dimensions of deprivation are considered.

The exploratory analysis derived from a simple factor analytic model suggests that welfare can be appropriately summarized by three dimensions. The first one is precisely captured by income, the second one by an average of the subjective welfare measures, and the third one by variables associated to "basic needs" (water, electricity). This is an interesting result as, on the one hand, it speaks about the importance of income-based assessments of welfare status, and, on the other, it shows that welfare is a truly multidimensional phenomenon that cannot be fully captured by income.

References

Arias, O., and W. Sosa Escudero. 2004. "Subjective and Objective Poverty in Bolivia." *2005 World Bank Bolivia Poverty Assessment.*

Attanasio, O., and M. Székely, eds. 2001. *Portrait of the Poor: An Assets-based Approach.* Washington, D.C.: IADB.

Bourguignon, F., N. Lustig, and F. Ferreira. 2004. *The Microeconomics of Income Distribution Dynamics.* Oxford University Press.

Brandolini, A., and G. D'Alessio. 1998. "Measuring Well-Being in the Functioning Space." General Conference of the International Association for Research in Income and Wealth, Cracow, Poland.

CEDLAS. 2007. A Guide to SEDLAC (www.depeco.econo.unlp.edu.ar/cedlas/sedlac).

Chen, S., and M. Ravallion. 2007. "Absolute Poverty Measures for the Developing World, 1981–2004." *PNAS* 104 (43): 16757–62.

Cleveland, W. 1993. *Visualizing Data.* Summit, N.J.: Hobart Press.

Deaton, A. 1997. *The analysis of household surveys. Microeconomic analysis for development policy.* Washington D.C.: World Bank.

———. 2003. "How to Monitor Poverty for the Millennium Development Goals." Working paper. Research Program in Development Studies. Princeton University.

———. 2007. "Income, Aging, Health and Wellbeing around the World: Evidence from the Gallup World Poll." Mimeo, Princeton University.

Deaton, A., and C. Paxson. 1998. "Poverty among the Elderly." In D. Wise, ed. *Inquiries in the Economics of Aging.* Chicago University Press for the National Bureau of Economic Research.

Gallup Poll. 2006. Gallup World Poll. Available at www.gallup.com/consulting/worldpoll/24046/about.aspx.

———. 2007. Gallup World Poll. Available at www.gallup.com/consulting/worldpoll/24046/about.aspx.

Gasparini, L., J. Alejo, F. Haimovich, S. Olivieri, and L. Tornarolli. 2007. "Poverty among the Elderly in Latin America and the Caribbean." Background paper for the *World Economic and Social Survey 2007.* The World Ageing Situation.

Gasparini, L., W. Sosa Escudero, M. Marchionni, and S. Olivieri. 2008. "Income, Deprivation, and Perceptions in Latin America and the Caribbean: New Evidence from the Gallup World Poll." CEDLAS, Universidad Nacional de La Plata.

Hardle, W. 1990. *Applied Non-parametric Regression.* Cambridge University Press.

Hardle, W., and L. Simar. 2007. *Applied Multivariate Statistical Analysis.* New York: Springer.

Johnson, R. A., and D. W. Wichern. 1998. *Applied Multivariate Analysis,* 4th ed. Englewood Cliffs, N.J.: Prentice Hall.

Menard, S. 2000. "Coefficients of Determination for Multiple Logistic Regression Analysis." *American Statistician* 54 (1): 17–24.

Osberg, L., and A. Sharpe. 2005. "How Should We Measure Well-being?" *Review of Income and Wealth* 51.

Ravallion, M., G. Datt, and D. van de Walle. 1991. "Quantifying Absolute Poverty in the Developing World." *Review of Income and Wealth* 37: 345–61.

Ravallion, M., and M. Lokshin. 2002. "Self-rated Economic Welfare in Russia." *Economic Review* 46: 1453–73.

Sen, A. 1984. "Rights and Capabilities." In A. Sen, ed., *Resources, Values and Development.* Oxford: Basil Blackwell.

———. 2000. "Social Justice and the Distribution of Income." In *Handbook of Income Distribution,* pp. 60–81. Amsterdam: Elsevier Science.

World Bank. 2004. *World Development Indicators.* Washington D.C.

3

The Conflictive Relationship between Satisfaction and Income

EDUARDO LORA AND JUAN CAMILO CHAPARRO

Income is the most revered variable in economics. At an aggregate level, the total income generated in a country is a measure of the size of its economy. Per capita income reflects the conditions of productivity and the purchasing power of the population, and the growth rate of this variable is the yardstick by which the material progress of a country is usually measured. On an individual level, personal disposable income represents the range of options that individuals have available to achieve maximum satisfaction. According to conventional economic theory, each increase in income makes possible an increase in satisfaction, albeit in ever-decreasing quantities as needs tend to become satiated.

However, when these theoretical predictions are matched against the opinions of people around the world, it becomes apparent that the relationship between income and satisfaction is more complex and less harmonious. Satisfaction in nearly all its dimensions tends to be on average greater in countries enjoying higher levels of per capita income. This chapter, however, demonstrates the existence of an "unhappy growth paradox": economic growth, instead of increasing, actually reduces satisfaction with various aspects of people's lives, especially in countries that have reached a certain standard of income and consumption.

Similarly, although higher individual earnings tend to be reflected in greater satisfaction, an increase in income for the social group to which an individual belongs produces the opposite effect (especially with the material dimensions of well-being). As a result, changes in expectations and aspirations can counteract the gains in satisfaction produced by increased income. This "aspiration treadmill" can lead to the paradox in which some of the most economically successful groups, with the highest aspirations, have lower levels of satisfaction than economically and socially marginalized groups with lower aspirations.

The complex relationship between income and satisfaction poses multiple political conflicts. Is economic growth desirable, even though it may reduce satisfaction—at least temporarily? Is it justifiable to keep people who lack aspirations in ignorance to prevent a decrease in satisfaction? Should efforts to improve quality of life be concentrated on people who suffer more due to the effect of comparisons and competition with others, and who are not usually the poorest? Since political decisions in a democratic system are the result of conflicts and negotiations between groups with different views and interests, the answers to these questions should be the result of a public debate on the conflictive relationship between income and satisfaction.

Satisfaction, Income, and Growth at Aggregate Level

Governments make tremendous efforts to track Gross Domestic Product (GDP), the best known measure of productive activity and the size of an economy. Although GDP per capita is usually considered a good indicator of a society's standard of living, it was not originally conceived with this end in mind. GDP does not take into account a number of activities that generate well-being, such as leisure, but it does include others that could well cause problems, such as depletion of nonrenewable natural resources or narcotics production (see Box 3.1). Despite these deficiencies, GDP does measure (after some accounting adjustments that need not be specified here)[1] the total income that people receive, and therefore does have a bearing on satisfaction because an individual's potential to consume is limited by income.

In the last few decades, the main objective of economic policy in Latin America and the Caribbean (LAC) has been to accelerate GDP growth. After the "lost decade" of the 1980s, governments in the LAC region embraced, to a greater or lesser extent, the dictates of the Washington Consensus, with its promises to raise growth rates in a sustainable manner by combining fiscal and monetary policies to guarantee macroeconomic stability with privatization and market deregulation to raise efficiency. Since then, growth has improved in the region, but the gains have been modest in comparison with other regions of the developing world, especially East Asia. In this decade, per capita income in the region has grown somewhat more quickly than in the developed world, but it is still a long

---

1. Personal disposable income is obtained by deducting from GDP the costs of capital depreciation, corporate retained earnings, government income from its own properties and enterprises, net transfers of income from families to government, and net transfers of income to the rest of the world.

Box 3-1. *Is GDP an Indicator of Well-Being?*

The idea of creating a system of accounts of domestic income and product arose from the Great Depression of the 1930s due to the need to monitor the level of productive activity. The idea was put into practice in the United States in 1942 to quantify the possibilities of production for the war period.

From the start, GDP was conceived as a measure of productive activity or, more exactly, of the market value of production of goods and services. Because its objective is not to measure well-being, it does not include goods such as leisure and the services that people provide in their own homes, while it does include everything that is produced through the market, whether or not it contributes to well-being, such as arms or drug production. As GDP only considers production and income flows, not changes in stocks of resources, it includes oil production but does not discount reduction of oil reserves. Nor does it consider other forms of depletion of natural resources or other losses of resources. As a result, when a country suffers a natural disaster, GDP can increase because of reconstruction activities despite deaths and loss of capital.

These deficiencies prevent comparisons of GDP between countries, between abundant and scarce nonrenewable natural resources, or between countries that conserve and those that destroy their natural resources, or between countries that have to devote a substantial part of their resources to combat crime and those that have a low crime rate. There are also problems of international comparability due to differences in currencies and relative prices, which are solved by valuing goods and services at common prices (in dollars at purchasing power parity).

In view of these limitations, numerous proposals have been made to adapt the GDP calculation. In the early 1970s, James Tobin (Nobel Prize for Economics in 1981) and William Nordhaus proposed that the value of household services and leisure be included, and certain "bad things" be deducted, such as pollution, and other activities, such as police services, which aim to correct social problems rather than generate goods. Similar considerations inspired the *Genuine Progress Indicator,* GPI, calculated by the private U.S. organization Redefining Progress, and *Measure of Domestic Progress,* MDP, produced by the New Economics Foundation in the United Kingdom. In both cases the traditional economic aggregates of consumption are adjusted by the value of environmental and social costs.

The United Nations, which since the 1950s has defined international standards for calculation of GDP, has expanded the initial system of national accounts to include the stocks of various types of capital and their changes. These expansions enrich the description of the economic system but do not offer good measures of well-being. The quality of health or education, the crime rate and political stability are important dimensions of the quality of life that cannot be captured in the national accounts.

---

way from recovering from the lag accumulated in previous decades. Whereas in the 1980s and 1990s per capita income in LAC countries was around 31 percent of income in developed countries, today it represents barely 25 percent (figures 3-1a and 3-1b).

However, Latin America and the Caribbean make up a highly heterogeneous region in relation to both economic growth and per capita income. In the current

Figure 3-1a. *Growth of Gross Domestic Product per Capita by Region and Decade, 1981–2006*

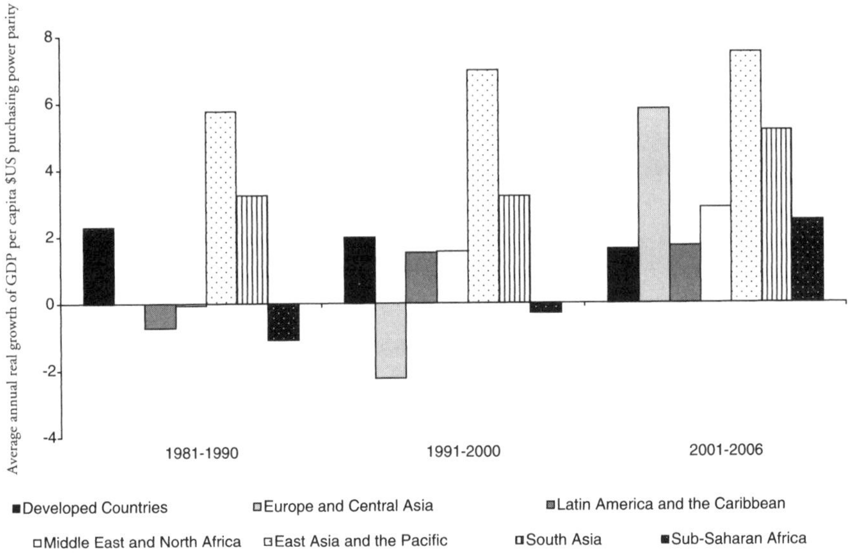

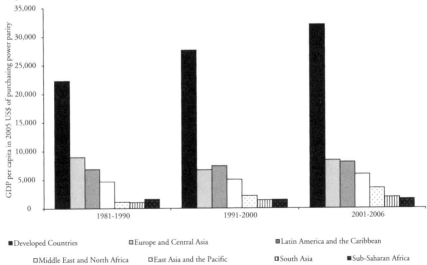

Source: Authors' calculations based on World Bank (2007).
Note: There are no comparable figures for Europe and Central Asia for the 1981–1990 decade.

Figure 3-1b. *Gross Domestic Product per capita by Region and Decade, 1981–2006*

Source: Authors' calculations based on World Bank (2007).

Figure 3-2a. *Growth of Gross Domestic Product per Capita, Average 2001–2006*

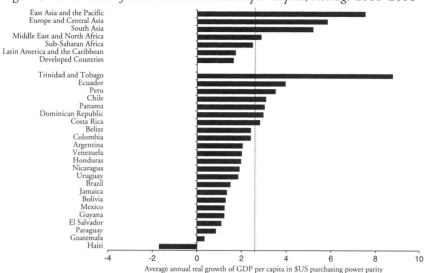

Source: Authors' calculations based on World Bank (2007).
Note: The vertical line represents the world median of economic growth 2001 to 2006 (2.65% average annual real).

decade, the richest country in the region, Trinidad and Tobago, has also had the highest growth, with rates comparable to India or China. The recent performance of Chile, the next country in line in income level, while not matching that of previous decades, is still respectable given the standards of the LAC region. In contrast, Mexico, which is next in the list by income level, has achieved only a modest growth rate. It is troubling to note that the countries with the lowest growth rates are also among the poorest in the region—such as Haiti, Guatemala, and Paraguay—where income per capita is comparable to average incomes in the poorest regions of the world (see figures 3-2a and 3-2b).

If the countries of the world were classified into two groups by level of per capita income, then the majority of Latin American and Caribbean countries would be in the high-income half. The only exceptions would be (in descending order of income) Guatemala, Paraguay, Bolivia, Guyana, Honduras, Nicaragua, and Haiti. But if the world were divided into two groups based on growth rate of per capita income during the 2001–2006 period, then most of the countries would be in the group of countries with slow growth. Only the following countries (in descending order) would remain in the group achieving rapid growth: Trinidad and Tobago, Ecuador, Peru, Chile, Panama, the Dominican Republic, and Costa Rica, and even some of these countries would be only temporary members of the high growth club.

Figure 3-2b. *Gross Domestic Product per Capita, Average 2001–2006*

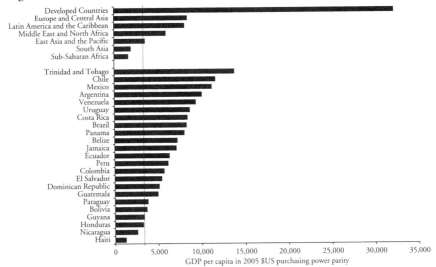

GDP per capita in 2005 $US purchasing power parity

Source: Authors' calculations based on World Bank (2007).

Note: The vertical line represents the world median of economic growth 2001 to 2006 (2.65% average annual real).

Satisfaction and Income per Capita

To quantify satisfaction, this chapter uses information recently collected by the most ambitious system of quality of life surveys: the Gallup World Poll. Since 2006 this company has conducted annual surveys in over 130 countries, which currently is the uniform source with the most extensive coverage on perceptions of quality of life.[2]

To analyze perceptions of quality of life, a distinction must first be made between individuals' perceptions of themselves and their personal living conditions. A second distinction must be made between the same individuals' perceptions of the circumstances in which they live and, more generally, their city or country. Using this distinction, table 3-1 provides the main questions included in the Gallup Poll on various aspects or "domains" of the quality of life analyzed in this chapter.

Judging by their own perceptions of the quality of life, Latin Americans[3] are not far from the world average in their perceptions of the various dimensions of their personal lives, based on the 2006 and 2007 Gallup Polls. On a scale of 0 to 10, the people of the region, on average, rate the quality of their own lives at 5.8, which is about the midpoint of all the world's regions (figures 3-3a to 3-3c). When

2. For a more detailed description of the Gallup World Poll, see chapter 1.

3. For the rest of this chapter, the term *Latin America* includes the Caribbean as well.

Table 3-1. *Questions on Satisfaction in the Gallup World Poll*

Domain	Perceptions of oneself and near environment	Perceptions of society and other external circumstances
General	"Please imagine a ladder with the steps numbered from zero to ten, where zero is the lowest step and ten the highest. Assume that the highest step represents the best life possible for you and the lowest step represents the worst. Which step of the ladder do you feel you are on at this time?"	"Imagine a ladder with the steps numbered from zero to ten, where zero is the lowest step and ten the highest. Assume that the highest step represents the best situation possible for your country and the lowest step represents the worst. Please tell me what number of step you think your country is on at this time."
Standard of living	"Are you satisfied or dissatisfied with your standard of living? That is, with all the things you can buy or do."	"Would you say that current economic conditions in your country are good or not?"
Health	"Are you satisfied or dissatisfied with your health?"	"Do you have confidence in the medical and health system of your country?"
Education	No questions on this domain	"In the city/area where you live, are you satisfied or dissatisfied with the education system and the schools?"
Work	"Are you satisfied or dissatisfied with your job or work?"	"Are you satisfied or dissatisfied with efforts to increase the number and quality of jobs in your country?"
Housing	"Are you satisfied or dissatisfied with your housing or place where you live at the moment?"	"In the city/area where you live, are you satisfied or dissatisfied with the availability of good housing at affordable prices?"

Source: Gallup World Poll (2006 and 2007).

people in the region are asked if they are satisfied with their personal economic situation, that is "all the things they can buy and do," 68 percent respond in the affirmative—a figure that might seem surprisingly high bearing in mind that over 35 percent of all Latin Americans are officially classified as poor. It is, however, close to the midway point between the percentage of satisfaction with personal economic situation in sub-Saharan Africa (39 percent) and Western Europe (86 percent) shown in figure 3-3b. A large majority of the region's population say they are satisfied with specific aspects of their lives: on average, about 80 percent are content with their health, job, or housing. Although these high levels of satisfaction might suggest an optimistic bias, even in the poorest parts of the world, the average rates of satisfaction with these dimensions of life is above 50 percent, and in the richer regions it is around 90 percent (figures 3-3c to 3-3f).[4]

4. Latin Americans are significantly more optimistic than the rest of the world only in job satisfaction.

Figure 3-3a. *Perceptions of Satisfaction with Life and the Situation of the Country*

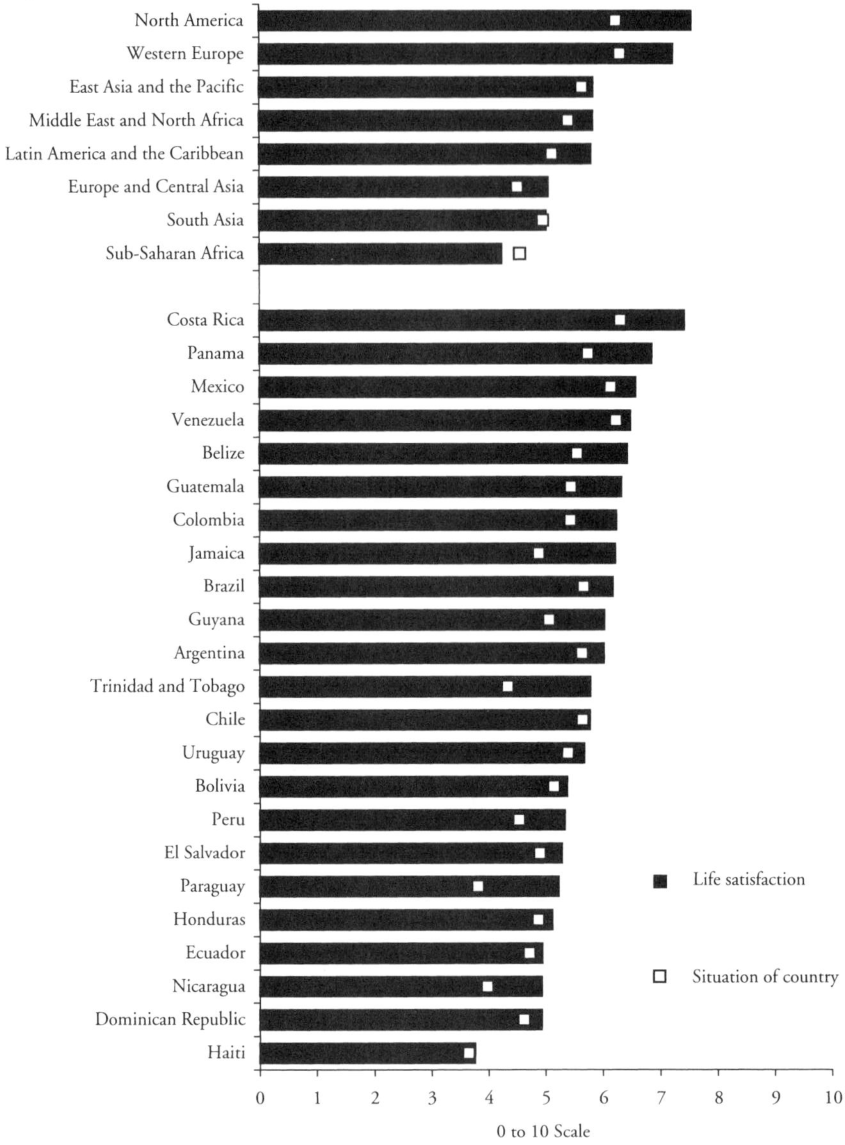

0 to 10 Scale

Source: Authors' calculations based on Gallup (2006 and 2007).

Figure 3-3b. *Perceptions of Personal Economic Situation and Economic Conditions of the Country*

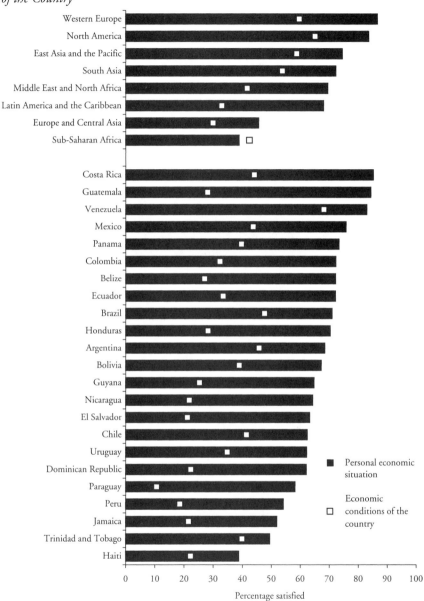

Source: Authors' calculations based on Gallup (2006 and 2007).

Figure 3-3c. *Perceptions of Own Health and National Health System*

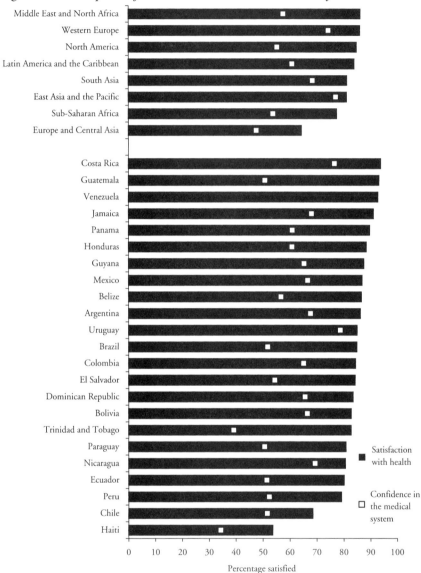

Percentage satisfied

Source: Authors' calculations based on Gallup (2006 and 2007).

Figure 3-3d. *Perceptions of the Education System*

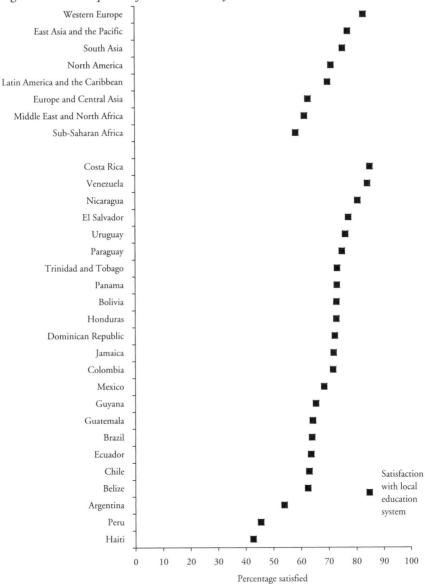

Figure 3-3e. *Perceptions of Employment and Labor Public Policy*

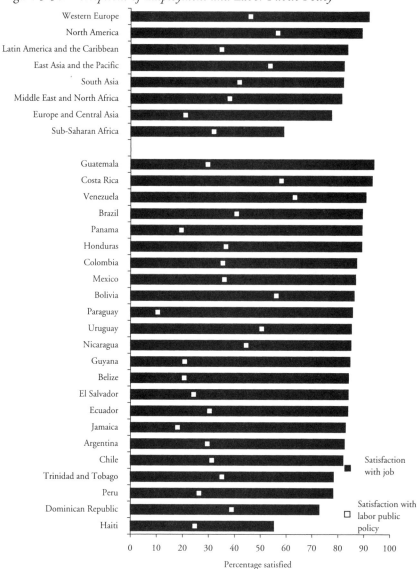

Source: Authors' calculations based on Gallup (2006 and 2007).

Figure 3-3f. *Perceptions of Own Housing and Housing Market*

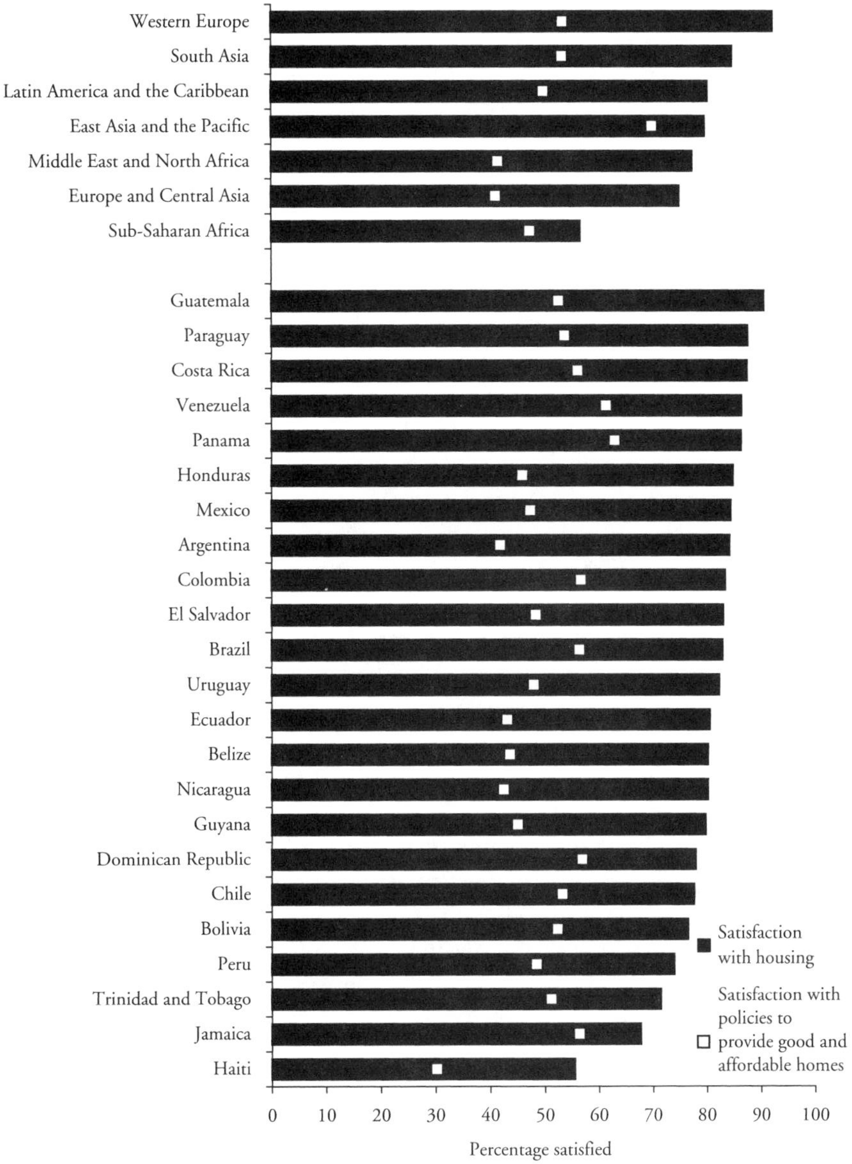

Percentage satisfied

Satisfaction with housing

Satisfaction with policies to provide good and affordable homes

Source: Authors' calculations based on Gallup (2006 and 2007).

Latin Americans rate more severely the various dimensions of the quality of life *of their own countries* (indicated by squares on the bars of each figure). In some aspects these differences are profound: although 83 percent of Latin Americans are satisfied with their job, only 35 percent believe that governments are doing as much as possible to create good jobs. But judging the situation of their countries or the quality of public policies more severely than their own living conditions is not a behavior exclusive to Latin Americans, whose perceptions of the living conditions of their countries is not appreciably different from the averages for all regions of the world.

According to the principles of economic theory, satisfaction expressed by individuals with various aspects of their lives and societies is greater on average in countries enjoying higher levels of per capita income. For example, figure 3-4a shows that the link between life satisfaction and per capita income around the world is very strong. A statistical analysis confirms that the relationship with income is significant in all domains of personal satisfaction, and in several of the collective aspects (table 3-2).[5] Latin American countries do not differ from the rest of the world in this linkage.[6]

Owing to the logarithmic method used in calculating per capita income, the results imply that increased income contributes to increased satisfaction (in its different aspects), but with diminishing returns. To increase average life satisfaction by one point (on a 0–10 scale) in a country with an annual per capita income of US$2,000 (approximately the average annual income of Latin American and Caribbean countries), per capita income would have to rise to US$7,500. To achieve the same increase of one point in life satisfaction in a developed country with a per capita income of US$10,000, a per capita income of US$36,000 would be needed. Similarly, an increase from US$2,000 to US$5,000 would be needed for a 10 percent increase in the proportion of the population satisfied with its material standard of living in an average Latin American country, whereas in a developed country per capita income would have to increase from US$10,000 to $25,000.

The coefficients of the personal satisfaction variables (except for the health domain) are higher than for the variables that rate country or city.[7] This implies

5. The econometric method used in Table 3.2 is ordinary least squares. Although the original dependent variables are binary (yes/no) or ordinal (steps from 0 to 10), here they are treated as current cardinal variables, so they are the averages for each country. Equally statistically significant variables are obtained if the regressions are run with individual data with the Probit or ordered Probit method and the same explanatory variables.

6. As mentioned in a previous footnote, Latin Americans are only more optimistic than the rest of the world in relation to employment. This result is obtained by including in table 3.2 regressions a dummy variable for the countries of Latin America and the Caribbean. The coefficient of that variable (0.067) is positive and significant at 1 percent for the regression with 122 countries.

7. The coefficients of the general satisfaction variables (satisfaction with life and the situation of the country) are not comparable with the coefficients of the other variables because the first set is measured on a 0–10 scale and the second set in percentages of satisfied individuals.

Figure 3-4a. *Relation between GDP per Capita and Life Satisfaction, 122 Countries*

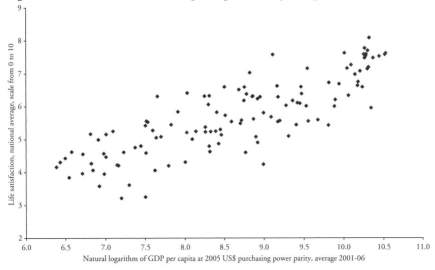

Source: Authors' calculations based on Gallup (2006 and 2007) and World Bank (2007).

that when opinions about dimensions of people's lives are compared, the differences between rich and poor countries are greater than when opinions on society in general are compared.

Previous studies, based on a smaller number of countries than in the Gallup World Polls on which these findings are based, have concluded that beyond a certain threshold, higher levels of per capita income do not result in improved well-being.[8] This conclusion can no longer be sustained in light of this new source of information. As Stevenson and Wolfers (2008) demonstrate in their detailed study, this conclusion is not supported by an analysis of the numerous existing databases covering many countries and periods (especially low and medium income).[9] It is also important to mention that the relation with income is stronger when a more framed question is used, such as the life satisfaction question on a 0–10 ladder included by the Gallup World Poll, than the less framed questions on happiness used by other surveys.

When the sample of countries is divided in two by level of per capita income, satisfaction with life is slightly *more* sensitive to income level in countries that are above average (although the difference is not statistically significant). If, however, instead of considering satisfaction with life, opinions are on the general situation

8. Diener and others (1993).

9. The inclusion of numerous low-income countries reinforces the linearity of the relation between income and satisfaction because it extends both variables downward, but it does not change in any way the original discussion on the existence of a high income threshold beyond which there is little or no gain in satisfaction.

Table 3-2. *Relation between Satisfaction, GDP per Capita, and Countries' Economic Growth*

		Life satisfaction	Situation of country	Standard of living	Economic situation of country
All countries	GDP per capita	0.733***	0.437***	0.096***	0.032
		(16.21)	(7.27)	(9.19)	(1.91)
	Economic growth	−0.075***	−0.016	−0.018***	0.012
		(−3.92)	(−0.61)	(−3.95)	(1.65)
	Constant	−0.607	1.384	−0.169	0.112
		(−1.5)	(2.58)	(−1.8)	(0.74)
	Number of observations	122	120	120	119
	R-squared adjusted	0.70	0.30	0.46	0.03
Poor countries below median GDP per capita	GDP per capita	0.629***	0.147	0.129***	−0.070
		(5.25)	(0.94)	(3.76)	(−1.58)
	Economic growth	−0.034	0.049	−0.007	0.024**
		(−1.47)	(1.65)	(−1.05)	(2.91)
	Constant	0.052	3.346	−0.427	0.844
		(0.06)	(2.92)	(−1.69)	(2.61)
	Number of observations	55	53	53	52
	R-squared adjusted	0.32	0.05	0.19	0.13
Rich countries above median GDP per capita	GDP per capita	0.843***	0.704***	0.125***	0.184***
		(6.7)	(4.24)	(6.17)	(4.17)
	Economic growth	−0.140***	−0.090	−0.039***	0.011
		(−3.97)	(−1.94)	(−6.84)	(0.88)
	Constant	−1.475	−0.971	−0.392	−1.360
		(−1.18)	(−0.59)	(−1.94)	(−3.09)
	Number of observations	67	67	67	67
	R-squared adjusted	0.57	0.31	0.66	0.19
Countries with growth below median	GDP per capita	0.846***	0.522***	0.114***	0.056*
		(16.34)	(6.95)	(9.58)	(2.54)
	Economic growth	0.062	0.208*	0.024	0.050
		(1.06)	(2.41)	(1.8)	(1.99)
	Constant	−1.722	0.360	−0.371	−0.136
		(−3.85)	(0.55)	(−3.6)	(−0.72)
	Number of observations	56	55	56	55
	R-squared adjusted	0.85	0.56	0.67	0.19
Countries with growth above median	GDP per capita	0.537***	0.254**	0.059***	−0.013
		(7.62)	(2.77)	(3.55)	(−0.48)
	Economic growth	−0.090**	−0.065	−0.025***	0.006
		(−3.04)	(−1.68)	(−3.59)	(0.55)
	Constant	1.097	3.197	0.185	0.516
		(1.75)	(3.92)	(1.25)	(2.21)
	Number of observations	66	65	64	64
	R-squared adjusted	0.51	0.12	0.28	0.01

Source: Authors' calculations based on Gallup World Poll (2007).

*Coefficient is statistically significant at the 10 percent level; **at the 5 percent level; ***at the 1 percent level; no asterisk means the coefficient is not different from zero with statistical significance.

Note: The econometric method used is ordinary least squares (OLS). The value in parenthesis is the t-statistic.

Satisfaction with health	Confidence in the medical system	Satisfaction with local education system	Job satisfaction	Satisfaction with job policies	Satisfaction with housing	Satisfaction with good and affordable homes
0.016**	0.032**	0.045***	0.070***	0.035**	0.078***	0.018
(2.68)	(2.9)	(4.86)	(10.68)	(2.87)	(10.55)	(1.52)
−0.016***	−0.011*	−0.004	−0.005	−0.006	−0.004	−0.006
(−6.2)	(−2.29)	(−0.98)	(−1.67)	(−1.07)	(−1.26)	(−1.18)
0.702	0.361	0.296	0.186	0.058	0.108	0.367
(12.91)	(3.7)	(3.57)	(3.16)	(0.53)	(1.66)	(3.6)
121	114	120	119	121	119	93
0.28	0.10	0.16	0.50	0.06	0.49	0.02
0.029	0.014	0.035	0.105***	−0.014	0.111***	0.005
(1.4)	(0.43)	(1.2)	(4.22)	(−0.42)	(4.28)	(0.17)
−0.011**	0.000	0.001	−0.004	0.003	−0.002	−0.002
(−2.92)	(−0.07)	(0.09)	(−0.82)	(0.51)	(−0.33)	(−0.26)
0.596	0.466	0.362	−0.068	0.409	−0.142	0.447
(3.98)	(1.98)	(1.67)	(−0.37)	(1.62)	(−0.74)	(1.92)
54	53	53	53	54	54	47
0.12	0.004	0.03	0.23	0.01	0.24	0.002
−0.006	0.051	0.080***	0.050***	0.121***	0.065***	0.027
(−0.49)	(1.75)	(3.53)	(4.62)	(3.8)	(4.68)	(0.82)
−0.029***	−0.029***	−0.008	−0.011***	−0.011	−0.012**	−0.012
(−7.94)	(−3.61)	(−1.33)	(−3.67)	(−1.25)	(−3.24)	(−1.39)
0.957	0.224	−0.030	0.397	−0.756	0.254	0.302
(7.47)	(0.77)	(−0.13)	(3.68)	(−2.39)	(1.86)	(0.93)
67	61	67	66	67	65	46
0.50	0.26	0.21	0.44	0.23	0.42	0.03
0.020**	0.053***	0.057***	0.072***	0.049**	0.083***	0.013
(3.36)	(4.13)	(5.42)	(8.14)	(3.29)	(8.38)	(0.81)
0.016	0.016	0.017	0.018	0.037	0.018	0.025
(2.43)	(1.12)	(1.46)	(1.83)	(2.17)	(1.64)	(1.11)
0.630	0.137	0.177	0.146	−0.105	0.035	0.354
(12.22)	(1.24)	(1.96)	(1.91)	(−0.82)	(0.41)	(2.76)
56	54	56	56	56	54	40
0.28	0.28	0.40	0.60	0.26	0.62	0.03
0.001	−0.004	0.022	0.059***	0.001	0.064***	0.014
(0.07)	(−0.21)	(1.37)	(5.91)	(0.07)	(5.81)	(0.79)
−0.023***	−0.020**	−0.005	−0.007	−0.010	−0.009	−0.015*
(−5.26)	(−2.76)	(−0.76)	(−1.7)	(−1.2)	(−1.87)	(−2.03)
0.867	0.716	0.495	0.288	0.357	0.246	0.464
(9.65)	(4.57)	(3.52)	(3.22)	(2.06)	(2.5)	(2.94)
65	60	64	63	65	65	53
0.29	0.09	0.01	0.37	0.02	0.36	0.05

in a country or its economic conditions, then this sensitivity is *significantly greater* in those countries with above-average income. In some specific dimensions of satisfaction with personal aspects of life, such as work or housing, sensitivity is lower with respect to income in countries in the above-average group, but in any event significant positive coefficients are obtained that are incompatible with the threshold hypothesis.

Consequently, at the aggregate level, the postulates of conventional economic theory on the relationship between the average *level* of per capita income and the various domains of satisfaction with people's lives, or with the country or city, are confirmed.

The "Unhappy Growth Paradox"

The relationship between income and satisfaction, however, is affected not only by the *level* but also the *growth* rate of per capita income. According to the simplest conventional economic theory, all things being equal, growth should not be expected to exert any *additional* influence on satisfaction levels over and above that already captured by income level. The empirical results presented in table 3-2 call this theoretical simplification into question since various dimensions of satisfaction *deteriorate* with economic growth. Figure 3-4b also suggests that life satisfaction and economic growth are inversely related.[10]

For each additional point of growth of per capita income (during the last five years) life satisfaction *falls* on average 0.07 points (on a scale of 0 to 10). The percentage of the population that is satisfied with its standard of living *declines* by 1.8 points, and the percentage who say they are satisfied with their health *falls* by 1.6 points. There are also negative coefficients in other dimensions on the perception of the quality of personal or community life, although those coefficients are less statistically significant.

The regressions of table 3-3 show that these results are not greatly affected when, instead of taking growth in the 2001–2006 period as has been done until now, a longer (1996–2006) or shorter (2005–06) period is considered. Given that the Gallup Poll dates back only to 2006, this source of information does not allow to test which is the best reference period. The long time series that exist for some countries would be more suitable for this purpose.[11]

Although the "unhappy growth paradox" implies that the relationship between income and satisfaction is more complex than basic economic theory suggests, it does not contradict the theory. One possible explanation for this is that satisfac-

---

10. The conclusions are practically the same whether or not the effect of income per capita on satisfaction is controlled, given that the correlation between economic growth and per capita income is practically nil (more accurately, 0.05 for income per capita growth during the 2001–06 period and the level of income per capita in 2006). Robustness tests appear later in this chapter.
11. With a variety of sources, for 11 developed countries there are time series that cover 25 years or more of information on life satisfaction (Veenhoven, 2007; Stevenson and Wolfers, 2008).

Figure 3-4b. *Relation between Economic Growth and Satisfaction with Life, 120 Countries*

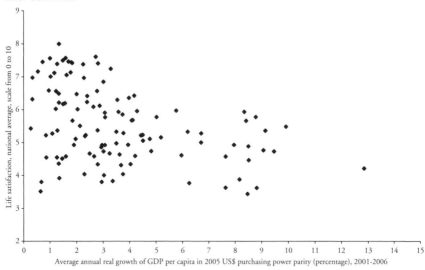

Source: Authors' calculations based on Gallup (2006 and 2007) and World Bank (2007).

tion depends not only on income (to the extent that it limits purchasing power), but also on consumer expectations. The fact that growth is linked more strongly and negatively with perceptions of individual quality of life than with perceptions of the standard of living of a country or a city suggests that growth increases expectations and extends the parameters within which individuals assess their own situation. If expectations and aspirations move in this direction, they are likely to do so more strongly in societies where the majority of the population has already overtaken the levels of consumption necessary to cover basic needs and where the options for consumption and emulation through spending are greater.[12]

This is exactly what is found in a comparison of the coefficients of the growth variable for countries that are above and below the median level of per capita income, as table 3-2 shows. In the relatively richer countries, which currently include most Latin American countries, growth is significantly and negatively associated with all personal aspects of the quality of life, and even with some community aspects (the situation of the country and confidence in the medical system). Among relatively poor countries, however, growth is only significantly (statistically) and negatively associated with one dimension of personal life: health. This relationship can reflect

12. Alternatively, growth could generate dissatisfaction by requiring changes in working practices or in people's lifestyles, which can have a detrimental effect on their forms of economic organization and cultural traditions. This kind of dissatisfaction should be strongest among poorer societies as they integrate into the market economy. This hypothesis, however, is not consistent with the results shown below. Alternative explanations are given at the end of this section.

Table 3-3. *Relation between Satisfaction, GDP per Capita, and Countries'*
Economic Growth: Robustness Tests with Different Growth Periods

All countries	Life satisfaction	Situation of country	Standard of living	Economic situation of country	Satisfaction with health
GDP per capita	0.733***	0.437***	0.096***	0.032	0.016**
	(16.21)	(7.27)	(9.19)	(1.91)	(2.68)
Growth, 2001–06	−0.075***	−0.016	−0.018***	0.012	−0.016***
	(−3.92)	(−0.61)	(−3.95)	(1.65)	(−6.2)
Constant	−0.607	1.384	−0.169	0.112	0.702
	(−1.5)	(2.58)	(−1.8)	(0.74)	(12.91)
Number of observations	122	120	120	119	121
R-squared adjusted	0.70	0.30	0.46	0.03	0.28
GDP per capita	0.741***	0.439***	0.098***	0.031	0.018**
	(15.94)	(7.31)	(9.01)	(1.89)	(2.69)
Growth, 2005–06	−0.045**	0.006	−0.009*	0.012*	−0.008***
	(−2.85)	(0.28)	(−2.38)	(2.21)	(−3.52)
Constant	−0.733	1.284*	−0.206*	0.105	0.667***
	(−1.78)	(2.41)	(−2.13)	(0.71)	(11.27)
Number of observations	122	120	120	119	121
R-squared ajdusted	0.69	0.30	0.42	0.05	0.13
GDP per capita	0.760***	0.441***	0.103***	0.027	0.022***
	(16.84)	(7.31)	(9.73)	(1.63)	(3.55)
Growth 1996–06	−0.098***	−0.013	−0.022***	0.018	−0.020***
	(−4.05)	(−0.4)	(−3.83)	(1.95)	(−5.85)
Constant	−0.804*	1.331*	−0.218*	0.141	0.656***
	(−2.04)	(2.53)	(−2.37)	(0.96)	(12.15)
Number of observations	122	120	120	119	121
R-squared adjusted	0.70	0.30	0.46	0.04	0.26

Source: Authors' calculations based on Gallup World Poll (2007).

*Coefficient is statistically significant at the 10 percent level; **at the 5 percent level; ***at the 1 percent level; no asterisk means the coefficient is not different from zero with statistical significance.

Note: The econometric method used is Ordinary Least Squares (OLS). The value in parentheses is the t-statistic.

both changes in the standards by which individuals judge their health, and genuine deterioration in health associated with growth, due to the effects of pollution, stress, or obesity.[13]

If expectations are the reason why growth leads to deteriorating satisfaction, the "unhappy growth paradox" should be observable when growth rates are high, but not when they are low or negative. If an economy enters recession,

13. In a study for the United States, Ruhm (2000) found a procyclical pattern in mortality rates, in 8 out of 10 cases analyzed, in tobacco consumption and the incidence of obesity. He also found that when the economy improves, physical activity decreases and less healthy foods are consumed. For a discussion of other studies on the subject, see Ruhm (2005).

Confidence in the medical system	Satisfaction with local education system	Job satisfaction	Satisfaction with job policies	Satisfaction with housing	Satisfaction with good and affordable homes
0.032**	0.045***	0.070***	0.035**	0.078***	0.018
(2.9)	(4.86)	(10.68)	(2.87)	(10.55)	(1.52)
−0.011*	−0.004	−0.005	−0.006	−0.004	−0.006
(−2.29)	(−0.98)	(−1.67)	(−1.07)	(−1.26)	(−1.18)
0.361	0.296	0.186	0.058	0.108	0.367
(3.7)	(3.57)	(3.16)	(0.53)	(1.66)	(3.6)
114	120	119	121	119	93
0.10	0.16	0.50	0.06	0.49	0.02
0.033**	0.045***	0.071***	0.036**	0.078***	0.017
(2.95)	(4.89)	(10.68)	(2.93)	(10.55)	(1.43)
−0.003	−0.002	−0.002	0.000	−0.001	0.000
(−0.89)	(−0.54)	(−1.02)	(0.12)	(−0.57)	(0.06)
0.329**	0.287***	0.176**	0.030	0.098	0.352***
(3.33)	(3.48)	(2.99)	(0.28)	(1.51)	(3.44)
114	120	119	121	119	93
0.06	0.16	0.49	0.05	0.48	0.001
0.035**	0.046***	0.072***	0.037**	0.079***	0.020
(3.16)	(4.92)	(10.96)	(3.03)	(10.68)	(1.63)
−0.011	−0.002	−0.007	−0.007	−0.005	−0.006
(−1.7)	(−0.41)	(−1.93)	(−1.07)	(−1.21)	(−1.04)
0.326***	0.282***	0.173**	0.043	0.098	0.351***
(3.38)	(3.46)	(3.02)	(0.4)	(1.53)	(3.46)
114	120	119	121	119	93
0.08	0.16	0.50	0.06	0.49	0.01

there is no reason to suppose that consumers are going to feel better, because they are not going to give up their expectations of material improvement. In fact, when the sample is divided between countries with growth per capita below and above the world average, the inverse relationship between satisfaction and growth is maintained only for high-growth countries (see the bottom grouping of countries in table 3-2).[14] In these countries, the higher the growth, the fewer

14. Due to the small number of countries with negative growth of income per capita (14) in the period utilized (2001–06), it is not convenient to divide the sample into countries with positive and negative growth. We have confirmed, however, that the influence of growth on satisfaction in countries with negative growth does not differ significantly (statistically) from the group of low-growth countries (for the effect we have included the interaction growth * Dummy of countries with negative growth in the regressions for the low-growth countries).

the people who say they are satisfied with their lives, with the things that they can do or buy, or with their health. Confidence in the medical system and in housing policy is also significantly reduced.[15] On the other hand, among low-growth countries, those with higher growth rates report higher levels of satisfaction in all aspects of private and public life. These higher levels are significant (statistically speaking) in relation to the opinions of people on the situation of the country, their own health, and the effectiveness of job creation policies.[16]

In sum, although satisfaction and income *level* demonstrate the relationship predicted by basic economic theory, economic growth seems to have a negative effect on various dimensions of individuals' satisfaction with themselves and their personal conditions (and sometimes even their satisfaction with community conditions). The explanation behind the "unhappy growth paradox" seems to be the increased expectations and aspirations generated by economic growth, especially in countries with relatively high income levels and high growth rates. This hypothesis will be examined later, when, instead of trying to explain the differences *between* countries, emphasis will be on the differences *within* countries. We will see how individuals' satisfaction depends not only on their income, but also on the income levels of others. However, the hypothesis of expectations does not rule out the existence of other factors that might help explain the negative effects of growth on some aspects of satisfaction, which will be discussed later. It should be mentioned that the experiences of certain countries can be different or change over time. For example, Stevenson and Wolfers (2008) find negative effects of growth on satisfaction in the early stages of the economic miracle of Ireland and South Korea, which disappear later (perhaps because of increased economic and social stability).

The "unhappy growth paradox" is consistent with popular opinion on the effects of structural reforms that accelerate growth. Initially the reforms, although they stimulate economic growth, produce feelings of unease, which, in this conceptual scheme, are caused by the effects of expectations but which in part can also result from the costs for many individuals of change of job or the need to adapt to new conditions of production that increase efficiency.[17] By their nature, some structural reforms, such as opening to international trade, generate

---

15. Rapid growth can require more frequent changes in labor skills and practices and increases labor instability. However, no reduction in job satisfaction is observed in the fastest-growing countries.

16. In the low-growth group, no differential effects of growth on any aspect of satisfaction were found for countries with negative growth.

17. This is a plausible hypothesis given that the phenomenon occurs only in countries with relatively rapid growth where people have to adapt at a faster pace so as to boost production. This would be consistent with the strong negative influence of economic growth on health in this group of countries. But, if this were the explanation, why should satisfaction with standard of living deteriorate?

redistribution of income between capital and labor, and between different types of labor, which also influences satisfaction (due to aversion to losses, individuals who lose income have a greater loss of well-being than the improvement of those who gain income).[18] If the reforms go into reverse, the country may return to its initial situation and avoid these losses of satisfaction, but it will sacrifice the possibility of a more rapid increase in future satisfaction rates once these initial losses are overcome.

Before going on to explore the hypothesis of expectations with information at the individual level, it is important to present some additional regression results based on country-level data in order to evaluate the robustness of the previous results and the possible influence of other factors on satisfaction with life in addition to income and growth.[19] The results, shown in table 3-4, are based on the basic regression described previously, which explains satisfaction with life based only on income and growth. Regressions 2 and 3 show that the coefficients of these two variables are not significantly influenced by their correlation (which is only 0.05). Regression 4 synthesizes the results on the differential influence of growth between poor and rich countries and between countries of slow and rapid growth. For this purpose, only the growth variables for rich countries and for countries of rapid growth are added to the basic regression. Both are significant and totally absorb the significance of the general growth variable.

The remaining regressions explore the possible influence of other variables and test the robustness of the coefficients of the income and growth variables.

Economic volatility (measured by the standard deviation of the growth rates of the last five years), inflation or income distribution are macroeconomic variables that could affect life satisfaction (or happiness), as various authors have analyzed.[20] Regression 5 does not support these ideas, as none of these variables is significant. Furthermore, our variables of interest retain their significance, and their coefficients are virtually unchanged.

Quality of institutions can also affect satisfaction, because for individuals *how much* their needs are met is just as important as *how* they are met. This "procedural utility" can be defined as the satisfaction of living and acting in institutionalized

18. The reforms can also cause disquiet for ideological reasons, or because the implementation process is not transparent or democratic. For a synthesis of public opinion on structural reforms in Latin America and its effects on production and growth, see Lora and others (2004). For a discussion of its political and electoral effects, see Lora and Olivera (2005).

19. Due to limitations of space, these additional exercises are focused on the life satisfaction variable. The results for the other aspects can be requested from the authors.

20. Di Tella, McCulloch and Oswald (2003) explore the empirical relation between inflation, unemployment and life satisfaction; Easterlin (1995) discusses the relation between life satisfaction, income distribution and economic growth.

Table 3-4. *Relation between Life Satisfaction and Various Country Variables*

Dependent variable: Life satisfaction, national average, scale from 0 to 10		1	2	3	4	5	6	7	8	9
Macroeconomic conditions	GDP per capita in constant 2005 dollars at purchasing power parity, average 2001–06	0.733*** (16.21)	0.745*** (15.58)	(14.02)	0.773***	0.720*** (13.48)	0.603*** (7.63)	0.680*** (8.70)	0.594*** (8.61)	0.542*** (6.82)
	Average annual economic growth, 2001–06	−0.075*** (−3.92)		−0.095** (−2.78)	0.075 (1.19)	−0.089*** (−3.93)	−0.055* (−2.56)	−0.071** (−2.74)	−0.021 (−0.94)	−0.061** (−2.23)
	Interaction between economic growth and dummy for countries with GDP per capita above world median				−0.068* (−2.19)					
	Interaction between economic growth and dummy for countries with growth above world median				−0.122* (−2.07)					
	Volatility (standard deviation) of economic growth, 2001–06					−0.010 (−0.31)				
	Gini coefficient, average 1995–2005					−0.173 (−0.23)				
	Average annual inflation rate, 2000–06					0.002 (0.23)				
Institutions	Voice and accountability, 2006						0.013 (0.02)			
	Political stability, 2006						−0.653 (−1.35)			
	Government effectiveness, 2006						2.417 (1.79)			
	Rule of law, 2006						0.884 (0.63)			
	Control of corruption, 2006						0.250 (0.21)			
	Quality of regulations, 2006						−2.497* (−2.39)			

Cultural and geographical characteristics									

	(1)	(2)	(3)	(4)	(5)	(6)	(7)	(8)	(9)
Cultural and geographical characteristics									
Ethnic fragmentation							0.507		
							(1.30)		
Linguistic fragmentation							−0.389		
							(−1.34)		
Percentage of population with monotheistic religious beliefs							0.002		
							(−1.10)		
Absolute value of latitude of center of country to the equator							0.327		
							(0.70)		
Cultural traits score							0.313***		0.263***
							(4.33)		(3.59)
Regional dummies									
Dummy for countries of East Asia and Pacific								−0.677**	−0.725**
								(−2.91)	(−2.23)
Dummy for countries of Europe and Central Asia								−1.154***	−0.780**
								(−4.9)	(−2.2)
Dummy for countries of the Middle East and North Africa								−0.721**	−0.596
								(−3.05)	(−1.33)
Dummy for countries of South Asia								−0.384	−1.187***
								(−1.08)	(−2.68)
Dummy for countries of Sub-Saharan Africa								−0.994***	−1.018***
								(−3.4)	(−2.71)
Dummy for countries of Latin America and the Caribbean								−0.450*	−0.401
								(−2.07)	(−1.38)
Constant	−0.607	−0.960*	5.787***	−0.995*	−0.334	0.540	−0.486	1.107	1.653*
	(−1.5)	(−2.3)	(37.42)	(−2.15)	(−0.51)	(0.92)	(−0.69)	(1.51)	(1.90)
R-squared adjusted	0.70	0.67	0.05	0.72	0.69	0.72	0.77	0.76	0.79
Number of countries	122	122	122	122	108	122	72	122	76

Source: Authors' calculations based on Gallup World Poll (2007).

*Coefficient is statistically significant at the 10 percent level; **at the 5 percent level; ***at the 1 percent level; no asterisk means the coefficient is not different from zero with statistical significance.

Note: The econometric method used is Ordinary Least Squares (OLS). The value in parenthesis is the t-statistic.

processes that contribute to satisfying the needs of autonomy, relatedness and competence.[21] Although there is abundant empirical evidence for this argument, our data do not confirm it. Regression 6 includes as explanatory variables the six synthetic measures of quality of public institutions produced by the World Bank.[22] These measurements consistently summarize all the information available on each of the most important aspects of public institutions, such as freedom of expression and accountability, political stability, effectiveness of the public administration, rule of law, control of corruption, and the quality of the regulatory framework for economic activities. Only the last of these quality measures of public institutions shows statistical significance, but with the incorrect sign. (This may be due to correlation with other measures because this unexpected relation disappears when the other institutional variables are taken out of the regression). The inclusion of this additional set of explanatory variables reduces, but does not eliminate, the significance of economic growth, while it keeps that of income per capita.

Regression 7 explores the possible influence of variables that can capture the effect of culture and collective behavior on life satisfaction. Most of the variables included are well known in the literature: ethnic and linguistic heterogeneity (which can affect social cohesion and possibilities of cooperation), the percentage of the population that professes a monotheistic religion and distance from the equator (with the presumption that attitude to life can be affected by these conditions).[23] None of these variables seem to have a robust influence on life satisfaction. Additionally, this set of variables includes a measure of cultural traits, which requires some explanation. As discussed by van Praag and Ferrer-i-Carbonell (2007), individual responses to subjective questions may be affected by psychological traits: given an equal set of objective circumstances, some individuals tend to respond to all subjective questions in a more positive way than others. This tendency can be isolated econometrically to produce an individual "psychological traits" variable.[24] We extend this method to produce a country-level "cultural traits" score.[25] This variable is a synthetic measure of the tendency (not attributable to objective variables) of the peoples of each country to respond affirmatively to the set of satisfaction (or, in general, subjec-

21. Frey, Benz and Stutzer (2003): "Procedural utility can thus be defined as the well-being people gain from living and acting under institutionalized processes as they contribute to a positive sense of self, addressing innate needs of autonomy, relatedness and competence."

22. Kaufman, Kraay and Mastruzzi (2006).

23. See Easterly, Ritzen and Woolcock (2006) for a deeper discussion.

24. The procedure involves two stages: in a first stage, regressions for all the available subjective variables at the individual level are run as functions of the relevant individual-level objective variables. Then, using principal component analysis, the errors of these regressions are used to produce the "psychological traits" variable for each individual.

25. In order to do this, the set of objective variables includes also relevant country-level objective variables. The country-level "psychological traits" variable will be the country averages of the individual "psychological traits" values.

tive) questions considered.[26] As shown in regression 7, culture traits, measured in this way, do influence the responses to the life satisfaction question. Although this is hardly surprising, what is relevant for our purposes is that the inclusion of the culture traits score does not affect the significance of our two main variables of interest: per capita income and growth.

Finally, regressions 8 and 9 include dummy variables by region, which attempt to capture the influence of omitted variables that may differ by region. Regression 8 shows that some of them are strongly significant and absorb the significance of the growth variable, indicating that growth is not randomly distributed across regions. As should be expected, culture traits also show regional patterns, as suggested by the fact that the significance of some of the regional dummies is reduced when the culture traits variable is included (regression 9). Notice, furthermore, that growth recovers its significance.

From the point of view of our variables of central interest, which are income and growth rates, this series of regressions shows that the central conclusions are robust: satisfaction has a strong and stable dependence on the (logarithm of) per capita income (with a coefficient estimated between 0.5 and 0.8, which is always very significant), and has negative dependence on the (percentage) growth rate of the per capita income, especially of the set of rich countries, and in most cases significantly. Only regional dummies weaken somewhat the associations between satisfaction and growth, especially when the influence of culture traits is not controlled for.

Hedonism, Envy or Solidarity?

The relation between levels of per capita income and the various domains of satisfaction holds true not only when comparing some countries with others, but also when comparing individuals within countries. This clearly requires the use of information on individual income levels, which, unfortunately, is not always accurately reported in the opinion polls. In the Gallup Poll, interviewees are only asked to state the income bracket of their family with very broad ranges (and not

26. The following set of questions were used: satisfaction with the life that a person expects to lead in five years' time; personal economic satisfaction; satisfaction with health; satisfaction with housing; satisfaction with the freedom to choose; satisfaction with the city; expectations held for the state of the country as a whole in five years' time; satisfaction with the national economic situation; confidence in the national medical system; satisfaction with the education system; satisfaction with efforts of the country to create jobs; and person feels safe walking alone at night. (Note that life satisfaction is not included as that would prevent the use of the resulting "cultural traits" variable as an independent variable to explain life satisfaction.) The set of individual objective variables was: age, age squared, gender, marital status, access to tap water, access to electricity, access to a land phone line, TV at home, and personal computer at home. The list of country-level objective variables was: log of GDP per capita 2005, average GDP per capita growth rate 2001–06, average inflation rate 2000–06, Polity IV rescaled score 2004, life expectancy, child mortality rate, education index of the Human Development Index (HDI) 2005, political stability score 2006, government effectiveness score 2006, regulatory quality score 2006, rule of law score 2006, and corruption control score 2006.

Table 3-5. *Relation between Satisfaction and Income of Individuals and of Others*

Variable	General		Economic situation	
	Life satisfaction (0–10 scale)	*Situation of country*	*Standard of living*	*Economic situation of country*
Gender (male = 1)	−0.168***	0.024	0.105	0.246**
	(−4.68)	(0.62)	(1.53)	(2.77)
Age	−0.045***	−0.030***	−0.077***	−0.001
	(−3.75)	(−3.65)	(−5.54)	(−0.11)
Age squared	0.000*	0.000***	0.001***	0.000
	(2.18)	(3.54)	(4.52)	(0.62)
Marital status, married	0.039	0.018	0.091*	0.043
	(0.57)	(0.26)	(2.35)	(0.64)
Marital status, divorced	−0.155	0.136	−0.148	−0.054
	(−1.3)	(1.33)	(−1.35)	(−0.45)
Marital status, widowed	0.030	−0.088	−0.027	0.284*
	(0.27)	(−0.58)	(−0.25)	(2.22)
Religion is important	0.223***	0.211**	0.202*	0.075
	(4.51)	(2.8)	(2.37)	(0.91)
Has friends to turn to	0.552***	0.278***	0.669***	0.309***
	(7.83)	(4.49)	(5.59)	(3.42)
Monthly income per capita of household, US$ PPP, natural log	0.410***	0.131***	0.370***	0.116***
	(13.81)	(3.7)	(11.82)	(3.35)
Average monthly income per capita of reference group, US$ PPP, natural log	0.254*	−0.077	−0.217*	−0.109
	(2.54)	(−1.16)	(−2.25)	(−1.07)
Number of observations	8593	8496	8525	8131
Pseudo-R²	0.047	0.034	0.065	0.074
Dummies for country	Yes	Yes	Yes	Yes

Source: Authors' calculations based on Gallup World Poll (2007).

*Coefficient is statistically significant at the 10 percent level; **at the 5 percent level; ***at the 1 percent level; no asterisk means the coefficient is not different from zero with statistical significance.

Note: Life satisfaction and the situation of the country are measured on a scale from 0 to 10 and the econometric method used is Ordered Logit. The other satisfaction variables are binary (yes/no), and the

easily comparable across countries). As explained by Leonardo Gasparini and coauthors in chapter 2, individual incomes can be generated by assigning random values to all the observations within each income bracket. Here we will make use of the income data generated by Gasparini, keeping in mind that because individual income levels are not accurately measured, it is difficult to know exactly what influence they have on quality of life perceptions. It is likely that the econometrically estimated coefficients are skewed downward (due to the "attenuation effect"), and that the sensitivity of satisfaction to individual income is therefore greater.

In spite of this limitation, as shown in table 3-5, income has a considerable and significant positive effect on all dimensions of satisfaction that relate to personal

	Health		Education	Employment		Housing	
	Satisfaction with health	Confidence in the medical system	Satisfaction with local education system	Job satisfaction	Satisfaction with job policies	Satisfaction with housing	Satisfaction with policies to provide good and affordable homes
	0.325***	0.000	0.026	−0.106	0.172***	0.170**	0.105*
	(6.2)	(0)	(0.54)	(−0.78)	(3.45)	(3.04)	(1.97)
	−0.046**	−0.028**	−0.021	0.023	−0.022*	−0.074***	−0.039***
	(−3.14)	(−2.73)	(−1.67)	(1.04)	(−2.41)	(−5.22)	(−3.63)
	0.000	0.000**	0.000	0.000	0.000	0.001***	0.001***
	(0.13)	(3.28)	(1.93)	(−1.12)	(1.9)	(6.01)	(3.72)
	−0.012	−0.089	−0.008	0.057	0.025	−0.092	−0.056
	(−0.09)	(−1.74)	(−0.13)	(0.46)	(0.47)	(−1.08)	(−1.23)
	−0.002	0.005	0.001	−0.013	0.093	−0.224*	−0.074
	(−0.01)	(0.05)	(0.01)	(−0.05)	(0.92)	(−2.05)	(−0.84)
	0.109	−0.285	0.184	0.253	0.128	0.207	0.124
	(0.75)	(−1.25)	(1.12)	(0.92)	(0.88)	(1.09)	(1.57)
	0.077	0.300***	0.237*	0.402**	0.109	0.126	0.254**
	(0.88)	(4.13)	(2.32)	(3.21)	(1.26)	(1.3)	(3.12)
	0.678***	0.230*	0.197*	0.490***	0.280**	0.516***	0.249**
	(8.56)	(2.16)	(2.24)	(4.52)	(2.89)	(5.21)	(2.61)
	0.196***	−0.035	−0.048	0.379***	0.005	0.261***	0.056
	(3.75)	(−1.03)	(−1.07)	(4.38)	(0.14)	(5.9)	(1.68)
	0.003	−0.348**	−0.390***	−0.429*	−0.397***	−0.236**	−0.278*
	(0.03)	(−3.2)	(−3.73)	(−2.23)	(−4.38)	(−3.11)	(−2.03)
	8588	7912	8345	3449	8405	8592	8095
	0.119	0.031	0.047	0.046	0.070	0.040	0.017
	Yes	Yes	Yes	Yes	Yes	Yes	Yes

econometric method used is Logit. Each person belongs to a reference group. The reference groups are people of the same gender, in the same country, of the same age range, and with similar education level. The value in parenthesis is the t-statistic

conditions.[27] Not surprisingly, the greatest influence is found in the aspects of people's lives that have most to do with their capacity to generate income and consume material goods, such as employment, standard of living, or housing. Nonetheless, income also seems to have an important influence on satisfaction with health and on life satisfaction in general. As might be expected, there is a looser relationship between individual income and satisfaction with community

27. All the regressions shown in tables 3–5 and following use the Logit or Ordered Logit estimation method, depending on whether the dependent variable is binary (yes/no) or takes discrete values (range 0–10). All the regressions include as additional controls the following variables that influence life satisfaction (see chapter 4 for a more detailed discussion): gender, age, age squared, married, divorced, widowed, religion is important, have friends to turn to.

dimensions of life. The relationship is positive and significant only in evaluation of the country's economic situation, which suggests that the personal economic situation might color judgments on the national economic situation.[28] However, for other collective aspects, income is not directly associated with satisfaction (for example, with policies on job creation or housing provision), or is associated inversely, which implies that individuals with higher incomes expect more from public policy (such as cases of confidence in health and education systems).

Consequently, people's opinions on personal aspects of their lives are consistent with the basic tenets of neoclassical economic theory, which predict that higher individual income will lead to higher utility derived from consumption of a combination of goods and services. But it is possible that, apart from having this effect, income might also exert an influence on satisfaction, depending on the extent to which tastes and aspirations alter.

Under the individualist approach of neoclassical economics, individual well-being is not influenced by the situation of others, or by their relative positions in society. This point of view contrasts with the sociological theories that have always held that behavior, evaluations, and aspirations are the result of interaction with society.[29] Although some economists as influential as Adam Smith and Karl Marx emphasized the relative positions of individuals and social groups, until recently the profession has largely ignored the subject.[30] However, in recent decades the topic has reemerged, thanks to the pioneering studies of Richard Easterlin (1974), who demonstrated that relative income is the explanation for the apparent paradox that differences in per capita income *between countries* are closely related to the average satisfaction levels of countries, whereas increases in income *over time* in a given country do little to improve the average levels of satisfaction of its inhabitants.[31]

According to Easterlin, the explanation is that individual satisfaction improves only when individuals move into a better position relative to their social group as a result of an increase in income. Other authors have confirmed that relative income does influence satisfaction.[32] They have also found that satisfaction

---

28. Since the regressions on which these conclusions are based include country dummies, the effect of the average income of all individuals in each country has already been isolated.

29. Merton (1957), Hyman (1960), Felson and Reed (1986), and Michalos (1985).

30. Two important exceptions are Veblen (1899), who emphasized the role of conspicuous consumption, and Duesenberry (1949), who showed that consumption and saving patterns are significantly influenced by relative income.

31. The United States clearly exemplifies this paradox. However, Easterlin's paradox has become rather blurred with the appearance of data covering more countries and more time periods. An exhaustive analysis of the available polls, carried out recently by Stevenson and Wolfers (2008), has concluded that no such paradox exists: not only is life satisfaction in general higher in richer countries, but the slope of that relationship is very similar to that found in time analysis or in comparisons between individuals within countries.

32. van Praag and Ferrer-i-Carbonell (2007), Ball and Chernova (2005), and Luttmer (2005).

depends on the "aspiration gap," meaning the difference between individuals' current income and the income they consider necessary to satisfy their needs, which tends to increase at the same rate as their current income. This "aspiration treadmill" means that a higher level of income (usually double an individual's current salary) is always seen as necessary; consequently, satisfaction does not increase (or increases much less than proportionally) with income.[33]

In practice, it is difficult to determine the social group that individuals compare themselves with in order to judge their own economic situation. According to some studies, the pertinent comparison is with people living in the same region;[34] others, with the country as a whole;[35] and others, colleagues in the same profession or a similar ethnic group.[36] The results are sensitive to how the reference group is defined. Kingdon and Knight find that satisfaction increases with the income of the reference group when this is defined as the ethnic group (South Africa) to which individuals belong, but decreases if a different reference ethnic group is considered. Graham and Pettinato (2002) find that the "frustrated achievers" result from their frustration of comparing themselves with others in the country, not with people in their community. Analyzing the subjective well-being of Latin Americans in cities of different sizes, Graham and Felton (2006) found that relative income is not a significant influence for people who live in small localities (up to 5,000 inhabitants), but it is for people who live in medium to large cities (positively for individuals with above-average income in their reference group, and negatively for those with below-average income). Following Ferrer-i-Carbonell (2005), this work defines the reference groups by age group and education, gender and country.[37] Because broad groups are involved, rather than ethnic or community groups, the effect of rivalry is likely to be stronger than solidarity.

When the influence of the average income of a reference group, defined in this way, is taken into account, it confirms that in the material aspects of personal life there is an effect of comparison—or envy—that reduces satisfaction. This occurs in satisfaction with everything that can be bought or done (personal economic situation) and with job and housing (as shown by the significant negative coefficients

---

33. Stutzer (2004), McBride (2005), and Senik (2006).
34. Stutzer (2004).
35. Ball and Chernova (2005).
36. Senik (2004) and Kingdon and Knight (2004).
37. More accurately, the results presented below are based on information from 19 Latin American and Caribbean countries. In each country, they distinguish six age groups by gender (ages 15 to 75, with ten year intervals each) and four groups by education (primary incomplete, primary completed, secondary incomplete, secondary completed, and higher incomplete and completed). A reference group is considered to have a sufficient number of observations to deduce statistical results if it contains at least 20 individuals. On this basis, between 182 and 258 reference groups are formed depending on the regression. Each individual belongs to only one reference group.

in the "reference group income" column in table 3-5).[38] In these aspects of life, individual satisfaction is strongly dependent on what others are seen to do and consume. As John Stuart Mill is said to have quipped, "men do not desire merely to be rich, but to be richer than other men."

When the income of the reference group increases at the same rate as the individual's, the improvement in satisfaction with standard of living that would normally accompany higher individual income is strongly counteracted by the comparison effect, and improvements in satisfaction with job or housing disappear completely. Accordingly, it could be said that employment and housing behave like "positional goods" in the sense that they generate satisfaction only to the extent that they are better than what the reference group has.[39] This does not happen with other aspects of personal life that are more difficult to display or compare, such as health or satisfaction with life in general. On the contrary, in this case the effect is one of solidarity rather than envy: life satisfaction in general increases with the average income of the members of the reference group.

Note that the effect of solidarity on life satisfaction at an individual level is inconsistent with the national-level result, where countries that grow more have less satisfaction, especially if they are rich. This suggests that the expectations (to which we have attributed this phenomenon) in relation to life satisfaction are not formed by comparison with the successes achieved by others, but possibly respond to economic growth through other channels. These channels do not correspond to any of the private or community dimensions of satisfaction analyzed in this article because all of them have a negative effect from the comparison with (the income of) others. This establishes a "life satisfaction paradox," which echoes Easterlin's paradox and to which there is no clear answer.

These results confirm that individual well-being depends not only on personal economic conditions, but also on the conditions of others. In the more material dimensions of personal well-being, there is an effect of competition with others, while in a more general assessment of personal life, there is a sense of empathy with the economic situation of other members of the social group.

What can be said on opinions about society? Do other people's incomes have an influence here too? With respect to satisfaction with community aspects of life, such as confidence in the health or education systems, satisfaction with government policy on job creation, or the availability of housing, the average income of

38. Average monthly income per capita of reference group, US$ purchasing power parity, natural logarithm.

39. Carlsson and collaborators (Alpízar and others, 2005; Carlsson and others, 2005) show that some consumer goods play a greater positional role than others: for example, television sets are highly positional, while length of vacation is not. Satisfaction from positional goods does not depend so much on their consumption but on their relative consumption; thus the utility from purchasing a larger television set may be nil if everyone in the neighborhood does the same, while the utility from an extra week of vacation does not depend on whether other people take short or long vacations.

the group to which each person belongs always has a significant negative influence. However, in this case the negative influence is not due to the competitive effect caused by comparison of personal income with the average income of the reference group. In fact, personal income has no bearing whatever on these opinions (once the influence of the average income of the group has been taken into account). In contrast, the negative influence of group income is consistent with the fact that groups with higher incomes are more demanding of public policy and collective results. Instead of an individualized mechanism of increasing aspirations with each person's income, there seems to be a group mechanism of aspirations that increases with the average income of all the members of the reference group. Consequently, opinions on community aspects of life are tainted not so much by the individual's personal conditions (at least, economically) but by the conditions and norms of the group to which the individual belongs.

Nevertheless, the assessment that individuals make of their countries in general and the economic situation seems to follow a different logic. Unlike the material aspects of personal life, evaluation of the country is not influenced by a competitive mechanism, or by a phenomenon of solidarity, as occurs with life satisfaction. In contrast with other collective aspects of life, this evaluation is not affected by a mechanism of the growing aspirations of a social group. The inhabitants of Latin America seem to assess their national situation based more on their own personal income than on the income of others. People seem to judge their country's situation by their pocketbooks, in which case opinions on the collective situation are heavily conditioned by personal considerations.

These conclusions are generalizations that assume that all socio-demographic groups behave in a similar way. But men and women, rich and poor, city and rural dwellers can all shape their terms of reference and expectations differently. Men are more susceptible than women to competition with their peers with respect to the material quality of life, while women are more susceptible than men to the performance of their peers in terms of satisfaction with job and housing. In comparison with the poor, rich people worry more when people from their own economic and socio-demographic group earn more than they do, which affects their satisfaction with what they can buy, their job, and even the situation in their country. However, as the reference group of poor people earns a higher income, they become more demanding about their own health, the medical system, and job creation policies.

In urban areas, people have more opportunities to consume and consequently more opportunities to compare consumption standards. Consequently, in cities improvements in the income of the reference group decreases satisfaction with personal economic situation and employment, which does not occur in rural areas. Also, in cities higher earnings are usually associated with lower satisfaction with education systems and with the policies to provide affordable housing (table 3-6). These results suggest that peer pressure and comparison with reference groups

Table 3-6. *Relation of Satisfaction to Income of Individuals and of Others: Differences by Gender, Income Level, and Area of Residence*
Natural logarithm US$ purchasing power parity

		Men	Women	Those with incomes above the regional median	Those with incomes below the regional median	Urban dwellers	Rural dwellers
General							
Life satisfaction	Coefficient	0.287*	0.259*	−0.129	0.549	0.149	0.500
	t-statistic	(2.3)	(2.47)	(−0.35)	(1.18)	(1.03)	(1.56)
	Observations	3,265	5,328	2,052	2,916	3,599	1,202
Situation of country	Coefficient	−0.103	−0.039	−0.482**	−0.040	0.011	0.019
	t-statistic	(−0.76)	(−0.48)	(−2.77)	(−0.15)	(0.12)	(0.1)
	Observations	3,241	5,255	2,038	2,881	3,574	1,177
Economic situation							
Standard of living	Coefficient	−0.330**	−0.174	−0.933***	−0.578***	−0.328*	0.044
	t-statistic	(−2.71)	(−1.34)	(−4.25)	(−3.37)	(−1.98)	(0.24)
	Observations	3,241	5,284	2,040	2,891	3,577	1,195
Economic situation of country	Coefficient	−0.157	−0.133	−0.163	0.101	0.088	0.050
	t-statistic	(−1.19)	(−1.1)	(−0.94)	(0.28)	(0.52)	(0.15)
	Observations	3,110	5,021	1,958	2,746	3,404	1,141
Health							
Satisfaction with health	Coefficient	−0.005	0.018	0.306	−0.921**	−0.014	−0.007
	t-statistic	(−0.03)	(0.13)	(1.2)	(−2.63)	(−0.09)	(−0.02)
	Observations	3,261	5,327	2,000	2,904	3,503	1,208
Confidence in the medical system	Coefficient	−0.372**	−0.341**	−0.218	−0.847***	−0.262	−0.336
	t-statistic	(−2.78)	(−2.75)	(−0.61)	(−3.41)	(−1.42)	(−1.73)
	Observations	3,051	4,861	1,970	2,643	3,390	1,177

Education							
Satisfaction with local education system	Coefficient	−0.418*	−0.370***	−0.585	−0.419	−0.409**	0.144
	t-statistic	(−2.56)	(−3.96)	(−1.6)	(−0.95)	(−3.02)	(0.38)
	Observations	3,183	5,162	1,984	2,868	3,487	1,187
Employment							
Job satisfaction	Coefficient	−0.361	−0.506***	−1.810***	−0.142	−0.847**	−0.609
	t-statistic	(−1.25)	(−3.85)	(−4.28)	(−0.16)	(−2.95)	(−1.07)
	Observations	1,912	1,498	983	936	1,531	366
Satisfaction with job policies	Coefficient	−0.394***	−0.397**	−0.377	−1.031**	−0.142	0.308
	t-statistic	(−3.75)	(−3.21)	(−1.24)	(−2.95)	(−0.99)	(1.03)
	Observations	3,210	5,195	2,017	2,852	3,516	1,175
Housing							
Satisfaction with housing	Coefficient	−0.121	−0.232*	−0.970*	−0.697**	−0.251	0.092
	t-statistic	(−0.87)	(−2.38)	(−2.51)	(−2.87)	(−1.22)	(0.32)
	Observations	3,264	5,328	2,047	2,925	3,586	1,206
Satisfaction with policies to provide good and affordable homes	Coefficient	−0.473**	−0.164	−1.232***	0.079	−0.436**	0.348
	t-statistic	(−2.75)	(−1.08)	(−6.31)	(0.21)	(−2.62)	(1.55)
	Observations	3,115	4,980	1,940	2,779	3,394	1,146

Source: Authors' calculations based on Gallup World Poll (2007).

*Coefficient is statiscally significant at the 10 percent level; **at the 5 percent level; ***at the 1 percent level; no asterisk means the coefficient is not different from zero with statiscal significance.

Note: This table shows only the coefficients for the independent variable "average monthly income per capita of reference group." Life satisfaction and the situation of the country are measured on a scale from 0 to 10 and the econometric method used is Ordered Logit. The other satisfaction variables are binary (yes/no), and the econometric method used is Logit. Each cell comes from a separated regression, which includes, in addition to income of the reference group, all the explanatory variables of the previous table. The value in parenthesis is the t-statistic.

may induce higher expectations for education and housing policies in the urban areas, which is not observed in rural areas.

There can also be differences between countries or groups of countries, since, as seen in an earlier section, growth does not have an equal effect on satisfaction in poor and rich countries, or in countries with weak growth and fast growth. But the results are less solid than those presented so far because of the smaller size of the samples and possible differences between individual countries.[40]

Political Economy Implications

One of the central questions of modern political economy is why so many democratic governments maintain policies that are damaging to economic growth and limit the incomes of the majority of the population. The adoption of the Washington Consensus by many countries provided an opportunity to answer this question. During the 1990s, various theories attempted to explain why these reforms (which included monetary and fiscal discipline measures, market liberalization and privatization) had not been adopted before, and why they were adopted at different times and with varying intensities by each country. The explanations revolved around the distributive conflicts that blocked progress on adoption of reforms until one group could force others to accept the costs. To speed up the reform process, it was thought convenient to simultaneously implement various reforms that offered cross-compensations to the groups holding veto power, given that promises to compensate losers from a single reform in the future would lack credibility.[41]

The evidence presented in this work suggests a simple but powerful mechanism of political obstruction to growth policies, which has received little attention in theoretical or empirical studies of political economy. This mechanism is the loss of satisfaction resulting from an increase in expectations and aspirations accompanying economic growth and improvements in the incomes of the reference groups of individuals. The most marked losses of satisfaction occur in the material domains of people's lives and tend to be strongest in the richest and most urbanized societies, as well as in the countries with the highest growth rates. It could be that the expansion of media and advertising also contributes to raising expectations, and there is some evidence to suggest that the most culturally and ethnically fragmented societies are those most likely to suffer the harmful effects of competition on satisfaction. The inverse association between satisfaction and reference group income levels is not limited to the private aspects of people's lives. In Latin

---

40. For reasons of space they are not presented, but can be requested from the authors.

41. For an introduction to these debates, see the brief summary and bibliographical recommendations in the entry "Washington Consensus" in *The Princeton Encyclopedia of the World Economy*, Reinert and Rajan, eds. (2008).

American societies, individuals with the highest income levels feel less satisfied with the results of government policies on health, education, job creation, and housing provision than more needy people.

In light of this evidence, a government strategy that focuses exclusively on improving efficiency and achieving economic growth may fall victim to its own success. This is especially true if, as occurred with the Washington Consensus, proponents tend to exaggerate potential benefits, which raises expectations. It is more feasible to garner political support with strategies that combine growth policies with strategies of economic and social inclusion, and with reforms of delivery of health, education, employment, and housing services. The majority of Latin American governments learned this lesson well in the 1990s. One visible consequence has been the notable increase in social expenditure from 8 percent to 11 percent of GDP and from US$257 per capita in 1990 to US$423 in 2005 (in year 2000 constant dollars).

However, strategies of inclusion and provision of social services that maximize political support are not necessarily the ones that produce the greatest improvements in the living conditions of poor people. An effective inclusion policy aimed at preventing loss of satisfaction might consist of reducing the income of families or individuals who are visible role models for the social groups that are most vulnerable to changes in expectations (in particular, the upwardly mobile urban middle class). Certain expropriations, price controls, or taxes might be very effective in achieving these goals. Similarly, a politically effective social policy could be based on concentrating improvements in coverage and quality of the services provided to the upwardly mobile middle and upper classes whose demands tend to increase as their income grows, while keeping the lower social groups uninformed because their expectations from social policy are more modest.

These obvious inconsistencies between what might be politically effective and what could contribute to improving income level or reducing poverty are clearly a constant dilemma for politicians and leaders in fragmented and unequal democracies such as those of Latin America. Given that, in a democratic system, political decisions are the result of conflicts and negotiations between groups holding different interests and views, these inconsistencies can rarely be resolved solely by technical arguments about which measures produce more growth or more poverty reduction. Likewise, they cannot be solved simply by adopting the measures that produce the greatest increase in immediate subjective individual well-being. Consequently, this chapter does not make the usual policy recommendations on what governments should do. The only policy implication is that the pubic debate would be more fruitful if opinion leaders, government economic advisors, and political organizations abandoned their simplistic thesis that all increases in income generate an increase in satisfaction (and thus political support) and, in its place, accept that the relationship between income and satisfaction is inherently conflictive.

References

Alpizar, F., F. Carlsson, and O. Johansson-Stenman. 2005. "How Much Do We Care about Absolute versus Relative Income and Consumption?" *Journal of Economic Behavior and Organization* 56: 405–21.

Ball, R., and K. Chernova. 2005. "Absolute Income, Relative Income, and Happiness." Haverford College. Unpublished.

Carlsson, F., G. Gupta, and O. Johansson-Stenman. 2005. "Keeping Up with the Vaishyas: Caste and Relative Standing." Working Paper in Economics 171. Göteborg, Sweden: Göteborg University.

Di Tella, R., R. McCulloch, and A. Oswald. 2003. "The Macroeconomics of Happiness." *Review of Economics and Statistics* 85 (4): 809–27.

Diener, E., and others. 1993. "The Relationship between Income and Subjective Well-Being: Relative or Absolute?" *Social Indicators Research* 28: 195–223.

Duesenberry, J. 1949. *Income, Saving and the Theory of Consumer Behavior.* Harvard University Press.

Easterlin, R. A. 1974. "Does Economic Growth Enhance the Human Lot? Some Empirical Evidence." In P. A. David and M. Reder, eds. *Nations and Households in Economic Growth: Essays in Honor of Moses Abramovitz.* Stanford University Press.

———. 1995. "Will Raising the Incomes of All Increase the Happiness of All?" *Journal of Economic Behavior and Organization* 27 (10): 35–48.

Easterly, W., J. Ritzen, and M. Woolcock. 2006. "Social Cohesion, Institutions, and Growth." *Economics and Politics* 18 (2): 103–20.

Felson, R., and M. Reed. 1986. "Reference Groups and Self-Appraisals of Academic Ability and Performance." *Social Psychology Quarterly* 49 (2): 103–09.

Ferrer-i-Carbonell, A. 2005. "Income and Well-being: An Empirical Analysis of the Comparison Income Effect." *Journal of Public Economics* 89 (5–6): 997–1019.

Frey, B. S., M. Benz, and A. Stutzer. 2003. "Introducing Procedural Utility: Not Only What, but Also How Matters." CREMA Working Paper 2003–02. Basel, Switzerland: Center for Research in Economics, Management and the Arts (CREMA).

Gallup Poll. 2006. Gallup World Poll. Available at www.gallup.com/consulting/worldpoll/24046/about.aspx.

———. 2007. Available at www.gallup.com/consulting/worldpoll/24046/about.aspx.

Graham, C., and A. Felton. 2006. "Does Inequality Matter to Individual Welfare? Some Insights from Latin America." *Journal of Economic Inequality* 6 (1): 107–22.

Graham, C., and S. Pettinato. 2002. *Happiness and Hardship: Opportunity and Insecurity in New Market Economies.* Brookings.

Hyman, H. H. 1960. "Reflections on Reference Groups." *Public Opinion Quarterly* 24 (3): 383–96.

Inter-American Development Bank. 2008. *Beyond Facts: Understanding Quality of Life.* Development in the Americas Report. Washington, D.C.

Kaufmann, D., A. Kraay, and M. Mastruzzi. 2006. "Governance Matters V: Aggregate and Individual Governance Indicators for 1996–2005." Washington, D.C.: World Bank.

Kingdon, G., and J. Knight. 2004. "Community, Comparisons and Subjective Well-being in a Divided Society." CSAE WPS/2004-21. Oxford, U.K.: Oxford University, Centre for the Study of African Economies.

Lora, E., and M. Olivera. 2005. "The Electoral Consequences of the Washington Consensus." *Economia* 5 (2): 1–61.

Lora, E., U. Panizza, and M. Quispe-Agnoli. 2004. "Reform Fatigue: Symptoms, Reasons, and Implications." *Federal Reserve Bank of Atlanta Economic Review* (2nd quarter): 1–28.

Luttmer, E. 2005. "Neighbors as Negatives: Relative Earnings and Well-Being." *Quarterly Journal of Economics* 120 (3): 963–1002.

McBride, M. 2005. "An Experimental Study of Happiness and Aspiration Formation." Manuscript.

Merton, R. 1957. *Social Theory and Social Structure.* Glencoe, Ill.: Free Press of Glencoe.

Michalos, A. 1985. "Multiple Discrepancies Theory." *Social Indicators Research* 16 (4): 347–413.

Reinert, K. A., and R. Rajan, eds. 2008. *The Princeton Encyclopedia of the World Economy.* Princeton University Press.

Ruhm, C. J. 2000. "Are Recessions Good for Your Health?" *Quarterly Journal of Economics* 115 (2): 617–50.

———. 2005. "Commentary: Mortality Increases During Economic Upturns." *International Journal of Epidemiology* 34 (6): 1206–11.

Senik, C. 2004. "Relativizing Relative Income." DELTA Working Paper 2004–17. Paris, France: Department and Laboratory of Applied and Theoretical Economics (DELTA).

———. 2006. "Is Man Doomed to Progress?" IZA Discussion Paper 2237. Bonn, Germany: IZA/Institute for the Study of Labor.

Stevenson, B., and J. Wolfers. 2008. "Economic Growth and Subjective Well-Being: Reassessing the Easterlin Paradox." Paper presented to the Brookings Panel on Economic Activity.

Stutzer, A. 2004. "The Role of Income Aspirations in Individual Happiness." *Journal of Economic Behavior and Organization* 54: 89–109.

van Praag, B. M. S., and A. Ferrer-i-Carbonell. 2007. *Happiness Quantified: A Satisfaction Calculus Approach.* Oxford University Press.

Veblen, T. 1899. *The Theory of the Leisure Class.* 1934 ed. New York: Modern Library.

Veenhoven, R. 2007. *World Database of Happiness, Trend in Nations.* Rotterdam: Erasmus University.

World Bank. 2007. World Development Indicators Online (http://publications.worldbank.org/ecommerce/catalog/product-detail?product_id=631625&).

4

Satisfaction beyond Income

EDUARDO LORA, JUAN CAMILO CHAPARRO,
AND MARÍA VICTORIA RODRÍGUEZ

A broadened understanding of satisfaction challenges the traditional economic theory that assumes that individuals maximize their well-being based on decisions that correctly predict basic well-being derived from consumption and from other key decisions, such as the allocation of time between work and leisure activities. In reality, human behavior does not adhere to such simple propositions.[1] The motivations that intervene in decisions are diverse and include momentary impulses, commitments, or simple routines that give rise to decisions that do not necessarily lead to achieving maximum satisfaction. A paradoxical conclusion of satisfaction studies is that the explicit pursuit of happiness can be counterproductive, because it affects individual aspirations and because people make systematic misjudgments about what produces happiness. In general, people fail to predict future utility or welfare effectively; thus they overestimate the effect of extrinsic attributes (particularly, the value of consumer goods) and underestimate the benefits of intrinsic attributes (friends, family, hobbies). In analyzing the factors that influence levels of satisfaction, it is apparent that beyond income and what can be obtained with it, other aspects of life have a greater impact on maintaining them.

---

1. The challenges that the "science of happiness" presents to economic theory are surveyed by Frey and Stutzer (2002); many of them were identified in the 1970s by the Leyden school (see van Praag, 1985) and by Brickman and Campbell (1971).

Since satisfaction depends on income, as well as other factors, the following mental experiment is pertinent: If a person undergoes a sudden critical change in some aspect of life, how much would his or her income have to be increased to maintain the same level of satisfaction? Although this concerns a completely hypothetical experiment, it is enlightening; it shows that greater income can hardly substitute for many of the most important facets of life, such as friendships or health. For example, for a Latin American,[2] the average "value" of friendship is nearly seven times his or her income, which gives support to the popular view, as many people have stated, that a good friendship is priceless.

The previous chapter analyzed how various domains of individual satisfaction relate to income. With a different focus, this chapter concentrates on life satisfaction in general to explore how it is affected by diverse factors, beyond income, and how the different dimensions of people's lives are reflected synthetically in their level of satisfaction. Life satisfaction in the Gallup World Polls—which are the source of information for this chapter—is measured according to the life satisfaction "ladder" question, which asks respondents, "On what step of the ladder do you feel you are currently" with "the highest step [10] representing the best possible life for you and the lowest step [0] representing the worst for you."[3] This method is only one out of many methods used to investigate life satisfaction and to measure its subjective utility (see box 4-1).

Individual Factors and Life Satisfaction

In surveys that use the "ladder" scale from 0 to 10 to determine a respondent's level of life satisfaction, the answers are concentrated mainly at the midpoint, but this does not mean the gradation lacks importance. Simply comparing the way in which answers are distributed in wealthy countries to their distribution in poor countries makes it clear that wealthier countries have a greater level of life satisfaction (as analyzed in chapter 3). Using this scale, a little more than 80 percent of the people surveyed in the poorest countries rate the quality of their current life between a 0 and a 5, whereas in the richest countries barely 25 percent of respondents give scores in this range (see figure 4-1). This would suggest that in order to understand life satisfaction, one must explain the differences *between* countries. Nonetheless, this route does not stretch very far; beyond the per capita income of the countries and the growth rate in past years, no other "national" variable makes a significant contribution to explaining the differences. Even if it did, it would not lead too far, since only a fraction (37 percent, to be exact) of the differences in levels of life satisfaction between some individuals and others is due to diversity among countries. The most effective gauges in analyzing life satisfaction are individuals, not countries.

---

2. In this chapter, the term *Latin America* (and its derivations) includes the Caribbean.
3. The complete text of the question appears in box 2-1 (general domain of self-perception).

Box 4-1. *Measurements of Subjective Well-Being*

In recent years, the use of surveys that investigate individual opinions of diverse aspects of life, including life satisfaction in general, has resurged. In Latin America, the annual Latinobarometro surveys, which cover 17 countries, have included this type of question since 1996. The World Poll of the Gallup Organization, applied in 23 Latin American countries and in more than 130 countries since 2006, includes numerous questions regarding life satisfaction. The World Values Surveys (WVS), which currently cover 80 countries, also explore life satisfaction. Based on diverse sources, for 11 developed countries, these surveys have gathered data concerning life satisfaction for 25 years or more.

In order to measure life satisfaction, respondents are asked to answer questions such as "Generally speaking, how happy are you with your life?" or "How satisfied are you with your life?" with answer options that range from four different levels to a scale of 0 to 10. Though psychologists usually prefer the question of "satisfaction" to that of "happiness," both are narrowly correlated. According to Blanchflower and Oswald (2004) and Graham and Pettinato (2002), the correlation coefficient between answers to both questions varies between 0.5 and 0.6. The "ladder" question employed in the Gallup World Poll is unusual in that it asks respondents to frame their evaluation of life satisfaction supposing "that the highest step represents the best possible life . . . and the lowest step the worst possible life," which imposes a certain comparative structure that does not exist in other life satisfaction measurement strategies.

Although these surveys are the best-known source of information on subjective welfare, there are other methods. The *experience sampling method* collects real-time data several times per day with regard to the respondents' feelings of well-being in their routine activities. This method has already been applied to representative populations in the United States, and studies have concluded that the most satisfactory daily activities include interactions with others and diverse leisure aspects, while some of the least satisfactory take place in work environments.

The *day reconstruction method* asks respondents how satisfied they are at different moments of the day. The U-index (for "unpleasant") of displeasure is equal to the portion of the day that an individual had unpleasant feelings. The *brain imaging method* measures brain activity associated with negative and positive feelings. These two last methods are quite costly and to date have only been applied in experimental form.

The broad consensus among academics is that subjective well-being is measurable to a certain degree of precision, moderately stable, and sensitive to changes in living conditions. The measurements are well correlated with diverse aspects of behavior associated with happiness, such as frequency of laughter in moments of social interaction. People who are happy according to such measurements are also considered happy by their friends and family; such individuals express positive emotions more frequently and are more optimistic, sociable, and extroverted. They also sleep better and are less likely to commit suicide.

Recently, a group of 50 notable academics proposed a system of *National Indicators of Subjective Well-Being and Ill-Being* (Diener, 2005; Kahneman and others, 2004). Such new ideas and methods to measure subjective well-being have revived the old dream of maximizing well-being, considered the final objective of the public policies

(continued)

Box 4-1. *Measurements of Subjective Well-Being (continued)*

by economists since the eighteenth century, such as Bentham (1781), and some as modern as Tinbergen (1956) and Theil (1964). In the past, this dream was considered unattainable because of obstacles in measuring well-being on a cardinal scale that allowed for comparisons between individuals and the difficulties in building a consistent social function starting with individual preferences and involving diverse outcome variables (Arrow's famous Impossibility Theorem).

Today, measurements of subjective well-being provide the cardinal scale and comparability among individuals that were lacking, and consequently, in principle they permit the construction of social well-being functions. For instance, the sum of happiness scores for individuals (that is, on a scale of 0–10) can be adopted as a simple and intuitive social welfare function; yet there are many objections to this hypothesis.

Sources: Frey and Stutzer (2007) and Veenhoven (2007).

Individual satisfaction levels differ according to age, sex, and employment status. Within these characteristics and many other differences among individuals (many of them impossible to measure) lies the great diversity that reveals satisfaction levels.

Age and Gender

In general, people from Latin America and the Caribbean (referred to herein simply as "Latin America") experience a slight reduction in their satisfaction level in

Figure 4-1. *Life Satisfaction in Rich and Poor Countries*

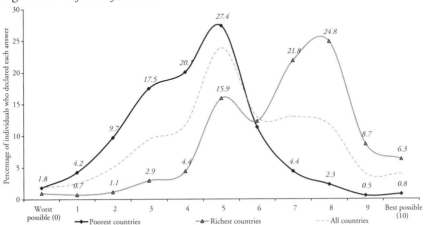

Source: Authors' calculations based on Gallup (2006 and 2007) and World Bank (2007).
Note: Income groups where built using the 2005 GDP per capita at US$ purchasing power parity (PPP). The total sample was split into four different groups with the same number of people. Poorest countries are those with GDP per capita below US$PPP 2,077. Richests countries have a GDP per captia above US$PPP 13,977.

the first years of their adult lives, and an increase in the latter years of their lives. The critical point seems to be reached at around age 56 for men and 60 for women, following a very stable trend, in spite of other factors that influence their satisfaction. Based on the Latinobarometro surveys, Graham and Pettinato (2000) have calculated that the lowest level of life satisfaction is reached at age 46. Many studies have found a U-shaped relation between age and satisfaction.[4] Both static studies (also called cross-sectional studies), like this one, and longitudinal studies (which evaluate information on people over time) have come to this same conclusion. Such studies do not account for differentiation among generations; thus they cannot predict how the level of satisfaction of the youngest generations surveyed will be affected when they reach more advanced ages. Nevertheless, studies in the United States indicate that in recent decades all new generations have lower levels of satisfaction than previous ones.[5]

Following a universal trend, Latin American women have declared themselves to be more satisfied with their lives, on average, than men, but the gender gap is more profound than a simple comparison of answers reveals; in fact, based on equivalent levels of income and other influential factors, which will be analyzed herein, women have indicated substantially higher levels of life satisfaction. For example, whereas a woman living under normal conditions has a 15 percent probability of giving a score of 8 (on a scale of 0 to 10) in terms of life satisfaction, this can reach 18 percent if the woman is in socioeconomic conditions similar to those of the average man. That said, although men usually have more favorable financial circumstances, it is women who feel more satisfied overall. This suggests that possibly their experiences are more intense or lasting.[6]

Beyond these demographic trends, there are numerous individual factors, which can be considered objective (in other words, externally observable), that are associated with life satisfaction. It is expedient to begin with the capacities of individuals and gradually expand the focus to encompass the environment that surrounds them.[7]

The Importance of Capabilities

Good health is the basis of all capabilities. It is important to recognize that there is no universally accepted objective measurement of individual health. Some

4. For example, Clark and Oswald (1994), Oswald (1997), and van Praag, Frijters, and Ferrer-i-Carbonell (2003).

5. Blanchflower and Oswald (2004).

6. Diener and others (1999).

7. Throughout this discussion, the direct impact of income has been kept isolated, as it has already been discussed in the previous chapter. There, the influence of the principal individual variables (gender, age, marital status, education, the significance of religion and friendships), which are discussed in the present chapter, is also controlled for. This approach is necessary because otherwise the impact of other variables that are correlated with income, which may have their own influence on life satisfaction (such as education), may be attributed to income.

known variables related to health, at least in the population (not for each individual separately), are height and body mass. The Gallup World Polls include a set of quasi-objective questions on basic individual health conditions (known as European Quality of Life-5 Dimensions Index [EQ-5D] and described in further detail in chapter 6). Based on an indicator composed on the basis of answers to those questions, it is apparent that those people with better health have, effectively, greater possibilities of declaring themselves more satisfied with life.[8] The effect is very strong and statistically very solid (see table 4-1). Take, for example, a Mexican woman who in all aspects apart from health is considered at the midpoint within her country's population; in other words, she is a "median" person (in a statistical sense)[9] who has median income and education levels and a median amount of material comforts. If this woman does not have any health deficiencies, she will most likely rate herself a 7 on the scale of satisfaction. If her health state corresponds to that of a median woman, her level of satisfaction will probably be reduced to a 5, and if her health status corresponds to that of the 25 percent of the Mexican women with health conditions worse than those of the median woman, her level could feasibly be a 4.

It is well-established that one's health status has a major impact on one's life satisfaction; in fact, the investigations of Dolan (2006) and Graham, Eggers, and Sukhtankar (2004) conclude that it is the *most* important determinant. Among the countries of the Organisation for Economic Co-operation and Development (OECD), where arterial hypertension is most common, it has been observed that the average happiness levels are lower.[10] Likewise, being obese increases the probability of leading a life with which one is less satisfied.[11]

Consequently, individuals with known health problems declare less satisfaction with their lives than healthy individuals. Most likely casualty relations exist in both directions, a question discussed in chapter 5. However, stronger than the link between life satisfaction and individuals' objective health indicators is the

8. The responses to the set of EQ-5D questions are converted into a single index using a formula that attaches a weight to each of the possible health states. The scoring algorithm is taken from Shaw, Johnson, and Coons (2005). For further details, see Lora (2008).

9. An explanation may be in order for those not versed in statistics: *median* and *average* are not the same thing. The *median* of a set of values is the value of the variable at the midpoint of all the values in the set, so that exactly half the values are above the median and half below, whereas the *average* is the sum of all the values divided by the number of values. Where the variable involved is "income," the *median* income is typically much less than the *average* income because the rich, though comparatively few in number, earn disproportionately large amounts, which distorts the average, inflating it well above the median value. (To give a crude example, consider a population of five individuals whose incomes are $100, $200, $300, $400, and $1,000,000; the median income for the population is $300, whereas the average income is a whopping $200,200.) Thus the median, rather than the average, individual is used to refer to the most typical or characteristic person within a particular population.

10. Blanchflower and Oswald (2007).

11. Graham and Felton (2005a) and (2005b) and Graham (2008).

Table 4-1. *Factors Related with Life Satisfaction*

		Latin America and the Caribbean		The world	
Dependent variable: life satisfaction (0–10)		1	2	3	4
Demographic characteristics	Male	-0.1690***	-0.2409***	-0.1567***	-0.1614***
	Age (years)	-0.0489***	-0.0569***	-0.0331***	-0.0364***
	Age squared	0.0004***	0.0005***	0.0003***	0.0003***
Human capital	Health Score (EQ-5D)[a]	1.2702***	0.9735***	n.a.	n.a.
	Complete primary education	0.0052	0.0425	n.a.	n.a.
	Complete secondary education	0.0766	0.1566	n.a.	n.a.
	Complete superior education	0.2541**	0.3954**	n.a.	n.a.
Relational goods	Married	-0.0216	0.0562	0.0768**	0.0792*
	Divorced	-0.0650	-0.0478	-0.2737***	-0.2633***
	Widowed	0.0651	0.1456	-0.2655***	-0.2545***
	Have one child	0.0043	-0.0255	0.0405	-0.0163
	Have two or more children	-0.0117	0.0084	0.0159	-0.0167
	Consider religion to be important	0.2536***	0.1783**	0.0589*	0.0811*
	Have friends	0.4325***	0.3613***	0.6495***	0.5117***
	Have employment	0.1046**	0.0583	0.2025***	0.1849***

Category		Col 1	Col 2	Col 3	Col 4
Material life conditions	Household income (monthly per capita in US$)	0.2225***	0.2209***	n.a.	n.a.
	Live in urban area	−0.0273	0.0368	0.1877***	0.1853***
	Access to running water service	0.0497	0.0821	n.a.	n.a.
	Access to electricity service	0.3551	0.1013	n.a.	n.a.
	Access to telephone service	0.1597**	0.1422**	n.a.	n.a.
	Assets index[b]	0.1368***	0.1539***	n.a.	n.a.
	Does not have shortage of income to cover food costs	0.4919***	0.4229***	0.7334***	0.6645***
	Does not have shortage of income to cover household costs	0.2232***	0.1499*	0.2840***	0.2236***
Personality trends	Individual optimism score		0.3069***		0.2953***
	Number of individuals	11,990	7,923	87,959	28,878
	Number of countries	19	17	97	51
	Fixed effects per country	Yes	Yes	Yes	Yes
	Pseudo-R squared	0.06	0.07	0.08	0.09

Source: Authors' calculations based on Gallup (2007).

a. European Quality of Life-5 Dimensions Index (EQ-5D) health score is a quantitative measure of health conditions based on five questions. A higher score indicates a better health status.

b. The assets included in the asset index are television, computer, automobile, washing machine, refrigerator, and DVD player.

n.a. = not available.

*Coefficient is statistically significant at the 10 percent level; **at the 5 percent level; ***at the 1 percent level; no asterisk means the coefficient is not different from zero with statistical significance.

Note: The coefficients indicate the effect of life satisfaction on an average individual, who is graded on a scale of 0 to 10.

relation between life satisfaction and health satisfaction, since both are influenced by traits of the individuals' personalities.[12]

The self-development capacity of any individual depends essentially not only on his or her health status, but also on his or her education level. There are serious limitations to conventional methods of measuring education based on the level of formal schooling attained or the overall years of education completed, especially in a region such as Latin America in which deficiencies in the quality of schooling are so pronounced.[13] Regardless of these limitations, surveys clearly show that the most-educated individuals tend to have greater life satisfaction levels. In the Gallup World Polls, respondents are asked only what level of education they have reached, and not the number of years spent in formal schooling. Nevertheless, the results clearly show that those individuals who have reached the tertiary level are more satisfied with their lives than those who have completed only secondary education, while at the same time the latter individuals declare greater life satisfaction than those who have finished only grade school or have no formal education.

Since this statistical analysis accounts for the relation between income and satisfaction separately, the significance of education in life satisfaction levels is implicit for other reasons. It is difficult to interpret the many reasons why individuals with higher levels of scholastic attainment feel better. In part, the root may be an inverse causality: those individuals with more positive attitudes and greater self-assurance achieve higher levels of education. Nevertheless, this explanation does not go far in countries such as those in Latin America, where education opportunities are so poorly distributed. There, it is more probable that the most scholarly individuals enjoy a higher social status and can seek jobs and activities that offer them enhanced personal enrichment opportunities. Also, it is likely that such individuals have a greater potential to appreciate the nonmaterial aspects in life, including their interpersonal relations.[14] In other words, more educated people have more options not only to satisfy their consumption needs (although perhaps subject to greater aspirations, as observed in the previous chapter), but also to feel more autonomous, capable, and connected.

Interpersonal Conditions

Family conditions, friendships, and other interpersonal relations constitute part of the objective bases of people's lives on which their self-development possibilities also depend. Happiness studies regularly conclude that when compared with single adults, married people feel better and divorcees and widows and widowers

---

12. van Praag, Frijters, and Ferrer-i-Carbonell (2003), Argyle (1999), and Diener and Seligman (2004).

13. Inter-American Development Bank (IDB) (2008), chapter 6.

14. Diener and others (1999).

feel worse.[15] Nevertheless, the dominating influence is unclear: whether having a stable partner enhances well-being or whether those individuals with a greater sense of life satisfaction have more possibilities in finding a partner and maintaining a stable relationship.[16] The estimates included in table 4-1 give partial support to these conclusions. In Latin America, only divorce seems to affect life satisfaction (and only once the influence of personality traits is isolated, as is discussed later in the chapter). Other marital statuses have no impact (in comparison to being single), whereas they do in the rest of the world.

Since having children is one of the most important decisions for any individual, it is conceivable that children contribute to life satisfaction; however, this is not what comes out of opinion surveys in Latin America or other parts of the world. Perhaps this sounds surprising, but diverse studies (though not the present one) have found that, based on the number of offspring per family, children can have a negative, although modest, effect on life satisfaction.[17] Nevertheless, no universal verdict exists on this subject. For example, whereas in western Germany children seem to diminish the level of life satisfaction, the opposite is found on the other side of the country.[18] Those who have conducted in-depth studies into the channels through which having children may affect life satisfaction have concluded that children can create dissatisfaction as they can augment levels of anxiety, stress, and depression, above all in the case of single parents. When such feelings manifest themselves, they have a stronger influence on the life satisfaction of men than women.[19] The impact children have on life satisfaction seems to depend on diverse conditions. The first child (and, in certain cultures, especially when it is male) produces greater satisfaction when the couple to whom it is born has a stable relationship than when that relationship is not stable. Teenage pregnancies or unwanted children tend to result in diminished satisfaction. Since econometric estimates of the influence of children on satisfaction, such those in table 4-1, use as comparator group those without children, and most of those people have selected to not have children, perhaps it is not so surprising to find no effect of children on satisfaction.

Beyond family structure, life satisfaction seems to depend mainly on the potential to interact with others and on spiritual beliefs.[20] Analysis of the Gallup World Polls confirms that people feel more satisfied when they consider friends and religion important factors. Compared to the rest of the world, for Latin Americans, being religious has a greater influence on life satisfaction, and having support from

---

15. Argyle (1999) and Oswald (1997).
16. Diener and others (2000).
17. Argyle (1999), Clark and Oswald (1994), Frey and Stutzer (1999), and van Praag, Frijters, and Ferrer-i-Carbonell (2003).
18. Frijters, Haisken-DeNew, and Shields (2004a) and (2004b).
19. Kohler, Behrman, and Skytthe (2005) and Ferrer-i-Carbonell and Frijters (2004)
20. Ellison (1991).

friends has a smaller impact. One's work environment provides an outlet for interpersonal development, and worldwide it plays a critical role in life satisfaction. In Latin America, the effect is less pronounced, but this does not mean that the noneconomic dimensions of employment have less importance for Latin American populations; on the contrary, IDB (2008)—chapter 7—shows that Latin Americans with paid employment especially value recognition and respect in the workplace, which confirms the importance of the relational dimension of the work environment. Nevertheless, many Latin Americans show a preference for self-employment because of the autonomy and flexibility it offers them.

It is important to keep in mind that when people express satisfaction with their lives and assert that religion or friendships are important factors, this may be a simple reflection of their personality and may not necessarily indicate that they dedicate more time or attention to activities that incorporate such factors. A method of testing whether personality is actually behind this correlation is to determine whether the level of satisfaction is maintained when a variable that synthesizes certain personality traits of each individual is considered.[21] As can be observed in table 4-1, the majority of the results are maintained; in particular, those people who consider religion and friendship important continue to express higher satisfaction with their lives when the personality traits variable is taken into account. On the other hand, the positive effect of being employed diminishes, which suggests that the association between life satisfaction and having a job is more complex: perhaps those who feel more satisfied with life have a predisposition toward having a job, or perhaps being employed contributes to a more favorable opinion overall.

Material Life Conditions

For most people, having access to a variety of goods and basic services is a prerequisite for life satisfaction, as pointed out clearly by Aristotle in *Nicomachean Ethics:* "Happiness . . . is the best, noblest, and most pleasant thing . . . yet evidently . . . it needs the external goods as well." The conditions of material life have been the focus of numerous studies and one of the main concerns of international development agencies since 1970. The most recent studies on happiness or life satisfaction support this position.

Clearly, income is the most obvious measure of people's economic capacity to satisfy their needs. However, even after income is accounted for, having access to specific goods and services contributes independently to life satisfaction. This could be the result of fluctuating income and the fact that some individuals lack access to credit or other financial assistance to satisfy their needs when their income is temporarily reduced, or because certain goods hold a value for people

---

21. This variable is simply the tendency (not explained by objective factors) of an individual to respond in a positive way to the set of perception questions included in the Gallup World Poll.

that surpasses their purchase price (or, more specifically, that such goods can sur-pass the satisfaction value that can be derived from other similarly priced goods).

From the Gallup World Polls, it has been observed that currently the life satis-faction levels of many people in Latin America are limited by their inability to cover their basic needs of food or housing (occasional or permanently). Some countries have reported alarming figures: 64 percent of those polled in Haiti declared that on some occasion in the preceding 12 months they lacked sufficient funds to buy food (see figure 4-2). In Nicaragua and El Salvador about half of respondents reported that in the preceding 12 months they had gone through periods in which they could not afford to pay for their homes. Food deprivation rates in various Latin American countries are abnormally high based on the income levels per capita in the region. Chapter 5 of this book discusses in greater detail the deleterious effects of food deprivation and other types of vulnerabilities on life satisfaction.

However, those goods traditionally considered essential (beyond individual income) are not the only ones that can affect life satisfaction. The statistical analy-ses summarized in table 4-1 indicate that life satisfaction for the average Latin American currently depends on having access to telephone service (fixed or mobile) and possessing a variety of durable assets, including a television, computer, auto-mobile, washing machine, refrigerator, and DVD player. It is impossible to obtain precise estimates as to which of these durable goods are the most essential, although it is clear that the more of these assets individuals have the greater level of satisfaction they assert. (Table 4-2 shows the possession rates for the services and

Figure 4-2. *Food Insecurity and per Capita Income*

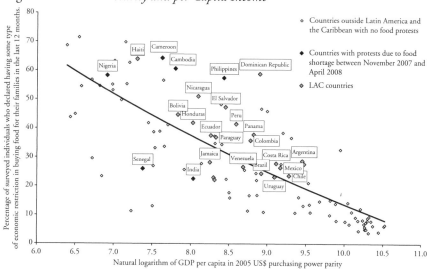

Source: Authors' calculations based on Gallup (2007) and World Bank (2007).

Table 4-2. *Asset Index and Components by Country*
Percentage of people owning each asset

Country (sorted by last column)	Television	Computer	Vehicle	Washing machine	Refrigerator	DVD player	Asset index, national average[a] Range: between −3 (own no asset) and 3 (own all assets)
Chile	98.5	44.2	35.9	91.3	89.4	64.2	1.15
Mexico	95.2	25.2	40.5	72.6	87.9	67.5	0.82
Panama	96.0	17.9	29.0	82.2	84.9	67.9	0.71
Costa Rica	97.3	31.9	34.8	62.1	90.7	57.8	0.70
Argentina	97.6	29.7	36.4	61.0	67.9	47.7	0.39
Colombia	95.7	24.0	13.4	49.3	84.0	45.4	0.13
Dominican Republic	88.7	17.6	23.6	77.3	77.9	28.5	0.13
Uruguay	96.7	29.5	30.1	61.1	50.7	39.8	0.10
Ecuador	94.4	23.1	17.3	30.7	83.2	53.7	0.04
Brazil	94.0	21.8	31.0	38.4	30.8	60.6	−0.21
Guatemala	92.7	28.7	26.2	19.2	59.6	45.2	−0.23
Paraguay	88.0	10.6	20.3	51.2	61.1	28.1	−0.37
Peru	90.3	21.0	10.8	20.0	49.8	52.7	−0.50
El Salvador	89.3	14.2	14.3	13.6	63.4	46.3	−0.53
Bolivia	85.9	19.2	19.3	6.8	43.9	42.8	−0.74
Nicaragua	80.6	11.4	14.0	6.2	42.9	38.1	−0.98
Honduras	69.6	13.1	16.0	7.0	44.0	23.5	−1.18

Source: Authors' calculations with support from Gallup (2007).

a. The asset index is the country average of individual-level asset scores. The score is constructed with the principal components statistical technique.

goods mentioned in this analysis and the synthetic index constructed to summarize them.)

Based on the impact of individual aspirations and comparisons of people regarding the satisfaction derived from consumption (see chapter 3), it could be presumed that life satisfaction depends not only on, or not greatly on, one's own possessions, but rather more on the goods possessed by those around one. Based on data from the Gallup World Polls, there is no evidence to support this hypothesis. Nevertheless, other studies have found several channels through which the conditions of others affect certain dimensions of satisfaction. For example, in Santiago, Chile, spatial segregation has an impact on the poor population's ambitions and levels of satisfaction with education: the most segregated have decreased ambitions and do not demand that education for their children meet the same standards as those who live near families with higher education levels.[22] In La Paz, Bolivia, homes located where there is a greater concentration of indigenous people have lower values, probably because this factor reduces the satisfaction that non-indigenous people have with their dwellings and neighborhoods.[23]

How Much Are Certain Sources of Satisfaction Worth?

An interesting digression is to recall previously discussed results in regard to "valuing" those personal capacities, interpersonal conditions, or goods that contribute to life satisfaction—for example, the value of friendship. Perhaps it is crass and ill-mannered to ask how much friendship is worth in monetary or other material terms, since the satisfaction derived from having friends is a value on its own. It is not necessary for friendships to generate material benefits or to be considered good business in order for them to be important in the lives of many people. Nevertheless, because of the satisfaction it offers, it is possible to compare friendship with income, which also produces satisfaction (directly or indirectly).

Consider a typical (or "median" in the statistical sense) Latin American woman who receives an income equivalent to US$163 per month and in all other aspects of her life is a typical person: she is 30 years old, lives in a city, has a secondary education, is married (her spouse has more or less the same income), has no children, considers her friends and religion important factors in her life, and lives in a modest home with all the basic services and an amount of household goods similar to that of other married women. She is in good health and does not suffer any serious economic limitations on her ability to pay for her housing or food.[24] If this woman lost her friendships, her life satisfaction level would crash, to a point at which if someone wanted to compensate her monetarily for this loss

22. Flores and Herrera (2008).
23. Hernani-Limarino and others (2008).
24. As attentive readers will have detected, these are all the significant variables that help explain life satisfaction for Latin Americans.

and make her feel the same level of life satisfaction again, that person would have to increase her income to US$1,246 per month. At that level, she would have the same probability of declaring the same level of life satisfaction as before.[25] This, of course, is a completely hypothetical exercise, but it reliably demonstrates that life satisfaction involves more fundamental factors than income.

This same method of appraisal is appropriate for other variables that have an impact on life satisfaction.[26] Health problems can also have a very large effect on satisfaction as discussed in greater detail in chapter 6. If the health status of the "average" Latin American woman described herein were to deteriorate to the point that 25 percent of the overall population was in worse health, her income would have to increase to US$581 per month for her to report an equivalent level of life satisfaction. In other words, her good health status is worth US$418 per month (the difference between US$581 and her actual income).

Figure 4-3 illustrates the valuation of other hypothetical life changes in this Latin American woman's life, such as facing divorce and losing her religious beliefs, her durable assets, or her job. It is important to remember that because one's assets or occupation are important factors in life satisfaction, in addition to income, this implies that their values surpass their effect directly related to income.[27] If this hypothetical woman were to lose her job, her income would have to increase to US$264 per month, a level almost US$100 over her current income, for her to report an equivalent level of life satisfaction, because her job is not only a source of income, but possibly a valuable source of interpersonal relationships and personal achievements. Similarly, if this hypothetical woman, a secondary school graduate, completed university studies, she could feel equally satisfied with life with a lesser income. Nevertheless, in this case it is important to bear in mind that this hypothetical exercise does not consider the possible effects of additional education on income and consumption aspirations. As discussed in chapter 3, shifts in aspirations can have a considerable impact on satisfaction.[28]

25. On a scale of 0 to 10, we have supposed that this woman's level of life satisfaction was originally rated a 6, the most probable level given her personal conditions. Conceptually, the calculation is very simple: it considers the income level required to equal the probability of reaching the same level of life satisfaction after another explanatory variable (in this case the dummy variable that says she has friends that she can rely on) is changed.

26. Note that the valuations herein measure the willingness to pay, not the ability to pay. In fact, several of these appraisals surpass the individuals' incomes and consequently are more than they would be able to pay. However, as a result of the attenuation bias (resulting from the measurement error) in the income coefficient, the valuations may de biased upwards.

27. If the price paid for some good corresponds to the equivalent satisfaction of the same amount spent on other things, then the good would not appear as an additional source of satisfaction in the regressions presented in table 4-1, as the entire effect would be captured by income. For a technical discussion, see van Praag and Ferrer-i-Carbonell (2007), chapter 11.

28. Here, comparison effects with the reference groups have not been considered because of the limitations imposed by group sizes in the estimations (see chapter 3).

Figure 4-3. *Amount of Extra Income Needed to Maintain an Individual's Initial Level of Satisfaction*

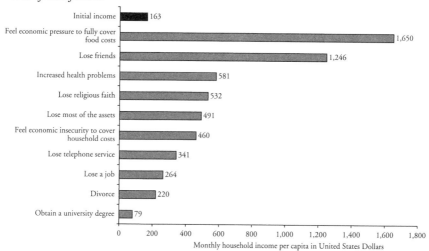

Source: Authors' calculations based on Gallup (2007).

Note: The person in this example is a married 30 year old Mexican woman, with no children, with a high school degree, employed, with friends and religious believes, that lives in a modest house with all public utilities. Each bar indicates the income this woman should receive in order to keep constant her life satisfaction if something occurs.

Life Satisfaction as a Synthesis of Different Life Dimensions

The previous section explored the relationship between life satisfaction and the diverse individual characteristics and conditions that can be observed externally or that respondents can presumably report with *some* objectivity. It is important to emphasize the word "some" because an individual can only judge, for example, whether he or she has pain or anguish, and whether its intensity is moderate or not (these are some of the health questions that form part of the EQ-5D survey mentioned previously), both of which imply subjective judgments, as well as to use personal judgment to decide whether friendships or religion are important.

In this section, an opposing approach is adopted; instead of trying to explain life satisfaction as a function of variables that are—to a certain point—objective, the approach here is to determine the importance that *subjective appreciations* of different aspects of individuals' lives have on life satisfaction. This assumes that when people evaluate their lives in responding to the "ladder" question, they implicitly assign a certain importance to each aspect of their lives. It is not necessary to ask the respondents directly how much importance they attribute to each dimension; it is sufficient to evaluate the statistical associations (quantified in table 4-3) between the answers to the "ladder" question and those regarding satisfaction with

Table 4-3. *Relationship between Life Satisfaction and Life Satisfaction with Different Life Aspects*

	Latin America and the Caribbean		The world		Latin America and the Caribbean: employed only	
	Employed people	*Employed and unemployed people*	*Employed people*	*Employed and unemployed people*	*Income above the regional median*	*Income below the regional median*
Economic satisfaction	0.7061***	0.7138***	0.7070***	0.7022***	0.6405***	0.4970***
Importance given to friendships	0.6532***	0.6219***	0.3885***	0.4549***	0.2573	0.7674***
Job satisfaction	0.3355***	n.a.	0.2853***	n.a.	0.2693*	0.2124
Health satisfaction	0.3183**	0.4216***	0.2898***	0.3468***	0.5520***	0.0941
Household satisfaction	0.1477*	0.2000**	0.0830*	0.1393***	-0.0623	0.1988
Personal liberty satisfaction	-0.0499	-0.0482	0.0837	0.0828*	-0.0269	-0.0766
Importance given to religion	0.0585	-0.0187	0.0735	0.0003	0.1063	0.1060
National economic conditions	0.0429	0.0244	0.1072*	0.0743*	-0.0470	0.1033
Trust in medical system	-0.1057	-0.0784	-0.0390	-0.0050	-0.1254	-0.0064
Satisfaction with labor public policies	-0.1232	-0.0476	-0.0426	-0.0168	-0.1382	-0.0559
Confidence in the educational system	-0.2380**	-0.2524***	-0.0608	-0.0369	-0.2695***	-0.1751
Satisfaction with city conditions	-0.2018*	-0.1155*	-0.0251	0.0085	0.0546	-0.3817***
Individual optimism score	0.2315***	0.2381***	0.1579***	0.1480***	0.2047***	0.2788***
Number of observations	4,669	10,941	23,075	52,218	2,232	1,485

Source: Authors' calculations based on Gallup (2007).

*Coefficient is statistically significant at the 10 percent level; **at the 5 percent level; ***at the 1 percent level; no asterisk means the coefficient is not different from zero with statistical significance.

Note: The coefficients indicate the effect of life satisfaction on an average individual, who is graded on a scale of 0 to 10. The independent variables, except optimism, have different scale values (yes = 1 or no = 0).

different realms. (According to some surveys that request explicit answers regarding the importance of the different realms, there is ample agreement between the two methods.)

Table 4-3 indicates that Latin Americans assign the greatest importance to satisfaction with their standard of living, more specifically, everything they can buy or do with their income. After this, the important factors are friendship, job and health satisfaction, and finally, satisfaction with their homes. (For those who are unemployed, job satisfaction is obviously not relevant, but the others are ranked similarly.) It is important to bear in mind that these are the topics of personal life covered in the Gallup World Polls.[29] Other private domains include satisfaction with individual autonomy and the importance of religion in one's personal life, but these two fields do not seem to have much weight for Latin Americans in evaluating their personal happiness. It is possible that other personal domains exist in which being or not being satisfied affects overall life satisfaction.

In contrast with the importance of the personal life aspects, most social or collective dimensions do not seem to have significant weight in the subjective appraisals of well-being. For example, no association has been found between satisfaction with a country's economic situation, its medical system, or its job creation policies and the residents' evaluation of life. Moreover, in the cases of satisfaction levels with the education system and city of residence, there is an inverse association with levels of well-being, possibly because as people satisfy their personal needs, they begin to worry about what surrounds them and their society and therefore become more critical about the deficiencies of certain policies (this assumes that in reality, the inverse association reflects a causality in the opposite direction—in other words, from life satisfaction to satisfaction with these public domains).

Perhaps what is stated above is not surprising, as it is to be expected that the appreciation each person has for his or her own life reflects, above all, his or her valuation of his or her personal conditions and interpersonal relations, more than a valuation of the environment where he or she lives. This is a significant conclusion that reveals that there are few individual motivations to influence public policies if they have no direct effect on personal conditions.

The relative importance that people of other regions assign to various private domains is similar to that which Latin Americans assign to those domains. Also, the conclusion that people attach little significance to public aspects in the valuation of their own lives is valid worldwide. In this sense, the only difference is that elsewhere in the world the level of satisfaction with the national economy seems to have a significant, although modest, importance (statistically) in the appreciation of life.

29. Actually, friendship is not a domain that can be judged in terms of satisfaction, rather in terms of importance. This is equally true of religion.

Where more profound differences can be noted is among Latin Americans who earn above and those who earn below the average income for the region (US$157 in monthly income per capita per household in terms of purchasing power parity).[30] When these two groups of workers are compared, it is clear that, in regard to private aspects of life, the wealthier groups consider health and job satisfaction more important than those with less income, for whom well-being depends solely on their satisfaction with their living standards and friendships. This difference suggests that in the case of the most affluent people, perhaps satisfactory employment supplies some of the needs otherwise supplied by interpersonal relations, whereas for those with fewer resources, friendships provide part of the economic security and protection mechanisms that employment provides for others.

In reference to the collective aspects of life, Latin Americans above the midpoint in terms of income level also function distinctly from those below. The inverse relation between life satisfaction and satisfaction with one's city of residence holds only among the poorest segment of the population, and the inverse relation between life satisfaction and satisfaction with the educational system arises only among the wealthiest. The interpretation given herein to such inverse associations suggests that the poorest tend to be conscious of deficiencies of the cities in which they live in direct relation to the level to which they have met their personal needs, while for the wealthiest, something similar occurs, but in relation to the education system.

A brief additional explanation with regard to the method employed in arriving at these conclusions may be useful for the more technically inclined reader. When correlation is sought between levels of life satisfaction and each of its domains, without consideration of the personality traits of individuals, many domains appear important. Clearly, this is because individuals' personality traits are reflected in their opinions on all aspects of life. Consequently, the estimations isolate this influence. If information were available for all the domains, the estimations should simply try to explain life satisfaction as a function of satisfaction with all domains and the variable that captures the personality traits, without including objective variables in the regression. Nevertheless, when information is lacking in some domains, there are debates over methods for capturing this information adequately to avoid biasing the other results. In the results documented in this chapter, consideration has been given to other variables for which there is some subjective information regarding overlooked domains (friendships, religion, security). It could be argued that one must also consider objective variables related to disregarded domains—for example, education variables, given that there is no information on people's satisfaction with their own education. The

---

30. This way of partitioning the sample is preferred to dividing the population based on the poverty lines to maintain more-balanced samples between the two groups, which facilitates the estimations.

problem is that the education variables can be correlated with many other things that are included (such as living standard satisfaction). In any case, the coefficients obtained for the domains with information are stable in terms of these options.[31]

The subsequent chapters explore some fundamental dimensions of the life of individuals: security in several dimensions (food, job, personal), health, education and employment. Throughout this chapter, it has been clear that subjective quality of life is associated with these dimensions, whether objective indicators are considered or an attempt is made to evaluate the weight that individuals subjectively assign to their satisfaction level with these domains. Nevertheless, the dimensions that are examined in the chapters that make up the remainder of the volume have not been selected because they are the most important for quality of life. In fact, it could be argued that friendships or religious beliefs have a more powerful influence on the subjective welfare of many people than the dimensions chosen for study here. However, these are not areas in which the government is able to, or should, intervene; rather they belong to a personal realm that should remain out of the public arena. On the other hand, security, health, education, and employment are amenable to government intervention. These are central areas for public policy, because what national and local governments do or do not do in these areas can affect quality of life.

Nevertheless, as discussed in chapter 1, this does not mean that the objective of public policies in these or other areas should be to maximize satisfaction with life in general or with specific life domains. But understanding people's opinions can contribute to improving the public debate, as well as to optimizing the design and implementation of public policies.

References

Argyle, M. 1999. "Causes and Correlates of Happiness." In D. Kahneman, E. Diener, and N. Schwartz, eds., *Well-Being: The Foundations of Hedonic Psychology.* New York: Russell Sage Foundation Publications.

Bentham, J. 1781. *An Introduction to the Principles of Morals and Legislation.* Available at http://socserv.mcmaster.ca/econ/ugcm/3ll3/bentham/morals.pdf.

Blanchflower, D., and Oswald, A. 2004. "Well-Being over Time in Britain and the USA." *Journal of Public Policies* 88 (7–8): 1359–87.

———. 2007. "Hypertension and Happiness across Nations." IZA Discussion Paper No. 2633. Institute for the Study of Labor (IZA), Bonn, Germany.

Brickman, P., and Campbell, D. 1971. "Hedonic Relativism and Planning the Good Society." In M. H. Appley, ed., *Adaptation-Level Theory: A Symposium.* New York: Academic Press.

Clark, A., and Oswald, A. 1994. "Unhappiness and Unemployment." *Economic Journal* 104 (424): 648–59.

---

31. For a detailed technical discussion, please see van Praag and Ferrer-i-Carbonell (2007), chapter 4.

Diener, E. 2005. "Guidelines for National Indicators of Subjective Well-Being and Ill-Being." *Social Indicators Network News (SINET)* 84: 4–6.

Diener, E., Gohm, C., Suh, E., and Oishi, S. 2000. "Similarity of the Relations between Marital Status and Subjective Well-Being across Cultures." *Journal of Cross-Cultural Psychology* 31 (4): 419–36.

Diener, E., and Seligman, M. 2004. "Beyond Money: Toward an Economy of Well-Being." *Psychological Science in the Public Interest* 5 (1): 1–31.

Diener, E., Suh, E., Lucas, R., and Smith, H. 1999. "Subjective Well-Being: Three Decades of Progress." *Psychological Bulletin* 125 (2): 276–302.

Dolan, P. 2006. "Happiness and Policy: A Review of the Literature." Report prepared for Department for Environment, Food and Rural Affairs (DEFRA), Whitehall, England.

Ellison, C. 1991. "Religious Involvement and Subjective Well-Being." *Journal of Health and Social Behavior* 32 (1): 80–99.

Ferrer-i-Carbonell, A., and Frijters, P. 2004. "How Important Is Methodology for Estimates of the Determinants of Happiness?" *Economic Journal* 114 (497): 641–59.

Flores, C., and Herrera, M. 2008. "Understanding Quality of Life in Latin America and the Caribbean: Satisfaction, Quality of Education, and Income Inequality." Latin American Research Network Paper. Inter-American Development Bank, Washington, D.C.

Frey, B., and Stutzer, A. 1999. "Measuring Preferences by Subjective Well-Being." *Journal of Institutional and Theoretical Economics* 155 (4): 755–78.

———. 2002. "What Can Economists Learn from Happiness Research?" *Journal of Economic Literature* 40 (2) (June): 402–35.

———. 2007. "Should National Happiness Be Maximized?" IEER Working Paper No. 306. Institute for Empirical Research in Economics, University of Zurich.

Frijters, P., Haisken-DeNew, J., and Shields, M. 2004a. "Money Does Matter! Evidence from Increasing Real Income and Life Satisfaction in East Germany Following Reunification." *American Economic Review* 94 (3): 730–40.

———. 2004b. "Investigating the Patterns and Determinants of Life Satisfaction in Germany Following Reunification." *Journal of Human Resources* 39 (3): 649–74.

Gallup. 2006. Gallup World Poll. Available at www.gallup.com/consulting/worldpoll/24046/about.aspx

———. 2007. Gallup World Poll. Available at www.gallup.com/consulting/worldpoll/24046/about.aspx

Graham, C. 2008. "Happiness and Health: Lessons—and Questions—for Public Policy." *Health Affairs* 27 (1): 72–87.

Graham, C., Eggers, A., and Sukhtankar, S. 2004. "Does Happiness Pay? An Initial Exploration Based on Panel Data from Russia." *Journal of Economic Behavior and Organization* 55 (3): 319–42.

Graham, C., and Felton, A. 2005a. "Does Inequality Matter to Individual Welfare? An Initial Exploration Based on Happiness Surveys from Latin America." CSED Working Paper No. 38. Brookings.

———. 2005b. "Variance in Obesity Incidence across Countries and Cohorts: A Norms Based Approach Using Happiness Surveys." CSED Working Paper No. 42. Brookings.

Graham, C., and Pettinato, S. 2000. "Happiness, Markets, and Democracy: Latin America in Comparative Perspective." CSED Working Paper No. 13. Brookings.

———. 2002. "Frustrated Achievers: Winners, Losers, and Subjective Well-Being in New Market Economies." *Journal of Development Studies* 38 (4): 100–40.

Hernani-Limarino, W., Jiménez, W., Arias, B., and Larrea, C. 2008. "The Quality of Life of Urban Neighborhoods in Bolivia: A Case of Study of the Great La Paz and Santa Cruz." Inter-American Development Bank, Washington, D.C. Unpublished.

Inter-American Development Bank (IDB). 2008. *Beyond Facts: Understanding Quality of Life.* Development in the Americas Report. Washington, D.C.

Kahneman, D., Krueger, A., Schkade, D., Schwarz, N., and A. Stone. 2004. "Toward National Well-Being Accounts." *American Economic Review* 94 (2): 429–34.

Kohler, H. P., Behrman, J., and Skytthe, A. 2005. "Partner + Children = Happiness? The Effects of Partnerships and Fertility on Well-Being." *Population and Development Review* 31 (3): 407–45.

Lora, E. 2008. "Percepciones de salud en América Latina." Background paper for *Beyond Facts: Understanding Quality of Life.* Development in the Americas 2009. Inter-American Development Bank, Washington, D.C. Unpublished.

Oswald, A. 1997. "Happiness and Economic Performance." *Economic Journal* 107 (445): 1815–31.

Shaw, J., Johnson, J., and Coons, S. 2005. "U.S. Valuation of the EQ-5D Health States: Development and Testing of the D1 Valuation Model." *Medical Care* 43 (3): 203–20.

Theil, H. 1964. *Optimal Decision Rules for Government and Industry.* Amsterdam: North-Holland

Tinbergen, J. 1956. *Economic Policy: Theory and Design.* Amsterdam: North-Holland.

van Praag, B. 1985. "Linking Economics with Psychology: An Economist's View." *Journal of Economic Psychology* 6 (3): 289–311.

van Praag, B., and Ferrer-i-Carbonell, A. 2007. *Happiness Quantified: A Satisfaction Calculus Approach.* Oxford University Press.

van Praag, B., Frijters, P., and Ferrer-i-Carbonell, A. 2003. "The Anatomy of Subjective Well-Being." *Journal of Economic Behavior and Organization* 51 (1): 29–49.

Veenhoven, R. 2007. "Measures of Gross National Happiness." Paper presented at OECD Conference on Measurability and Policy Relevance of Happiness, April 2–3, Rome.

World Bank. 2007. World Development Indicators Online (http://publications.worldbank.org/ecommerce/catalog/product-detail?product_id=631625&).

5

Vulnerabilities and Subjective Well-Being

MAURICIO CÁRDENAS, CAROLINA MEJÍA,
AND VINCENZO DI MARO

Economists like to study people on the basis of what they do (choices). However, human beings are much more complex and many aspects of their well-being are not necessarily reflected in observable choices, but are embedded in intangibles such as wishes, perceptions and expectations. As Amartya Sen (1986, p.18) puts it, "the popularity of this view [individual utility only depends on tangible goods, services and leisure and it is inferred from behaviour, or revealed preferences] in economics may be due to a mixture of an obsessive concern with observability and a peculiar belief that choice is the only human aspect that can be observed."

The "Economics of Happiness" has been trying to challenge these narrow assumptions combining economists' and psychologists' techniques and complementing standard income-based measures of welfare with broader measures of well-being. The ultimate objective is to gain a better understanding of "Quality of Life" (QoL) in order to design successful policies for improving living conditions.

Research on QoL, or perceived well-being in general, focuses on its interrelationships with income, inequality, macro and micro policies, political arrangements, and social capital. As noted by Graham (2008), one particularly appealing feature of happiness research is that "there are certain questions to which revealed preferences cannot provide answers, but happiness surveys (based on expressed preferences) can provide some insights. These include the welfare effect of macro and institutional arrangements that individuals are powerless to change (inequality is one example), and behavior that is driven by norms, addiction, or self-control problems."

This chapter aims to contribute to the study of the link between deprivation and well-being. Deprivation can relate to most aspects of human life, including psychological, physical and economical ones. The focus of this chapter is on the vulnerability of individuals and households to situations and occurrences that can potentially lead to deprivation and, ultimately, adversely affect well-being. In particular, the chapter narrows down the concept of vulnerability focusing on three types of insecurity: nutritional, personal, and job-related. This set of insecurities seems rich enough to encompass several potentially important aspects of one's life and, therefore, is able to capture the broader concept of deprivation. In addition to this, these different types of insecurity can be studied in comparison to each other so as to highlight their relative importance in explaining perceived well-being.

The idea that the relationship between deprivation and QoL is a particularly complex one is supported by several well established results in the happiness literature, some of them already mentioned in previous chapters, such as the well known Easterlin paradox. Although within countries wealthier people are, on average, happier than poor ones, the relationship between per capita income and average happiness level across countries is much weaker.[1] In particular, wealthier countries (as a group) are found to be happier than poor ones (as a group), but happiness seems to rise with income only up to a point and not beyond it. There is now some controversy on the existence of this paradox. Anthony and Charles Kenny (2006) argue that welfare, represented by objective indicators such as life expectancy, infant mortality, literacy, and housing, has a weak relationship with income, either absolute or relative. Recent work by Angus Deaton (2007), which makes use of the 2006 Gallup World Poll, shows that across countries average happiness is strongly related to per capita national income. Moreover, this effect holds across the range of international incomes, ruling out the existence of a critical level of per capita income above which income has no further effect on happiness.

Even the strong positive relationship between income and happiness within countries is now challenged by many additional findings. After basic needs are met, other factors such as rising aspirations, relative income differences, and the security of gains become increasingly important in explaining happiness. It has been argued that humans are on a "hedonic treadmill": aspirations increase along with income and, after basic needs are met, relative rather than absolute levels matter to well-being.[2] Interestingly, some studies on Latin America show how inequality can undermine the positive welfare effects of living in developing countries with higher average income.[3]

---

1. In regard to the affirmation that, whithin countries, wealthier people are, on average, happier than poor ones, see Easterlin (1974); see also Oswald (1997) and Diener and others (1993).

2. See Easterlin (2003).

3. See Graham (2008) and Graham and Felton (2006).

More specifically on the relationship between deprivation and QoL, it is commonly found that deprivation in general, and abject poverty in particular, tend to reduce happiness, but at the same time it is also true that very poor people can be happier than other groups. This can happen when the poor have low expectations or simply do not perceive themselves as poor.[4] In addition, the well-being of those who escaped poverty is often undermined by insecurity associated to the risk of falling back to poverty. This can explain why happiness data show that income has strong negative effects on welfare among this group. Unless panel data are used, income data alone do not reveal the vulnerability of these individuals. Indeed, their reported well-being is often lower than that of the poor.[5] Some anecdotal evidence from South Africa supports this point: people who came out of apartheid with much better economic conditions and much better educational opportunities are now reporting that they are very much afraid of their kids reverting to the past situation. This kind of "intergenerational" insecurity seems to have adverse effects on the appraisal of their own life satisfaction.[6]

Another seminal issue in the happiness literature is adaptation. Level and changes of life satisfaction are potentially very dependent on how adaptable an individual is to the occurrences of life. For instance, according to the psychologists' "set point" theory, every person has a happiness level to which he or she goes back over time, even after experiencing major events, such as winning the lottery or getting divorced.[7] However, even if the happiness level will eventually adapt to this longer-term equilibrium, it has been shown that individuals adapt more in the pecuniary dimension than in the non-pecuniary dimension. This means that events such as bereavement, illness or unemployment can have a lasting effect on life satisfaction.[8] It follows from this that policy conclusions based only on pecuniary measures of well-being can be misleading.

Adaptation and policy are linked in at least one other way, which refers to the way "demands for changes" are transmitted from individuals to policymakers. For example, in case people adapt faster to specific types of insecurity (some evidence that individuals seem to adapt better to personal insecurity issues will be shown below) they might tend to underestimate these issues when expressing their demands to policymakers. These issues might nonetheless be very important, and adaptation to them does not necessarily mean that they do not hinder improvements of objective living conditions. Policymakers might have to support other ways to elicit demands from individuals in these cases.

In this chapter the main research question is whether and to what extent insecurity (vulnerability) has an effect on perceived well-being. From a policy perspec-

---

4. Rojas (2004).
5. Graham and Pettinato (2002).
6. "Survey: South Africa," *The Economist,* April 6, 2006.
7. Easterlin (2003).
8. Easterlin (2001).

tive, the study of the types of insecurity in a unified framework should be preferred to studies in which measures of insecurity are studied in isolation. However, there are many problems when an estimation approach that considers all the proxies of insecurities at the same time is employed: interconnections between measures of insecurity (likely to confound results), data limitations and selection issues (job insecurity proxies are defined only for those who work). With these caveats in mind, the chapter studies in a unified framework the relative importance of different types of insecurity (nutritional, personal and job-related) in terms of their effects on well-being.

The first type of insecurity analyzed in this chapter is nutritional insecurity. The link between poor nutrition, worse adult labour market and educational outcomes, and poor health status has been clearly established in the literature.[9] Previous research on QoL has been devoted mainly to the general relationship between perceived well-being and physical health (of which nutrition is a major determinant). In general, positive states of well-being correlate with better physical health.[10] While the correlations between objective physical health and well-being are lower (in part because people appear to adapt over time to many illnesses and because most people are relatively healthy), certain illnesses that interfere with daily functioning produce marked decrements in well-being. Direction of causality is not fully understood. Not surprisingly, self-reported health affects well-being as well as objective health does, at least in case of severe health problems.[11] However, there is also evidence that causality might run from well-being to health.[12]

The second type of insecurity analyzed is job-related insecurity (fear of unemployment). The relationship between job insecurity and perceived well-being has been extensively studied, and a negative effect of job insecurity on life satisfaction is well established.[13]

Regarding personal insecurity, the third type of insecurity studied, the presence of violent crime and conflict is a crucial aspect of well-being, particularly for lower income countries. Without doubt, constant fear, widespread criminal activity and violent attacks on the civil population reduce welfare. The literature on the effects of crime and, more generally, of violent confrontation provides solid conclusions on the negative effect of these factors on almost every aspect of society.[14] As Chen, Loayza and Reynal-Querol (2007) emphasize, violence and crime destroy human capital and infrastructure, fracture social cohesion, weaken institutions and deter

9. See, among others, Strauss and Thomas (1998) and Behrman (1996).
10. See Hilleras, Jorm, Herlitz, and Winblad (1998), Murrell, Salsman, and Meeks (2003) and Ostir, Markides, Black, and Goodwin (2000).
11. On how self-reported health affects well-being, see Okun, Stock, Haring, and Witter (1984). To see how objective health affects well-being, see Brief, Butcher, George, and Link (1993) and Okun and George (1984).
12. See Diener and Seligman (2004), p.13.
13. For a review of the results see Diener and Seligman (2004), and Frey and Stutzer (2002).
14. For a thorough review on the costs of civil war see Collier and others (2003).

investment enterprises. Similarly, Londoño and Guerrero (1999) summarize the findings of six case studies on the social and economic costs of violence in Latin America concluding that, by the end of the last decade, conflict and war cost around 14.5 percent of the Latin American GDP per year, with dire consequences for human capital formation, investment and social norms.[15]

The estimation of happiness functions, in addition to the usual methodological concerns, raises some additional challenges. In general, these regressions yield quite low R^2s reflecting the extent to which emotions and other unobserved components of true well-being are driving the results. Interestingly, recent research in psychology has found that one's level of happiness is related to one's genetic endowment. Genes may control half of the personality traits that determine one's level of happiness, with the other half linked to lifestyle, career and relationships.[16]

The presence of unobserved psychological traits (for example, optimism vs. pessimism or bad/good mood in the day of the interview) might be codetermining satisfaction, and bias the results. The availability of different measures of perceived well-being (related to perceptions on different points in time) allows this chapter to deal with this issue. Another methodological issue arises when measuring perceived well-being based on the so-called "ladder" question already mentioned in previous chapters (a 0–10 scale used to capture the individual's satisfaction). Care should be exercised when using an ordinal variable in the estimations.[17] This chapter will deal with both issues in what follows using the estimation approaches proposed by van Praag and Ferrer-i-Carbonell (2008).

The organization of the chapter is as follows. First, the data used are described and the methodological issues discussed. This is followed by a description of the measures of insecurity and perceived well-being used. Then the results about the relationship between types of insecurity and perceived well-being are presented and discussed. Finally, some concluding remarks are drawn and policy implications of the results are discussed.

Data and Methodological Issues

The data source of this chapter is the Gallup World Poll.[18] Respondents in 132 countries are asked about a wide range of life satisfaction dimensions (overall satisfaction with life, satisfaction with one's standard of living, satisfaction with freedom to choose what to do with one's life and health satisfaction, among others).

---

15. See Cárdenas (2007) for the effects on growth. There is a vast literature on the effects of violence on development in Colombia, surveyed in Ibáñez and Jaramillo (2006).

16. See Weiss, Bates, and Luciano (2008).

17. For example, if somebody evaluates his or her satisfaction level by a 7, it does not imply that his satisfaction is exactly equal to 7. The exact evaluation might be 6.75 or 7.25, but because of the necessary discreteness of the question we have to round it off to 7.

18. For more details, see www.gallupworldpoll.com/content/24046/About.aspx.

In addition to this, and key for the purposes of the chapter, several measures of nutritional, personal, and job insecurity are available. As well two waves of data are available: 2006 (data for all 132 countries) and 2007 (data only for Latin America and the Caribbean—LAC—countries and Canada and the United States). Respondents are not the same individuals and do not belong to the same household in the two waves (that is, this is not a panel of individuals or households). Specific questions are discussed in more detail in the sections below.

Regarding the methodology, the estimation of happiness functions, in addition to the usual concerns, raises new challenges. As mentioned, one major issue is the presence of an unobserved psychological trait that might bias the results. Ideally, one would like to account for it via individual fixed effects in case panel data were available. However, the availability of different measures of perceived well-being allows this chapter to deal with this issue. The followed procedure is based on van Praag and Ferrer-i-Carbonell (2008) and draws on the intuition that when different questions about different satisfaction domains are posed to the same respondent, then his/her psychological trait will affect all of his/her answers to the different domains (for example, the optimism of a person is likely to affect both his/her answer to the life satisfaction and to the health satisfaction questions). Hence, it is possible to extract the personality factor from the correlation of these answers.

In more detail, each satisfaction domain variable is regressed against the same set of explanatory variables. Under the assumption that the most important omitted variable in the life satisfaction regressions is the personality trait factor, then one would expect the correlation among the residuals of these regressions to be very high and the common psychological trait to be the common effect that is responsible for the sizeable correlation. Accordingly, this common factor can be isolated by application of a principal-components analysis on the residual covariance matrix. In particular, the loadings (score) with respect to the first principal component of the variance/covariance matrix of the residuals are used as proxy of the psychological trait factor.

Several satisfaction variables are present in the Gallup World Poll. However, it would not be viable to use all of them as they are based on very different classifications, such as "ladder question," dummy and verbal categories. In addition to this, it is likely that the common personality effect shows up more clearly in questions that have several categories or numerical values.[19] With this in mind, the chapter uses the following 6 variables as life satisfaction domains: current, past and future life satisfaction "ladder" question and current, past and future perception

---

19. For example, if the respondent on the day of the interview was in a very good mood, he or she might have given a 7 as answer to the ladder question even if his or her "true" life satisfaction was only 5. However, if the categories are very spaced or they are dichotomous then the mood of the respondent might not have any effect on the respondent's answer.

of the country's situation "ladder" question.[20] The unique opportunity of using these 6 variables is that they have exactly the same format. In addition to this, within each group of questions (two groups: three questions for life satisfaction and three for country situation) the only difference is time of reference.

It is not clear a priori which kinds of psychological traits the generated variable is capturing (and it is beyond the scope of this chapter to investigate this issue). This means that it is not clear how to interpret values of this variable or, for example, differences between average country values. However, the country average values of the generated psychological trait factor are depicted in figure 5-1. Under the quite strong assumption that this variable is capturing only "optimism/pessimism" of individuals, then figure 5-1 suggests than in 2007 people in Argentina, Chile, Paraguay and Uruguay were the most "pessimistic" (higher negative values) and those in Belize, Colombia, Costa Rica and Venezuela the most "optimistic" (higher positive values). Another simpler way of controlling for the personality trait bias is to include in the specification life satisfaction in the past (or future) as a regressor. However, it can be shown that with this approach the bias does not completely disappear.[21]

Another methodological issue refers specifically to the fact that the main life satisfaction measure of this study is a "ladder" question with a scale from 0 to 10. Specifications with variables of this kind as dependent variable are commonly estimated with ordered probit or logit. However, van Praag and Ferrer-i-Carbonell (2008) show that coefficients estimated with OLS and ordered probit for happiness functions are remarkably very similar and suggest using their own estimators—Cardinal Ordinary Least Squares (COLS) and Probit Ordinary Least Squares (POLS)— which are basically a less computing-intensive alternative to ordered probit.[22]

In particular, the COLS estimator permits the use of the cardinal information in the life satisfaction "ladder" question. For instance, even if the possible answers to this question are only integers, a response '7' can refer to any number between 6.55 and 7.45. The COLS basically "cardinalizes" the original satisfaction variable. In particular, it is first assumed that any of the responses can correspond to a unit interval (for example, answer 5 corresponds to the interval [4.5,5.5], answer 6 to

---

20. In particular, the questions' format is as follows: "Please imagine a ladder with steps numbered from zero at the bottom to ten at the top. Suppose we say that the top of the ladder represents the best possible status for you or your country and the bottom of the ladder represents the worst possible life for you or your country. On which step of the ladder would you say you personally feel you or your country stand at this time, assuming that the higher the step the better you feel about your life or your country, and the lower the step the worse you feel about it? Which step comes closest to the way you feel?; On which step would you say you stood five years ago?; Just your best guess, on which step do you think you will stand in the future, say about five years from now?"

21. It can be shown that while the bias is reduced with this approach, it does not completely disappear. Ideally one would like to estimate a specification in which both the Ys and the Xs are expressed as difference between current and lagged variable. However, in the Gallup data only the lagged life satisfaction (Y) is available.

22. For more details on COLS and POLS see chapters 2, 3, and 4 in van Praag and Ferrer-i-Carbonell (2008).

Figure 5-1. *Personality Trait Factor*

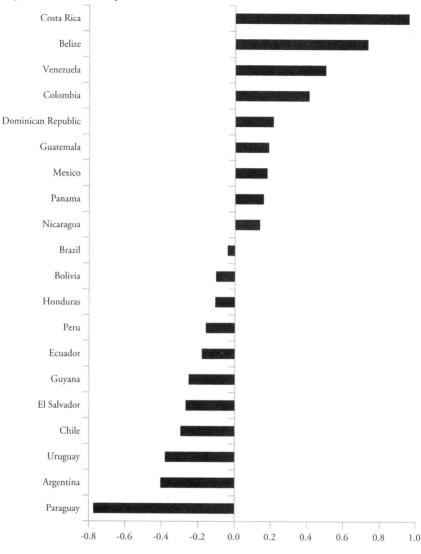

Mean of factor loading of the principal component

Source: Authors' calculations based on Gallup World Poll (2007).

[5.5,6.5] and so on; extreme values are treated as follows: 1 corresponds to [0,0.5] and 10 to [9.5,10]). Then it is possible to construct a variable Z_{COLS} as follows: $Z_{COLS} = E[Z|u_{i-1}<Z<u_i)$, where Z is N(0,1) distributed and the u_i comes from the interval values as defined above. Finally, it is possible to use this constructed variable as a dependent variable in place of the original life satisfaction measure.

In practice Z is the original life satisfaction variable standardized (mean and standard deviation by country and time); this is to be kept in mind when interpreting the coefficients of the COLS estimation. Obviously, the COLS estimator is heavily dependent on the assumption of individuals interpreting the ladder question in a cardinal way, an assumption that is undoubtedly quite strong, which this study would wish to avoid. Nevertheless, COLS results can be useful as comparison benchmark with the other estimators.

Types of Insecurity and Well-Being

As stressed in the introduction, this chapter focuses on three types of insecurity: nutritional, personal and job-related. In the Gallup World Poll, several proxies of insecurity are available. The full wording of the questions about insecurity that will be used below (the abbreviations that are going to be used to refer to them in text are indicated in parenthesis) is presented here:

Nutritional Insecurity

Have there been times in the past twelve months when you did not have enough money to buy food that you or your family needed? ["not enough money" or NI money].

Have there been times in the past 12 months when you or your family have gone hungry? ["gone hungry" or NI hungry].

Job Insecurity

Do you think you could lose your job in the next six months? [only for 2007, "job insecurity"]

Personal Insecurity

Do you feel safe walking alone at night in the city or area where you live? ["safe walking"]

Have you had money or property stolen from you or another household member within the past 12 months? ["stolen"]

Have you been assaulted or mugged within the past 12 months? ["mugged"]

Are there gangs in the area where you live? [only for 2007, "gangs"]

Are there illicit drug trafficking or drug sales in the area where you live? [only for 2007, "drug"]

Based on Gallup's 2007 wave, figure 5-2 summarizes the average incidence of the different types of insecurity in LAC as a whole. Remarkable figures are that only 50 percent of respondents think that it is safe walking in the area where they live and that more than 30 percent have nutritional problems (not enough

Figure 5-2. *Types of Insecurity in Latin America and the Caribbean—Total Incidence*

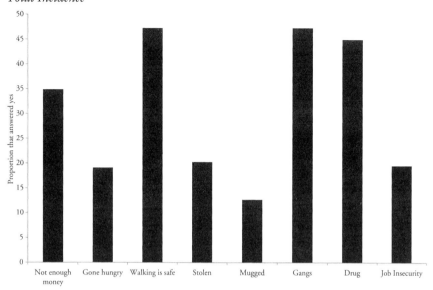

Source: Authors' calculations based on Gallup World Poll (2007).

money); as a comparison, the figures for the United States are 74.7 percent and 6.5 percent, respectively. The incidence of each type of insecurity across LAC countries is presented in figures 5-3 to 5-5.

As regards personal security, rates are generally quite high for all LAC countries. However, in countries like Bolivia, Ecuador and Venezuela, it is particularly likely for the respondent to have been mugged or to have had property stolen (see figure 5-3a). Presence of gangs and/or drug trafficking is quite widespread across LAC countries with Argentina, Belize, Costa Rica and Uruguay showing the highest values (see figure 5-3b).

In terms of the nutritional insecurity patterns (see figure 5-3c), the picture is somewhat more varied: some countries like Brazil, El Salvador and Uruguay display lower incidence of nutritional insecurity, but still notably higher than the United States and Canada, while others show extremely high rates, like Dominican Republic, Mexico, and Panama. Job insecurity is more prevalent in countries like Belize, Chile, and Honduras.

In order to gain more insights on the incidence of insecurities in LAC, the insecurity variables are grouped together in an indicator of intensity of insecurity occurrence. This indicator ranges from 0 for individuals that did not experience any of the insecurity events considered here ("completely secure"), to 7 for individuals that experienced all of the insecurity forms ("not secure at all"). When this

Figure 5-3a. *Incidence of Different Types of Insecurities: Assault, Muggings, Street Safety*

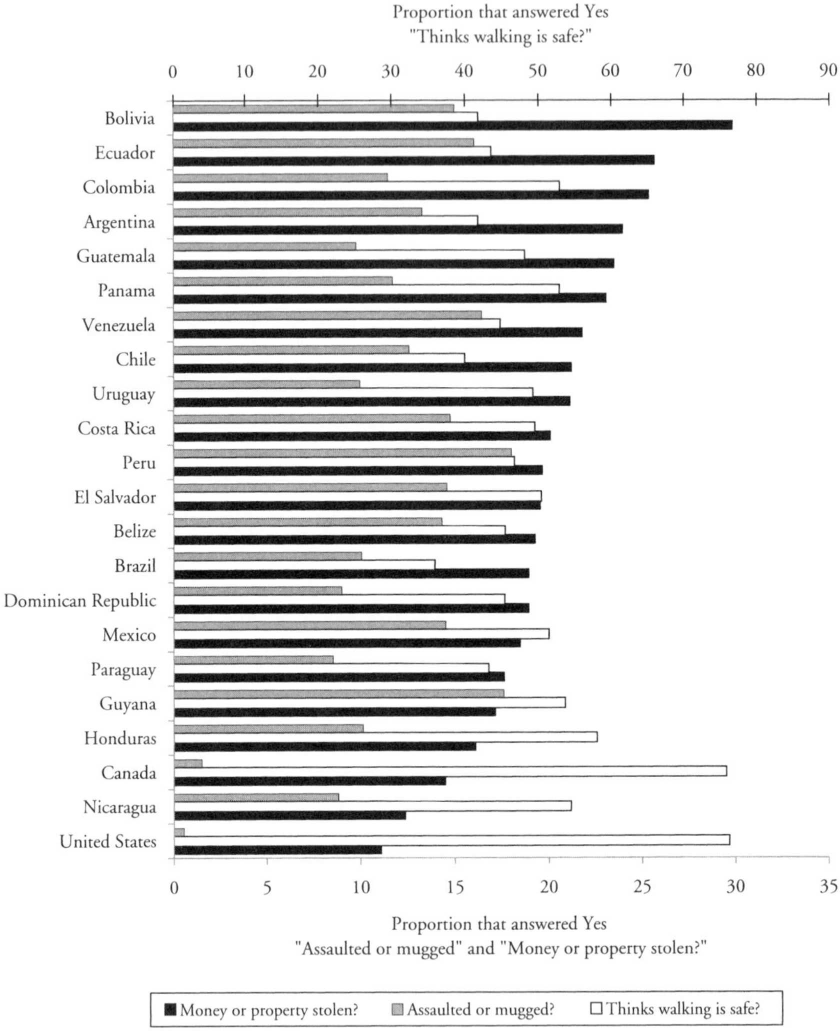

Source: Authors' calculations based on Gallup World Poll (2007).

indicator is plotted for the LAC region as a whole (see figure 5-4), one can notice that around 23 percent of respondents were "completely secure" and less than 1 percent were "not secure at all." Most of the respondents experienced between one to three insecurity occurrences, with the percentage of those experiencing four events still being quite high at more than 5 percent.

The focus of the chapter is now narrowed down, comparing LAC countries in terms of percentage of respondents "completely secure" and of those "less secure"

Figure 5-3b. *Incidence of Different Types of Insecurities: Gangs and Drugs*

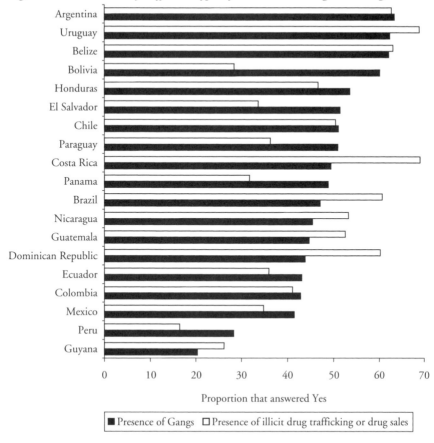

Source: Authors' calculations based on Gallup World Poll (2007).

(that is, proxied as percentage of respondents having experienced 5 or more insecurity occurrences). These two indicators are plotted for each country in figure 5-5.

One interesting pattern is that, for some countries, both percentages, of "completely secure" and "less secure," are quite high. Clustering of people at these extreme values might be a consequence of inequality in these countries: many people are able to completely avoid insecurity; however, they coexist with another big group of people that is very exposed to insecurity. An additional potential explanation is that, in some countries, pockets of ungovernable areas (with very high violence levels) coexist with much safer areas (or areas that managed to reduce the high violence in the recent past). One particularly fitting example is Colombia, where major metropolitan areas (namely Bogota and Medellin) made remarkable progress in reducing violence while other small areas are still cursed with high violence.[23]

23. See Soares and Naritomi (2007).

Figure 5-3c. *Incidence of Different Types of Insecurities: Nutritional and Job Insecurity*

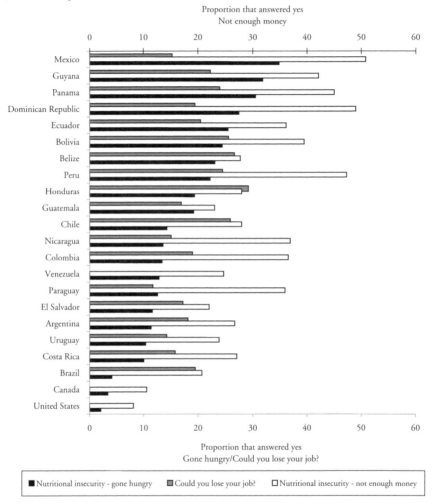

Proportion that answered yes
Not enough money

Proportion that answered yes
Gone hungry/Could you lose your job?

■ Nutritional insecurity - gone hungry   ▨ Could you lose your job?   □ Nutritional insecurity - not enough money

Source: Authors' calculations based on Gallup World Poll (2007).
Note: No data available for Canada, Venezuela and USA for "Could you lose your job?"

Another exercise is to assess the incidence of these types of insecurity changes by income quintiles and educational level. In figure 5-6, nutritional and job insecurity are graphed against the five income quintiles while in figure 5-7 the same is done for personal insecurity proxies. As regards these latter measures, it seems that their incidence is not dramatically different across income quintiles. On the contrary, quite marked differences arise in terms of job insecurity and, particularly, nutritional insecurity.

Figure 5-4. *Intensity of Insecurity in Latin America and the Caribbean*

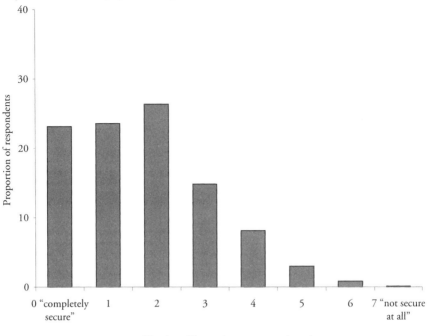

Number of insecurity events experienced

Source: Authors' calculations based on Gallup World Poll (2007).
Note: Venezuela not included as not all the insecurity proxies are available for this country.

As regards educational level, nutritional and job insecurity are, not surprisingly, clustered particularly among individuals with low levels of education (see figure 5-8). However, when incidence of personal insecurity is considered (in figure 5-9), it seems that insecurity spreads across educational levels in a much more "equal" way.

With regards to the perceived well-being measures, four different proxies are used. Their full wording is reported here:

Life satisfaction "ladder" question

Please imagine a ladder with steps numbered from zero at the bottom to ten at the top. Suppose we say that the top of the ladder represents the best possible life for you and the bottom of the ladder represents the worst possible life for you. On which step of the ladder would you say you personally feel you stand at this time, assuming that the higher the step the better you feel about your life, and the lower the step the worse you feel about it? Which step comes closest to the way you feel?; On which step would you say you stood five years ago?; Just your best guess, on which step do you think you will stand in the future, say about five years from now?

Figure 5-5. *Percentage of Respondents: "Completely Secure" vs. "Not Secure at All"*

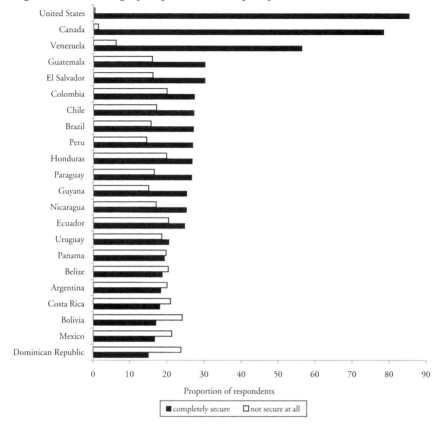

Source: Authors' calculations based on Gallup World Poll (2007).

Notes: For Canada, Venezuela and USA the maximum number of possible insecurity events is 5 (as "gangs", "drug" and "job insec" are not available), as such percentages are not directly comparable to those for the other countries (for which themaximum number is 7).

Satisfaction with standard of living

Are you satisfied or dissatisfied with your standard of living, all the things you can buy and do?; Right now, do you feel your standard of living is getting better or getting worse?

Satisfaction with choosing what to do with one's life

Are you satisfied or dissatisfied with your freedom to choose what you do with your life?

Figure 5-10 reports the average response to the life satisfaction "ladder" question for LAC countries in 2007. According to this figure, the most satisfied individuals

Figure 5-6. *Nutritional and Job Insecurity by Income Quintiles in Latin America and the Caribbean*

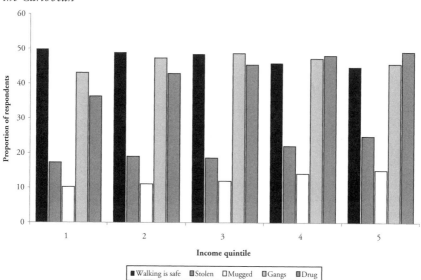

Source: Authors' calculations based on Gallup World Poll (2007).

Figure 5-7. *Victimization Measures by Income Quintiles in Latin America and the Caribbean*

Source: Authors' calculations based on Gallup World Poll (2007).

Figure 5-8. *Nutritional and Job Insecurity by Educational Attainment in Latin America and the Caribbean*

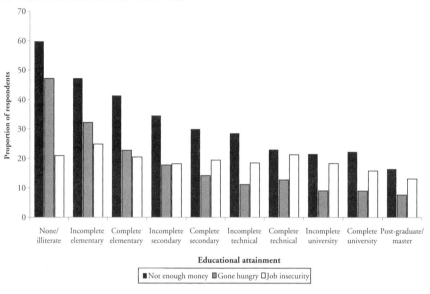

Source: Authors' calculations based on Gallup World Poll (2007).

Figure 5-9. *Victimization Measures by Educational Attainment in Latin America and the Caribbean*

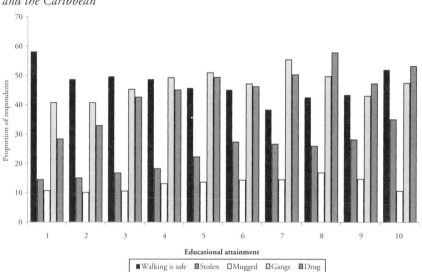

Source: Authors' calculations based on Gallup World Poll (2007).

Figure 5-10. *Life Satisfaction Measure: "Ladder" Question*

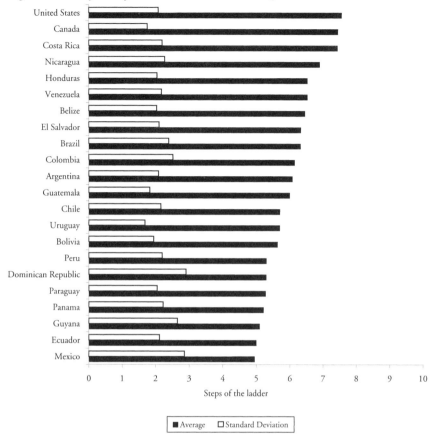

Steps of the ladder

■ Average ☐ Standard Deviation

Source: Authors' calculations based on Gallup World Poll (2007).

in the LAC region live in Costa Rica, Honduras and Nicaragua, while Ecuador and Mexico present the lowest levels of satisfaction. Interestingly, in terms of satisfaction with one's standard of living (see figure 5-11), average values are generally very high and the peaks are for Costa Rica, El Salvador, and Venezuela (notably, they have levels comparable to the United States). Figure 5-12 reports the average satisfaction with freedom to choose what to do with one's life.

Relative Importance of Types of Insecurity

From a policy perspective, one would like to learn something about the relative importance of different types of insecurity in terms of their effects on well-being. However, in the present context, this is not an easy exercise because several difficulties arise in estimating a regression with all the proxies of insecurities included

Figure 5-11. *Satisfaction with Standard of Living*

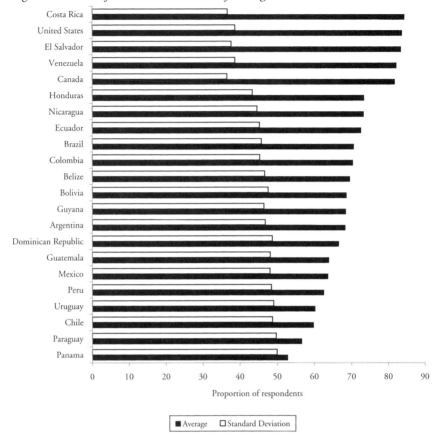

Proportion of respondents

■ Average   □ Standard Deviation

Source: Authors' calculations based on Gallup World Poll (2007).

jointly. First, there might be interdependence between the different types of insecurities (for example, between job insecurity and not having enough money to buy
food), which is likely to confound the results. In addition to this, data limitations
play a role as the three types of insecurity are available at the same time only in the
2007 wave of the Gallup World Poll. Also, there is only one measure of job insecurity in the Gallup data, with this meaning that this dimension might not be
completely captured. Finally, selection issues are relevant as the job insecurity
proxy ("Do you feel you could lose your job in the next six months?") is intended
only for those who are working, while the proxies for the other insecurities are
generally applicable.

    With this caveat in mind, this section tries to assess the relative importance of
each type of insecurity compared to the others. The analysis is restricted to LAC

Figure 5-12. *Satisfaction with Choosing What to Do with One's Life*

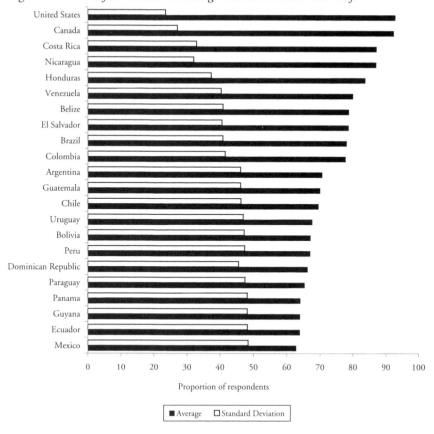

Proportion of respondents

■ Average ☐ Standard Deviation

Source: Authors' calculations based on Gallup World Poll (2007).

countries and Gallup wave 2007 so as to have all the insecurity proxies available. To compare all the available proxies of personal insecurity to other measures of insecurity, two strategies are used: to use all victimization variables in the same regression (except for "safe walking"), or to include "intensity" of victimization (as dummies for each number of victimization events) and add dummies for "stolen" and/or "mugged" and one for "gangs" and/or "drug trafficking" as single variables in separate regressions.

The regression model estimated here is based on specification (1) where i refers to individuals within each country, Y is the measure of well-being and NUT refers to either the "not having enough money" or the "gone hungry" proxy of nutritional insecurity, JOB refers to the proxy of job insecurity and $VICT$ to the one of personal insecurity. Determinants of perceived well-being, alternative to nutritional insecurity, are included in EXP. This set includes variables that have been proved to be important determinants of subjective well-being in the literature. In particular, the variables included are income, availability of social networks (dummy =1 if the respondent has friends ready to help in case of need) and dummies if respondent is unemployed, has had health problems, thinks religion is important, is married, is widowed or has experienced depression. In addition to this, the personality trait factor is included (estimated with the procedure discussed in the previous section) as a major determinant of perceived well-being when the latter is measured by the "ladder" question. Finally, a set of controls is included in X; these controls are: age categories, country income groups and dummies for country.

$$Y_i = \beta_0 + \beta_1 NUT_i + \beta_2 JOB_i + \beta_3 VICT_i + \beta_4 EXP_i + \beta_5 X_i + e_i \qquad (1)$$

In table 5-1, the results are reported using the life satisfaction "ladder" question as dependent variable. As far as personal insecurity proxies are concerned, one general finding is that they do not seem to play a role comparable to nutritional and job insecurity. However, the occurrence of only one victimization event is negatively and significantly associated with life satisfaction (see column 4).

If the results in column 4 of table 5-1 are considered as benchmark (in which we proxy personal insecurity with dummies for the number of victimization forms and we control for the personality trait factor), then it can be concluded that, for the same increase in life satisfaction, a 1-percentage-point decrease in the incidence of nutritional insecurity is marginally equivalent to a 3.9-percentage-point decrease in job insecurity and a 4.8-percentage-point decrease in personal insecurity.[24]

The role of the three types of insecurity on the additional measures of life satisfaction is studied ahead (see results in table 5-2). First, it seems that the role of insecurity is generally larger on satisfaction with one's standard of living than with "freedom." Another interesting result is that the role of personal insecurity is much more pronounced now. No matter which proxy of personal insecurity is used, coefficients are negative and significant (with the exception of 1 victimization event, for satisfaction with standard of living, and 1 and 2 victimization events, for satisfaction with freedom to choose life, which are negative but not significant).

In addition to this, when "freedom" is the dependent variable, the importance of personal insecurity becomes predominant with respect to the other types of insecurity.

A discussion of the trade-off ratios between types of insecurity can clarify these points. If the specification with stolen and/or mugged as proxy of personal insecurity is used as benchmark for the standard of living (see column 2), the terms are: 1-percentage-point decrease in nutritional insecurity is equivalent to

---

24. For this comparison, the coefficient of "1 victimization event" (−0.151) is being used as proxy of the effect of personal insecurity on life satisfaction.

Table 5-1. *Life Satisfaction and Types of Insecurity*
Life satisfaction proxy: ladder question

	1 OLS[a]	2 OLS[a] controlling for personality traits	3 COLS[b]	4 OLS[a] controlling for personality traits	5 OLS[a] controlling for personality traits	6 OLS[a] controlling for personality traits
Nutritional insecurity	-0.690***	-0.721***	-0.283***	-0.728***	-0.720***	-0.721***
	(0.11)	(0.08)	(0.05)	(0.08)	(0.08)	(0.08)
Job insecurity	-0.390***	-0.223**	-0.159***	-0.186**	-0.186**	-0.190**
	(0.10)	(0.09)	(0.04)	(0.09)	(0.09)	(0.08)
Property stolen	-0.001	-0.001	-0.002			
	(0.06)	(0.05)	(0.03)			
Mugged	0.017	0.036	0.007			
	(0.14)	(0.11)	(0.06)			
Presence of gangs	0.029	0.003	0.012			
	(0.08)	(0.04)	(0.03)			
Presence of drug trafficking/sales	-0.077	0.064	-0.032			
	(0.07)	(0.05)	(0.03)			
One victimization event				-0.151**		
				(0.05)		
Two victimization events				-0.012		
				(0.06)		
Three victimization events				0.075		
				(0.10)		

(continued)

Table 5-1. *Life Satisfaction and Types of Insecurity (continued)*
Life satisfaction proxy: ladder question

	1 OLS[a]	2 OLS[a] controlling for personality traits	3 COLS[b]	4 OLS[a] controlling for personality traits	5 OLS[a] controlling for personality traits	6 OLS[a] controlling for personality traits
Four victimization events				0.152 (0.12)		
Stolen and/or mugged					0.021 (0.06)	
Gangs and/or drug trafficking						−0.002 (0.05)
Number of observations	3,855	3,254	3,855	3,859	3,85	3,737
R-squared	0.222	0.605	0.223	0.61	0.609	0.607

Source: Authors' calculations using Gallup World Poll (2007).

*Coefficient is statistically significant at the 10 percent level; **at the 5 percent level; ***at the 1 percent level; no asterisk means the coefficient is not different from zero with statistical significance.

Notes: Standard errors in parentheses. Country fixed effects were included and standard errors are clustered at country level. Controls included age categories and income from Gallup World Poll 2007.

a. Ordinary Least Squares.
b. Cardinalized ordinary least squares.

Table 5-2. *Other Dimension of Life Satisfaction Question and Types of Insecurity*

	Satisfaction with					
	Standard of living (probit)			Freedom to choose life (probit)		
	1	2	3	4	5	6
Nutritional insecurity	−0.188***	−0.187***	−0.189***	−0.042**	−0.043**	−0.044**
	(0.016)	(0.016)	(0.018)	(0.018)	(0.018)	(0.019)
Job insecurity	−0.094***	−0.096***	−0.100***	−0.039**	−0.042**	−0.036**
	(0.025)	(0.025)	(0.025)	(0.016)	(0.017)	(0.016)
One victimization event	−0.007			−0.028		
	(0.019)			(0.021)		
Two victimization events	−0.015			−0.051***		
	(0.017)			(0.018)		
Three victimization events	−0.105***			−0.089***		
	(0.027)			(0.021)		
Four victimization events	−0.128***			−0.148***		
	(0.043)			(0.047)		
Stolen and/or mugged		−0.072***			−0.057***	
		(0.019)			(0.017)	
Gangs and/or drug trafficking			−0.032**			−0.055***
			(0.014)			(0.012)
Number of observations	4.648	4.639	4.488	4.555	4.548	4.403
R-squared	0.117	0.116	0.116	0.057	0.054	0.054

Source: Authors' calculations based on Gallup World Poll (2007).

*Coefficient is statistically significant at the 10 percent level; **at the 5 percent level; ***at the 1 percent level; no asterisk means the coefficient is not different from zero with statistical significance.

Notes: Standard errors in parentheses. Country fixed effects were included and standard errors are clustered at country level. Controls included age categories and income from Gallup World Poll 2007.

a 1.95-percentage-point decrease in job insecurity and a 2.59-percentage-point decrease in personal insecurity. The same comparison for "freedom" (see column 5) gives: 1-percentage-point decrease in nutritional insecurity is equivalent also to a 1-percentage-point decrease in job insecurity and to a 0.75-percentage-point decrease in personal insecurity.

In search of stories that might explain this set of results, one possibility is that victimization's dimensions become more relevant only when a definition of perceived well-being more focused on economic circumstances is used (as it is the perception of standard of living) as compared to a more general assessment of one's life (as it is the life satisfaction "ladder" question). This seems quite consistent with the idea of adaptation to insecurity. In particular, people might adapt faster to crime or violence, which might then have a smaller impact on their individual level of general happiness but still a marked impact when it comes to more specific features of one's lifestyle (as those that the perception of standard of living question is supposedly capturing). In addition to this, it seems that the perception of freedom to choose what to do with one's life is more associated to some underlying long-term satisfaction level and, therefore, less responsive to the presence of nutritional and job insecurity. However, the role of personal insecurity on this dimension of life satisfaction becomes more important, suggesting that freedom to choose is related to lack of crime and conflict.

Results above suggest that the ladder question is capturing a quite different concept of life satisfaction than the other measures of life satisfaction employed: the ladder question seems more related to a general appraisal of current happiness; satisfaction with standard of living is the narrowest concept of the three and seems to be more related to specific economic circumstances; satisfaction with freedom to choose what to do with one's life seems more related to aspirations and, therefore, more related not only to current but also to expected life satisfaction.

As far as questions about life satisfaction are concerned, one general point is that the framing of these questions can affect the measured relationship between income and happiness. Graham, Chattopadhyay and Picon (2008), also using the Gallup World Poll, compare different types of life satisfaction questions and find that questions that provide more of a frame for respondents (as the ladder question) seem to have a closer relationship with income than questions that are vaguer and more open-ended (as the satisfaction with freedom to choose life).

Another result potentially related to the issue of adaptation arises when personal insecurity is proxied with the number of victimization events experienced. In the case of the ladder question, having experienced only one victimization event lowers life satisfaction as compared to the case of "no victimization issues" (the omitted category), but the same does not happen when more than one victimization occurrence is experienced (see table 5-1, column 4). This result is consistent with the idea of people adapting soon to victimization issues. Having experienced more than one victimization event might be indication of a context in which personal insecurity is a common feature and, therefore, individual perception of life satisfaction might not respond when an additional victimization event occurs. On the other hand, having experienced only one victimization event might indicate that the context is not adapted to personal insecurity; with this meaning that even one single event has a strong negative impact on life satisfaction.

When it comes to satisfaction with standard of living and freedom to choose life, the results are different. The more victimization events experienced, the more negative is the association with life satisfaction (see table 5-2, columns 1 and 4).

Following the definition of the three measures of life satisfaction proposed above, results in table 5-1 and 5-2 suggest that there might be a certain degree of adaptation to victimization in terms of current happiness (ladder question), but not when it comes to satisfaction with a specific economic situation (satisfaction with standard of living) and aspirations (satisfaction with freedom to choose what to do with one's life).

A closer look at the issue of adaptation to personal insecurity can be attained studying if there are differential patterns between the sample of LAC countries with very "high violence" (that we proxy as being in the top 20 percent of the homicide rate distribution) and the sample with "low violence" (those in the bottom 20 percent of the homicide rate distribution). As a way of clarifying the interpretation of this exercise, it is probably worth spelling out the priors considered.[25] It was found that, in terms of current happiness (ladder question), there seems to be a certain degree of adaptation, as one would expect this to be more evident in "high violence" countries (in which violence might be a common daily experience). On the contrary, evidence of adaptation in terms of aspirations was not found (satisfaction with freedom to choose life). It is difficult to form a prior here: this could reflect that adaptation of aspirations works only in "high violence" countries, or that neither in "low" nor in "high" violence countries there is a manifest adaptation pattern. In this last case, additional victimization events would be expected to have a more negative effect in "low violence" countries, with this supporting the idea of some degree of adaptation in "high violence" areas.

A specification in which nutritional insecurity and the number of victimization events are included (grouping three or four events in one category) is estimated next. Job insecurity is excluded in order to have enough observations to run the estimation on the restricted samples of countries. Table 5-3 reports results for the estimation of this specification (OLS controlling for the personality trait factor) for the sample of "all LAC countries" (LAC), "high violence" and "low violence" countries. In particular, "high violence" countries in the sample are Belize, Bolivia, Brazil, Colombia, El Salvador, Guatemala, Honduras, and Venezuela. "Low violence" countries in the sample include Chile, Peru, and Uruguay.

---

25. In other terms, a story that might be consistent with the issue of adaptation is being proposed. Obviously, it is not argued that this is the only story; there might be many others, either in favor or against the adaptation hypothesis.

Table 5-3. *Life Satisfaction and Types of Insecurity in "Low" and "High" Violence Countries*

	Ladder question			Satisfaction with					
				Standard of living			Freedom to choose life		
	Latin America and the Caribbean	High violence	Low violence	Latin America and the Caribbean	High violence	Low violence	Latin America and the Caribbean	High violence	Low violence
	OLSª controlling for personality traits	OLSª controlling for personality traits	OLSª controlling for personality traits	Probit	Probit	Probit	Probit	Probit	Probit
	1	2	3	4	5	6	7	8	9
Nutritional insecurity	-0.795***	-0.754***	-0.783***	-0.181***	-0.176***	-0.171***	-0.035**	-0.069***	-0.023
	(0.047)	(0.026)	(0.029)	(0.016)	(0.024)	(0.062)	(0.014)	(0.022)	(0.051)
One victimization issue	-0.094**	-0.105**	-0.114*	-0.019	-0.055	0.023	-0.022**	-0.027	-0.047***
	(0.039)	(0.045)	(0.058)	(0.018)	(0.041)	(0.023)	(0.011)	(0.024)	(0.010)
Two victimization events	-0.038	0.032	-0.1	-0.022	-0.03	0.007	-0.056***	-0.049**	-0.056***
	(0.054)	(0.041)	(0.121)	(0.014)	(0.033)	(0.061)	(0.016)	(0.024)	(0.017)
Three or more victimization events	0.056	0.065	-0.013	-0.093***	-0.121**	-0.046	-0.101***	-0.084***	-0.109*
	(0.054)	(0.099)	(0.051)	(0.020)	(0.048)	(0.070)	(0.013)	(0.026)	(0.058)
Number of observations	10,145	3,848	1,684	12,706	4,680	2,091	12,393	4,575	2,036
R-squared	0.605	0.579	0.583	0.102	0.083	0.087	0.047	0.021	0.051

Source: Authors' calculations based on Gallup World Poll (2007).

*Coefficient is statistically significant at the 10 percent level; **at the 5 percent level; ***at the 1 percent level; no asterisk means the coefficient is not different from zero with statistical significance.

Notes: Standard errors in parenthesis. Country fixed effects were included and standard errors are clustered at country level. Controls included age categories and income from Gallup World Poll 2007. "High" violence countries include Belize, Bolivia, Brazil, Colombia, El Salvador, Guatemala, Honduras, and Venezuela; "Low" violence countries include Chile, Peru, and Uruguay.

a. Ordinary Least Squares.

In terms of the ladder question, both in "high" and "low" violence countries, experiencing only one victimization issue is associated with a lower life satisfaction than "no victimization episodes" (the omitted category), with the negative correlation being slightly higher for the low violence country sample. Interestingly, the dummy for "2 victimization events" is very close to zero and not significant for the "high violence" sample but negative and sizeable (but still not significant) for the "low violence" sample.

This evidence seems to suggest that individuals in "low violence countries" manage to deal with personal insecurity in terms of consequences on their standard of living (additional victimization events do not lower satisfaction; see column 6 in table 5-3) while in "high violence countries" having experienced "3 or more victimization events" would decrease life satisfaction (see column 5).

Satisfaction with freedom to choose life seems to be negatively affected by victimization both in "high" and in "low" violence countries. However, the estimated coefficients for number of victimization events variables are larger for the "low violence" sample and the dummy for "1 victimization event" is only significant for the "low violence" sample (see columns 8 and 9 in table 5-3). Even if these results are not conclusive, they are nevertheless supporting the existence of a certain degree of adaptation to victimization.

Regarding the effect of insecurity on perceived well-being for individuals that are in different parts of the income distribution, this chapter tries to assess the issue in two different ways: considering the group of households with income below US$ 5 PPP a day and the group of households that are in the top 10 percent of the income distribution (in each country), and more generally, considering the households grouped by income quintiles (in each country).

Table 5-4 reports the results of the estimation of a specification in which the insecurity proxies with the dummies "below US$ 5 PPP a day" and "top 10 percent income distribution" are interacted. Personal insecurity is proxied with a dummy for "stolen" and/or "mugged."

Evidence shows that individuals both at the very bottom and at the very top of the income distribution do not show any differential response to the three types of insecurity. This result suggests that response of life satisfaction to insecurity is quite constant along income distribution.

When interactions with income quintiles are considered, in table 5-5, there is some evidence that those at the very top of the income distribution manage to partly offset the negative effect of nutritional insecurity in terms of life satisfaction "ladder" measure (see the interaction with income quintile 5 in column 1). However, this is not true for the other types of insecurity, for which there is no clear pattern arising from results in table 5-5. However, a small sample issue arises with this type of exercise as there might be only very few occurrences of insecurity for those at top quintiles of the income distribution.

Table 5-4. *Life Satisfaction and Types of Insecurity by Income Groups*

| | Ladder question | | Satisfaction with | | | |
| | OLS[a] controlling for personality traits | | Standard of living (probit) | | Freedom to choose life (probit) | |
	1	2	3	4	5	6
Nutritional insecurity	-0.720***	-0.733***	-0.186***	-0.042**	-0.186***	-0.041**
	(0.081)	(0.080)	(0.019)	(0.019)	(0.016)	(0.020)
Income below US$ 5 PPP a day	-0.025		-0.032		-0.023	
	(0.196)		(0.053)		(0.051)	
Top 10% income distribution		0.12		-0.02		-0.021
		(0.137)		(0.075)		(0.055)
Job insecurity	-0.186**	-0.171*	-0.096***	-0.039**	-0.103***	-0.043**
	(0.083)	(0.086)	(0.024)	(0.018)	(0.025)	(0.017)
Income below US$ 5 PPP a day	-0.046		-0.01		-0.066	
	(0.340)		(0.055)		(0.061)	
Top 10% income distribution		-0.126		0.067		0.006
		(0.148)		(0.055)		(0.051)

Personal insecurity						
Income below US$ 5 PPP a day	0.015	0.028	−0.074***	−0.061***	−0.065***	−0.061***
	(0.061)	(0.072)	(0.019)	(0.016)	(0.019)	(0.021)
Top 10% income distribution	0.193	−0.041	0.043	−0.049	0.074	0.02
	(0.159)	(0.133)	(0.065)	(0.059)	(0.053)	(0.045)
Income below US$ 5 PPP a day	−0.203		0.011		−0.089	
	(0.187)		(0.050)		(0.068)	
Top 10% income distribution		0.017		0.006	0	
		(0.105)		(0.054)	(0.058)	
Number of observations	3.85	3.85	4.639	4.548	4.639	4.548
R-squared	0.609	0.609	0.117	0.055	0.117	0.055

Source: Authors' calculations based on Gallup World Poll (2007).

*Coefficient is statistically significant at the 10 percent level; **at the 5 percent level; ***at the 1 percent level; no asterisk means the coefficient is not different from zero with statistical significance.

Notes: Standard errors in parentheses. Country fixed effects were included and standard errors are clustered at country level. Controls included age categories and income from Gallup World Poll 2007.

a. Ordinary Least Squares.

Table 5-5. *Life Satisfaction and Types of Insecurity by Income Quintiles*

	1 Ladder question OLS[a] controlling for personality traits	2 Satisfaction with standard of living (probit)	3 Satisfaction with freedom to choose life (probit)
Nutritional insecurity	−0.805***	−0.189***	−0.051
	(0.157)	(0.030)	(0.036)
Income quintile 2	0.107	−0.035	0.042
	(0.170)	(0.044)	(0.055)
Income quintile 3	0.156	0.032	−0.001
	(0.175)	(0.035)	(0.043)
Income quintile 4	0.024	−0.03	0.011
	(0.174)	(0.054)	(0.040)
Income quintile 5	0.352**	0.075	0.012
	(0.129)	(0.046)	(0.038)
Job insecurity	−0.228	−0.093**	−0.031
	(0.181)	(0.037)	(0.048)
Income quintile 2	−0.172	0.024	−0.036
	(0.203)	(0.041)	(0.053)
Income quintile 3	0.019	0.016	−0.008
	(0.212)	(0.053)	(0.057)
Income quintile 4	0.473**	0.052	−0.072
	(0.205)	(0.032)	(0.049)
Income quintile 5	−0.028	0.019	0.007
	(0.213)	(0.046)	(0.045)
Personal insecurity	0.196	−0.083*	−0.022
	(0.162)	(0.044)	(0.033)
Income quintile 2	−0.005	−0.04	−0.079
	(0.184)	(0.053)	(0.055)
Income quintile 3	−0.293*	−0.023	0.008
	(0.155)	(0.045)	(0.041)
Income quintile 4	−0.258	0.03	−0.007
	(0.180)	(0.044)	(0.054)
Income quintile 5	−0.137	0.011	−0.021
	(0.145)	(0.051)	(0.051)
Number of observations	3,794	3,794	3,733
R-squared	0.62	0.153	0.073

Source: Authors' calculations based on Gallup World Poll (2007).

*Coefficient is statistically significant at the 10 percent level; **at the 5 percent level; ***at the 1 percent level; no asterisk means the coefficient is no different from zero with statistical significance.

Notes: Standard errors in parentheses. Country fixed effects were included and standard errors are clustered at country level. Controls included age categories and income from Gallup World Poll 2007.

a. Ordinary Least Squares.

One last question refers to whether, and to what extent, the effect of insecurity on perceived well-being is different for individuals with different educational levels. Two exercises are performed: table 5-6 reports the estimation results of a specification in which the insecurity proxy is interacted with a dummy for having "low educational level" (illiterate and complete/incomplete primary) and a dummy for having "university" studies (complete/incomplete university studies or postgraduate/master). Being at the extremes of the educational level scale does not seem to make a difference in terms of response of life satisfaction to insecurity: coefficients of interactions are not significant.

In table 5-7, results of a specification that includes interactions with all the observed educational levels are reported; the omitted category is "complete secondary school." The inclusion of all the educational level variables comes at the price of having only few observations for some of the groups. For clarity, coefficients of the interactions with the types of insecurity are presented in different columns (that is, coefficients in columns 1, 2, and 3 come from the same regression, and the same applies to columns "4, 5, 6" and "7, 8, 9"). Being illiterate seems to lead to a more negative response of life satisfaction "ladder" question to nutritional insecurity (see column 1) but not of other measures of life satisfaction (see columns 4 and 7). As regards job insecurity, having an educational level higher than "complete secondary school" seems to partly offset the negative effect on life satisfaction "ladder" question (see column 2; all coefficients are positive but the one of "post-graduate studies," for which the caveat of having only few observations is particularly relevant). Once again, the same results are not found for the other measures of life satisfaction (see columns 5 and 8).

Overall, the results above seem to suggest that the response of life satisfaction to insecurity is remarkably constant across income and educational level, at least for satisfaction with standard of living and freedom to choose life. However, some differential responses arise when it comes to response to nutritional insecurity in terms of the ladder question. Perhaps not surprisingly, individuals that are a priori less vulnerable to insecurity (such as individuals living in households that are the richest of each country, at the top income quintile) manage to partly offset the negative response to nutritional insecurity, whereas groups a priori more vulnerable to nutritional insecurity (as illiterates are) show a more negative response to this type of insecurity as compared to more educated groups.

Conclusions

The narrow view that choice is the only aspect of human life that can be observed (and so the only determinant of individual utility) has been challenged by a new literature that is trying to add psychologists' techniques to the tools of economics. In particular, the Quality of Life approach goes beyond income-based measures of welfare and tries to incorporate broader measures of well-being.

Table 5-6. *Life Satisfaction and Types of Insecurity by Education Groups*

| | Ladder question | | Satisfaction with | | | |
| | OLS[a] controlling for personality traits | | Standard of living (probit) | | Freedom to choose life (probit) | |
	1	2	3	4	5	6
Nutritional insecurity	−0.678***	−0.717***	−0.180***	−0.188***	−0.034**	−0.044**
	(0.091)	(0.085)	(0.022)	(0.018)	(0.016)	(0.022)
Low educational level	−0.116		−0.024		−0.034	
	(0.126)		(0.033)		(0.023)	
Attended university		0.019		−0.002		−0.003
		(0.094)		(0.033)		(0.045)
Job insecurity	−0.191*	−0.194**	−0.096***	−0.095***	−0.061***	−0.032
	(0.098)	(0.092)	(0.031)	(0.031)	(0.021)	(0.021)
Low educational level	0.036		−0.006		0.055**	
	(0.110)		(0.033)		(0.023)	
Attended university		0.044		−0.006		−0.047
		(0.090)		(0.065)		(0.045)

Personal insecurity						
0.07	0.008	−0.077***	−0.080***	−0.062***	−0.057***
(0.070)	(0.064)	(0.022)	(0.023)	(0.018)	(0.022)
Low educational level						
−0.209		0.026		0.025	
(0.132)		(0.044)		(0.031)	
Attended university						
	0.002		0.041		0.007
	(0.118)		(0.045)		(0.037)
Low educational level						
−0.083		0.04		0.022	
(0.067)		(0.034)		(0.022)	
Attended university						
0.272***		−0.035		0.022	
(0.094)		(0.030)		(0.022)	
	0.272***		−0.035		−0.018
	(0.094)		(0.030)		(0.013)
Number of observations						
3.842	3.842	4.63	4.63	4.54	4.54
R-squared						
0.609	0.611	0.117	0.117	0.055	0.055

Source: Authors' calculations based on Gallup World Poll (2007).

*Coefficient is statistically significant at the 10 percent level; **at the 5 percent level; ***at the 1 percent level; no asterisk means the coefficient is not different from zero with statistical significance.

Notes: Standard errors in parentheses. Country fixed effects were included and standard errors are clustered at country level. Controls included age categories and income from Gallup World Poll 2007.

a. Ordinary Least Squares.

Table 5-7. *Life Satisfaction and Types of Insecurity by Educational Levels*

	Ladder question			Standard of living			Freedom to choose		
	OLS[a] *controlling for personality traits*			*OLS*[a] *controlling for personality traits*			*OLS*[a] *controlling for personality traits*		
	Nutritional insecurity	*Job insecurity*	*Personal insecurity*	*Nutritional insecurity*	*Job insecurity*	*Personal insecurity*	*Nutritional insecurity*	*Job insecurity*	*Personal insecurity*
	1	*2*	*3*	*4*	*5*	*6*	*7*	*8*	*9*
Insecurity	-0.556***	-0.267*	0.097	-0.158***	-0.047	-0.107***	-0.057***	-0.041	-0.065**
	(0.120)	(0.141)	(0.111)	(0.027)	(0.046)	(0.039)	(0.027)	(0.040)	(0.033)
Illiterate	-0.495*	-0.068	-0.12	-0.005	-0.016	0.104	0.038	0.034	0.06
	(0.265)	(0.260)	(0.463)	(0.062)	(0.103)	(0.112)	(0.044)	(0.058)	(0.080)
Incomplete primary	-0.099	0.166	0.134	-0.077	-0.03	0.084	0.022	0.053	0.055
	(0.266)	(0.213)	(0.266)	(0.056)	(0.053)	(0.084)	(0.041)	(0.060)	(0.062)
Complete primary	-0.224	0.131	-0.324**	-0.034	-0.075*	0.053	-0.037	0.039	0.029
	(0.180)	(0.183)	(0.157)	(0.040)	(0.045)	(0.051)	(0.037)	(0.036)	(0.032)
Incomplete secondary school	-0.244	0.076	-0.043	-0.03	-0.083	0.043	0.057*	-0.007	-0.002
	(0.233)	(0.249)	(0.257)	(0.049)	(0.053)	(0.056)	(0.034)	(0.048)	(0.042)

	(1)	(2)	(3)	(4)	(5)	(6)	(7)	(8)	(9)
Incomplete technical school	0.347**	0.705**	−0.168	−0.01	0.095	0.141***	0.108**	0.037	0.061
	(0.162)	(0.335)	(0.276)	(0.124)	(0.143)	(0.028)	(0.046)	(0.054)	(0.048)
Complete technical school	0.19	0.303	−0.067	−0.119**	−0.148	0.002	0.056	−0.062	−0.004
	(0.192)	(0.290)	(0.284)	(0.051)	(0.102)	(0.077)	(0.078)	(0.062)	(0.060)
Incomplete university studies	−0.077	0.117	0.237	0.061	0.001	0.028	0.03	−0.121*	0.011
	(0.175)	(0.165)	(0.215)	(0.057)	(0.094)	(0.047)	(0.062)	(0.067)	(0.071)
Complete university studies	−0.132	0.146	−0.272***	−0.045	−0.084	0.089*	0.005	0.04	0.007
	(0.178)	(0.155)	(0.097)	(0.048)	(0.093)	(0.050)	(0.077)	(0.054)	(0.058)
Post-graduate studies	0.242	−0.186	−0.301	−0.455***	−0.092	−0.026	−0.005	−0.18	0.130*
	(0.608)	(0.397)	(0.358)	(0.144)	(0.111)	(0.183)	(0.211)	(0.158)	(0.072)
Number of observations		3.842			4.584			4495	
R-squared		0.624			0.135			0.064	

Source: Authors' calculations based on Gallup World Poll (2007).

*Coefficient is statistically significant at the 10 percent level; **at the 5 percent level; ***at the 1 percent level; no asterisk means the coefficient is not different from zero with statistical significance.

Notes: Standard errors in parentheses. Country fixed effects were included and standard errors are clustered at country level. Controls included age categories and income from Gallup World Poll 2007.

a. Ordinary Least Squares.

Within this broader approach, this chapter studied the link between deprivation and QoL. Several well-established results in the happiness literature support the idea that this relationship is a particularly complex one. This chapter tried to focus on the vulnerability of individuals and households to situations and occurrences that could potentially lead to deprivation and, ultimately, adversely affect well-being. The proxies of vulnerability used throughout this chapter were measures of nutritional, personal and job insecurity. From a policy perspective, the study of the types of insecurity jointly should be preferred to studies in which measures of insecurity are studied in isolation. However, considering all the insecurity types at the same time poses some problems: interconnections between measures of insecurity (likely to confound results), data limitations and selection issues (job insecurity proxies are defined only for those who work). With this caveat in mind, this chapter studied the importance of insecurities in explaining life satisfaction compared to each other.

It has been shown that, overall, the incidence of insecurity is quite widespread across LAC countries. When the measures of insecurity used in this chapter were grouped in one indicator, it was noticed that only around 23 percent of respondents in LAC as a whole could be considered as "completely secure" (that is, they did not experience any of the insecurity occurrences considered here). Most of the respondents experienced between one and three insecurity issues; the percentage of those experiencing four events was still quite high at more than 5 percent. Notably, more than 30 percent of respondents in LAC as a whole reported that there had been times in the past 12 months in which they did not have enough money to buy food (as a comparison, the figure for the United States is 6.5 percent), and less than 50 percent of respondents in LAC thought that it was safe walking alone in the streets at night (the United States, 74.7 percent). Not surprisingly, there is quite a lot of variability between LAC countries, especially in terms of nutritional insecurity.

Overall, the findings suggest that nutritional insecurity is playing the leading role in explaining life satisfaction. Job insecurity has generally a significant and negative, but smaller, effect on perceived well-being. Personal insecurity seems to have an effect only on some measures of life satisfaction. This is very in line with a situation in which additional factors (such as rising aspirations, relative income differences, and security of gains) become relevant only after basic needs are met.[26] The benchmark results show that, for the same increase in life satisfaction, a 1-percentage-point decrease in the incidence of nutritional insecurity is marginally equivalent to a 3.9-percentage-point decrease in job insecurity and to a 4.8-percentage-point decrease in the measure of personal insecurity.

---

26. Nutritional insecurity seems a much closer proxy of basic needs than job and personal insecurity.

As regards the role of personal insecurity, the findings of this chapter show that while it is not associated with the life satisfaction "ladder" question, it is a strong predictor of satisfaction with one's standard of living. One interpretation is that personal insecurity might become relevant only when a definition of perceived well-being more focused on economic circumstances is used (as it is the perception of one's standard of living) as compared to a more general assessment of one's life (as it is the life satisfaction "ladder" question).

Interestingly, when the measure of life satisfaction employed is satisfaction with freedom to choose what to do with one's life, the effect of insecurity is still significant, but smaller in magnitude. In addition to this, the role of personal security on this dimension of life satisfaction becomes more important (a 1-percentage-point decrease in nutritional insecurity equivalent to a 0.75-percentage-point decrease in personal insecurity) than the ones of the other types of insecurity. This set of results suggests that perception of freedom to choose what to do with one's life is more associated to some underlying long-term satisfaction level and, therefore, it is overall less responsive to the presence of insecurity, but relatively more responsive to personal insecurity.

The study also finds some evidence of individuals adapting faster to some types of insecurity. Adaptation and policy are linked in several ways, with an important one being the way "demands for changes" are transmitted from individuals to policymakers. For example, in the case where people adapt faster to a specific type of insecurity, people might tend to underestimate these insecurities when having to express their demands to policymakers. These issues might nonetheless be very important, and adaptation to them does not necessarily mean that they do not hinder improvements of objective living conditions. Policymakers might have to support other ways to elicit demands from individuals in cases like this.

In particular, when proxying for personal insecurity with an indicator of its intensity (by the number of victimization events for each respondent, maximum is 4 if respondent experienced "stolen," "mugged," "presence of gangs" and "presence of drug trafficking/sales") it is found that only having experienced one single victimization occurrence is negatively associated with life satisfaction. This result is consistent with the idea of people adapting soon to victimization issues. Having experienced more than one victimization event might be an indication of a context in which personal insecurity is a common feature, something not new, and therefore individual perception of life satisfaction might not respond when an additional victimization event occurs. On the other hand, having experienced only one victimization event might suggest low adaptation to an insecure environment and, therefore, a strong negative impact on life satisfaction.

In regard to the effects of insecurity on perceived well-being according to different levels of income and education, this chapter finds that individuals at the very top of the income distribution manage to partly offset the negative consequences of nutritional insecurity in terms of the life satisfaction "ladder" measure.

As far as educational levels are concerned, being illiterate seems to lead to a more negative response of life satisfaction to nutritional insecurity. For the other types of insecurity and the other measures of life satisfaction, the results presented in this chapter do not show a clear pattern. Overall, the results indicate that response of life satisfaction to insecurity is not dramatically different along income distribution and educational levels.

References

Behrman, J. R. 1996. "The Impact of Health and Nutrition on Education." *World Bank Research Observer* 11 (1): 23–37. Oxford University Press.

Brief, A. P., A. H. Butcher, J. M. George, and K. E. Link. 1993. "Integrating Bottom-up and Top-down Theories of Subjective Well-Being: The Case of Health." *Journal of Personality and Social Psychology* 64: 646–53.

Cárdenas, M. 2007. "Economic Growth in Colombia: A Reversal of Fortune." In *Ensayos Sobre Política Económica y Social*. Banco de la República, forthcoming.

Chen, S., N. V. Loayza, and M. Reynal-Querol. 2007. "The Aftermath of Civil War." World Bank Policy Research Working Paper 4190, April 2007.

Collier, P., H. Hegre, A. Hoeffler, V. L. Elliott, M. Reynal-Querol, and N. Sambanis. 2003. *Breaking the Conflict Trap: Civil War and Development Policy*. World Bank Publication. Oxford Universty Press.

Deaton, A. 2007. "Income, Aging, Health and Wellbeing around the World: Evidence from the Gallup World Poll." Mimeo, Princeton University.

Diener, E., and M. Seligman. 2004. "Beyond Money: Toward an Economy of Well-Being." *Psychological Science in the Public Interest* 5 (1): 1–31.

Diener, E., E. Sandvik, L. Seidlitz, and M. Diener. 1993. "The Relationship Between Income and Subjective Well-Being: Relative or Absolute?" *Social Indicators Research* 28: 195–223.

Easterlin, R. 1974. "Does Economic Growth Enhance the Human Lot? Some Empirical Evidence." In P. David and M. Reder, eds. *Nations and Households in Economic Growth: Essays in Honor of Moses Abramovitz*. Stanford University Press.

———. 2001. "Income and Happiness: Towards a Unified Theory." *Economic Journal* 111 (473): 465–84.

———. 2003. "Explaining happiness." *Proceedings of the National Academy of Sciences* 100 (19): 11176–83.

Frey, B., and A. Stutzer. 2002. "What Can Economists Learn from Happiness Research?" *Journal of Economic Literature* 40 (2): 402–35.

Gallup World Poll. 2006. Available at www.gallup.com/consulting/worldpoll/24046/about.aspx.

———. 2007. Available at www.gallup.com/consulting/worldpoll/24046/about.aspx.

Graham, C. 2008. "Happiness and Health: Lessons—and Questions—for Public Policy." *Health Affairs* 27 (1): 72–87.

Graham, C., S. Chattopadhyay, and M. Picon. 2008. "The Easterlin and Other Paradoxes: Why Both Sides of the Debate May be Correct." Paper prepared for the Princeton Conference on International Differences in Well Being, Princeton, N.J.

Graham, C., and A. Felton. 2006. "Inequality and Happiness: Insights from Latin America." *Journal of Economic Inequality* 4 (1): 107–122.

Graham, C., and S. Pettinato. 2002. *Happiness and Hardship: Opportunity and Insecurity in New Market Economies*. Brookings.

Hilleras, P. K., A. F. Jorm, A. Herlitz, and B. Winblad. 1998. "Negative and Positive Affect among the Very Old: A Survey on a Sample Age 90 Years or Older." *Research on Aging* 20: 593–610.

Ibáñez, A. M., and C. Jaramillo. 2006. "Oportunidades de desarrollo económico en el post-conflicto: propuesta de política." *Coyuntura Económica* 36 (2). Fedesarrollo.

Kenny, A., and C. Kenny. 2006. *Life, Liberty and the Pursuit of Utility.* Exeter, U.K.: Imprint Academic.

Londoño, J. L., and R. Guerrero. 1999. "Violencia en América Latina—Epidemiología y Costos." Documento de Trabajo R-375. Washington, D.C.: Inter-American Development Bank.

Murrell, S. A., N. L. Salsman, and S. Meeks. 2003. "Educational Attainment, Positive Psychological Mediators, and Resources for Health and Vitality in Older Adults." *Journal of Aging and Health* 15: 591–615.

Okun, M. A., and L. K. George. 1984. "Physician- and Self-ratings of Health, Neuroticism and Subjective Well-Being among Men and Women." *Personality and Individual Differences* 5: 533–39.

Okun, M. A., W. A. Stock, M. J. Haring, and R. A. Witter. 1984. "The Social Activity/Subjective Well-Being Relation: A Quantitative Synthesis." *Research on Aging* 6: 45–65.

Ostir, G. V., K. S. Markides, S. A. Black, and J. S. Goodwin. 2000. "Emotional Well-Being Predicts Subsequent Functional Independence and Survival." *Journal of the American Geriatrics Society* 48: 473–478.

Oswald, A. 1997. "Happiness and economic performance." *Economic Journal* 107: 1815–31.

Rojas, M. 2004. "Well-being and the Complexity of Poverty." Research Paper No. 2004/29. Helsinki: World Institute for Development Research.

Sen, A. 1986. "The Standard of Living." In S. McMurrin, ed. *Tanner Lectures on Human Values,* vol. VII. Cambridge University Press.

Soares, R., and J. Naritomi. 2007. "Understanding High Crime Rates in Latin America: The Role of Social and Policy Factors." In Rafael Di Tella, Sebastian Edwards, and Ernesto Schargrodsky, eds., *NBER Inter-American Seminar on Economics 2007.* NBER and University of Chicago Press, forthcoming.

Strauss, J., and D. Thomas. 1998. "Health, Nutrition and Economic Development." *Journal of Economic Literature* 36 (2): 766–817.

van Praag, B., and A. Ferrer-i-Carbonell. 2008. *Happiness Quantified: A Satisfaction Calculus Approach.* Rev ed. Oxford University Press.

Weiss, A., T. C. Bates, and M. Luciano. 2008. "Happiness is a Personal(ity) Thing: The Genetics of Personality and Well-Being in a Representative Sample." *Psychological Science* 19: 205–10.

6

Health Perceptions and Quality of Life in Latin America

CAROL GRAHAM AND EDUARDO LORA

Health is widely recognized as a life dimension that is central to individual happiness, to quality of life, and to economic welfare. Yet our ability to measure health status—and how it varies across individuals and societies—is limited. Life expectancy and mortality are the two most commonly used measures of societal health and serve as important benchmark indicators. Yet health is much more than what these indicators gauge. Illness, functional limitations, and other conditions that limit physical or mental welfare are crucial dimensions of health, but they are much more difficult to measure; most of the tools that we have for assessing their welfare effects are crude or imprecise.

This chapter focuses on the potential of survey data—and in particular subjective assessments of health status and satisfaction—to contribute to understanding of various aspects of health. It also highlights the limitations of these data and discusses their relation to other forms of measurement. Although the information garnered from perceptions data is not always consistent with objective indicators, it provides novel and relevant information—including what the gaps between subjective and objective measures tell us. Perceptions data provide a useful instrument for better understanding the values that individuals attach to various aspects of their health; the variance in aspirations and norms about what is or is not good health; and the attitudes about public health policies.

This analysis finds very clear gaps between perceived and objective indicators of health, some of which echo the broader themes that run throughout the book (such as generally lower expectations among the poor), and some of which are more specific to health. Indicators of perceived health are more evenly distributed across socioeconomic cohorts than are either objective indicators of health or perceived income indicators. This could be for several reasons. First, due to the links between mental and physical health, unobserved personality traits may be even more important in the determinants of health perceptions than they are in other quality of life domains, such as education or job satisfaction. Second, the low expectations of the poor are particularly pronounced in the health arena, as the poor adapt to and/or tolerate ill health. Third, mental health and uncertainty seem to have different effects on perceived health status than do physical health conditions.

This chapter analyzes the relation between subjective health assessments and objective health indicators from alternative perspectives. This analysis provides an overview of the general health perceptions data and its relation to objective indicators for a large region—a wide sample of respondents in Latin America and the Caribbean (LAC).[1] The chapter then explores how individuals value different health states, via an analysis of the relationship between health status indicators (as measured by a standardized instrument known as EQ-5D–European Quality of Life 5 Dimension Index) and health and life satisfaction scores. Finally, findings are placed in the context of the more general relationship between happiness and health, across countries and across individuals over time. Significant evidence is found regarding adaptation as health standards improve, which is analogous to the adaptation that characterizes the income and happiness relationship. While this analysis is exploratory, it contributes to better understanding the gaps between objective and subjective health indicators, which in turn is important to health policy and to understanding how different cohorts process and respond to policy messages.

What We Know from the Literature

There is little theoretical basis to understand how health perceptions are formed and how they relate to the individual's objective health status. However, self-rated health and subjective assessment of health conditions are valuable sources of information. Self-rated health is usually elicited through a single question such as "are you satisfied with your health?" Subjective assessment of health conditions require more specific questions to measure the prevalence, and sometimes the severity, of disability, pain, anxiety or other health-related limitations or symptoms.

Self-rated health is a good predictor of subsequent health outcomes. In a well-known study, Mossey and Shapiro (1982) found that self-rated health (by people

1. In this chapter, the term *Latin America* includes a small sample of Caribbean countries as well. Thus, *Latin America* encapsulates Latin America and the Caribbean (LAC) for the rest of this chapter.

aged 65 and older) is a predictor of mortality independent of objective health status. Controlling for objective health status, age, sex, life satisfaction, income and urban/rural residence, the risk of early mortality and late mortality for persons whose self-rated health was poor was nearly three times that of those whose self-rated health was excellent. Furthermore, the increased risk of death associated with poor self-rated health was greater than that associated with poor objective health status. Idler and Angel (1990) assessed the ability of self-rated health status to predict mortality in a wider age group (25–74 years). They found that, net of its association with medical diagnoses, demographic factors, and health-related behaviors, self-rated health is a good predictor of mortality over the 12-year follow-up period among middle-aged males, but not among elderly males or females of any age. Idler and Benyamini (1997) examined 27 studies that assessed the ability of self-rated health to predict mortality and found that in nearly all of the studies it was a good predictor, despite the inclusion of numerous specific health status indicators and other relevant covariates known to predict mortality.

Self-rated health has also proven to be a relatively good measure of health status.[2] In the countries surveyed by the European Foundation for the Improvement of Living and Working Conditions (EFILWC) perceived health tended to reflect morbidity rates.[3] Women tend to report poorer health than men. Self-rated health declines with age, but is higher for those with more education and higher incomes. Based on the Gallup World Poll, which is also our main data source, Deaton (2008) has confirmed that satisfaction with health declines with age, but the rate of decline is steeper in poorer countries. In some rich countries, like the United States, health satisfaction increases beyond a certain age.

Self-rated health is subject to important criticisms. Upon assessing the correlates of health satisfaction in the cross country sample of the Gallup World Poll, Deaton (2008) concluded that health satisfaction should not be used as an indicator of health status, since it does not correlate well with life expectancy, infant mortality or prevalence of HIV/AIDS at the country level. Several authors have shown that self-rated health is often subject to cultural and other biases that render self-reported health measures difficult to compare across groups of individuals. Jürges (2007) has found that an important part of cross country differences in self-reported health in 10 European countries can be attributed to cultural differences in response styles. Groot (2000) analyzes the impact of age biases in the United States and finds that the scale of reference of a subjective health measure changes with age. And while perhaps not a criticism as much as an observation, Graham (2008) notes the strong and consistent correlation between self-reported health and happiness and other measures of reported well-being.

2. Robine and others (2003).
3. EFILWC (2004).

Danny Kahneman (2000) has explored how framing effects can affect individual assessments across a range of domains, including health. Dolan and Kahneman (2008) examine how different concepts of utility—which can vary starkly across the rich and the poor, for example—can affect health valuations. Previously, Dolan (1997) introduced the concept of time trade-offs for assessing different health states. This is an interview-based method in which individuals who report various health states are asked how many healthy life years they would trade-off in exchange for not having the condition, with the possible responses ranging from a few months to more life years than are available (in which health states are assessed as worse than death).

Accepting limitations, subjective evaluations of health states are a valuable source of information that compare favorably with objective evaluations as predictors of morbidity. In contrast to the objective morbidity measures on which an external observer establishes the occurrence or otherwise of a certain illness based on a specific method that can be repeated with some consistency, self-perceived morbidity is based on subjective judgment. In some aspects of health, such as pain or suffering, the subjective perception is the only valid source of information. In other aspects, external observation and individual perception can coincide or provide supplementary information. Other health problems or deficiencies, such as hypertension, cannot be perceived and are only detectable by external observation. Therefore, to fully characterize morbidity, both self-perception and external observation are essential.

An important note of caution is that the use of self-perceived morbidity is a function of the pathological burden of the individual's social and cultural context. A very common pattern is that as the transition to better health standards in a country or community moves ahead, self-perceived morbidity increases although observed morbidity falls, because knowledge of illnesses or health problems improves and health expectations rise. Murray and Chen (1992) and Sen (2002) show that in India, Kerala state reported (in 1972–73) much higher prevalence rates (reported by the population) of chronic illnesses than other states of India, despite being the state with the highest life expectation and education levels. In turn, self-reported morbidity of the same illnesses in the United States was much higher than in Kerala. Similarly, it is very common to find that self-perceived morbidity rates at any given time in a country are high among the upper income groups.[4]

As Murray and Chen (1992) conclude: "if the interpretation of self-reported morbidity is so problematic, of what use are measures of self-perceived morbidity? First and perhaps most importantly, perceived illness is by itself a major social phenomenon. If more and more people in a society feel ill, this would be important to anyone concerned with well-being. Second, self-perceived morbidity provides critical information on the relevance of disease to the individual. Only through

---

4. Murray and Chen (1992) cite the cases of Ivory Coast, Ghana, and Peru.

the individual can we learn about the true burden of pain and suffering. For a health planner concerned with community health, such information is vital. . . . Third . . . , sudden changes in self-perceived morbidity probably reflect changes in the burden of pathology. Longer-term changes, on the other hand, could equally be due to changing pathology or to social and cultural factors affecting illness perception" (p. 493).

Health perceptions of the general populations of the Latin American countries have been the subject of very few studies. Suárez-Berenguela (2001) calculated socio-economic gradients of self-assessed health status in Brazil, Jamaica, and Mexico and of self-reported symptoms of illness or accident in those same countries, plus Ecuador and Peru. While he found the expected relationship between socio-economic status and better self-assessed health, the slope of that relationship was substantially less steep than that for socioeconomic status and objective indicators of morbidity or mortality. Dachs and others (2002) studied inequalities in self-reported health problems in 11 Latin American countries. They found that inequalities (by quintiles) were small, which they attributed to cultural and social differences across socio-economic groups in the perception of health. They concluded that "it is important to develop regional projects aimed at improving the questions on self-reported health in household interview surveys so that determinants of the inequalities in health can be studied in depth." This chapter follows that advice.

The studies reported above and throughout the chapter note variance across various health conditions as well as across age, income, and education cohorts. Our research highlights, in particular, the wide variance related to different norms and expectations across socioeconomic cohorts and cultures, in addition to different health conditions. This is an area where there is a great deal unknown; we bring new methodological approaches and marshal empirical evidence to approach these questions. Our aim is to enhance the understanding of how objective conditions, individual perceptions, and shared cultural and social norms influence the objective and perceived health states of thousands of individuals in Latin America.

The Health Perception Data

The main source of information for this chapter is the World Gallup Polls, applied in over 100 countries in 2006 and 2007, which provide the most extensive coverage of perceptions of quality of life. In the 2007 poll, for the 20 countries of Latin America covered additional questions were included on health perceptions and conditions of access to health services (see box 6-1). Health conditions are assessed through a method of health self-evaluation known as European Quality of Life-5 Dimensions Index (EQ-5D), a standardized instrument originally designed to complement other instruments but now increasingly used as a "stand

Box 6-1. *Health Perceptions*

This chapter makes use of survey data collected through the 2006 and 2007 rounds of the Gallup Polls, which covered over 100 countries from all the regions of the world. The Gallup Polls surveyed three aspects of health perceptions: overall self evaluation of health, self-perceived morbidity and conditions of access to health services. To assess overall health the Gallup World Poll uses the following question: "Are you satisfied or dissatisfied with your help?" (henceforth "health satisfaction"). For the 20 Latin American and Caribbean (LAC) countries included in the 2007 round of the Gallup survey an additional question is included: "Using a scale from 0 to 10, on which the best state you can imagine is marked 10 and the worst state you can imagine is marked 0, indicate how good or bad your own health is today" (henceforth "health state"). Self-perceived morbidity in the 20 LAC countries is assessed through the set of EQ-D5 questions that go verbatim as follows:

I am going to ask you a few simple questions about your health today. Please indicate which statements describe your own health today:

• *Mobility* (your ability to walk around; select only one): I have no problems in walking around / I have some problems in walking around / I am confined to bed.

• *Self-care* (ability to take care of yourself; select only one): I have no problems with self-care / I have some problems washing or dressing myself / I am unable to wash or dress myself.

• *Usual activities* (work, study, housework, family, or leisure activities; select only one): I have no problems with performing my usual activities / I have some problems performing my usual activities / I am unable to perform my usual activities.

• *Pain/discomfort* (select only one): I have no pain or discomfort / I have moderate pain or discomfort / I have extreme pain or discomfort.

• *Anxiety/depression* (select only one): I am not anxious or depressed / I am moderately anxious or depressed / I am extremely anxious or depressed.

In this chapter we refer to each of three answer options as no problem / moderate condition / extreme condition. The World Poll included three questions on perceived health problems that partly overlap with the EQ-5D and are not used in this study. The 2006 and 2007 World Polls included also a few questions about conditions of access to, and satisfaction with, health services, which are not discussed here.

alone" measure, which has been used extensively in Europe and the United States. This is the first instance that we know of its application in a large sample of developing countries, and surely one as wide ranging in per capita income levels as those in Latin America. The responses to the set of EQ-5D questions can be used to produce a single index value for health status, which may be calculated by applying a formula that essentially attaches a weight to each of the levels in each dimension. This formula is based on the valuation of EQ-5D health states from general population samples using a time trade-off method (described in detail in the section on valuation of health states below). Shaw and others (2005) have developed a scoring algorithm based on modeling work for the U.S. general population. With the system of weights implied in this algorithm, the EQ-5D index ranges from −0.11 to 1.0 on a scale where 0.0 = death and 1.0 = perfect health. We make use of the algorithm in the analysis below.

The percentage of Latin Americans who say they are satisfied with their health seems very high—85 percent according to the 2007 polls—but it is not significantly different from other regions of the world, with the notable exception of Eastern Europe and Central Asia.[5] The surprising similarity between percentages of satisfaction in the large regions of the world is a phenomenon that challenges simplistic interpretations on how health perceptions are formed. Countries with very different income levels or with appreciably different objective health conditions report similar percentages of health satisfaction. Figures 6-1a and 6-1b show the low association (without controlling for other variables) in national data between health satisfaction and income levels or life expectation.

In Latin America, Guatemala is one of the countries with the highest levels of health satisfaction, despite its deficient mortality indicators and its enormous gaps in various health indicators, especially between the indigenous and non-indigenous populations. With a health satisfaction score of 0.93,[6] Guatemalans evaluate their health better than people in almost any other country in the world, with only two exceptions: Kuwaitis and Costa Ricans. Among the countries of Latin America covered by the 2007 poll, Chileans are the least satisfied with their health, even though objective health indicators in Chile are among the region's best. Beyond Latin America, it is even more intriguing that some of the countries most affected by the HIV-AIDS epidemic—such as Tanzania, Zimbabwe, Botswana, South Africa, and Kenya—report health satisfaction coefficients of 70 percent or more. The satisfaction coefficient for Kenya (82 percent) is equal to Britain's and is one percentage point higher than the one for the United States.[7]

The EQ-5D questions revealed that at the time of the poll 25 percent of Latin Americans suffered from pain, 18.5 percent suffered anxiety, about 10 percent were not able to perform normal activities for persons of their age, 9.5 percent said they had physical limitations in their daily activities and 3.8 percent had problems with looking after themselves. Since this is the first time, to our knowledge, that the EQ-5D questions have been applied to a general population, it is not possible to offer adequate comparisons with other regions. However, the prevalence rate of anxiety is very close to that estimated for the United States using different methods: about 18.1 percent of American adults ages 18 or older have an anxiety disorder.[8]

5. The same result is reported by Clifton and Gingrich (2007).
6. See table 6-2. Health satisfaction ranges from 0 (no one is satisfied) to 1 (everyone is satisfied).
7. Deaton (2008).
8. In the United States, mental disorders are diagnosed based on the *Diagnostic and Statistical Manual of Mental Disorders,* 4th ed. (DSM-IV). See NIMH (2009).

Figure 6-1a. *Self-Reported Health Satisfaction and GDP per Capita*

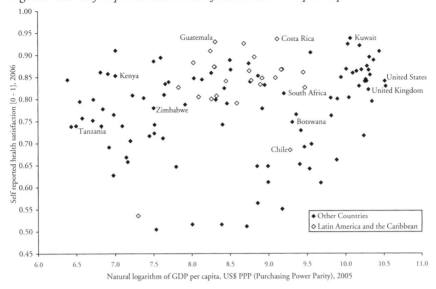

Source: Authors' calculations based on Gallup World Poll 2006-2007, and World Bank (2007).

Figure 6-1b. *Self-Reported Health Satisfaction and Life Expectancy*

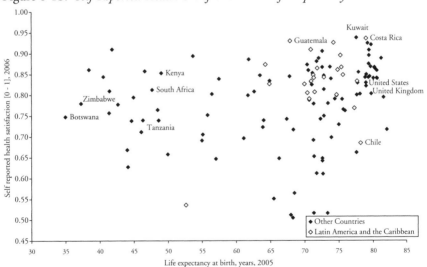

Source: Authors' calculations based on Gallup World Poll 2006-07, and World Bank (2007).

Figure 6-2. *Health Satisfaction—Three Alternative Measures*

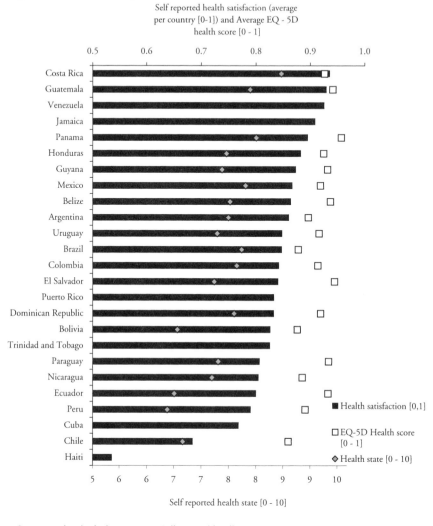

Self reported health satisfaction (average per country [0-1]) and Average EQ - 5D health score [0 - 1]

Self reported health state [0 - 10]

Source: Authors' calculations using Gallup World Poll 2007.
Note: EQ-5D = European Quality of Life-5 Dimensions Index. Health state and EQ-5D not available for Cuba, Haiti, Jamaica, Trinidad and Tobago and Venezuela.

Figure 6-2 shows three alternative global evaluation measures of the health of the populations of LAC. The first measure is the percentage of the population that expresses satisfaction with its health in the 2007 polls, which we have used so far (including some Caribbean countries that were not covered in 2007 but are in the 2006 poll). The second measure is the average of the responses to the question on self-evaluation of health states on a scale from zero to 10, which was only asked in the 2007 poll. The third measure is evaluation of the health

Figure 6-3. *Relation between Two Measures of Self-Reported Health: Health Satisfaction and Health State, Chile and Guatemala*

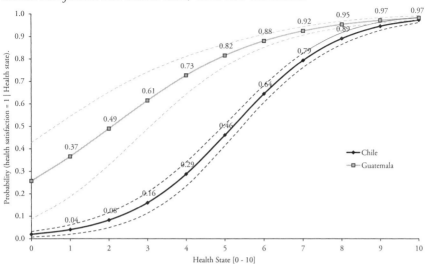

Source: Authors' calculations using Gallup World Poll 2007.
Note: Dotted lines are 95% confidence intervals.

states reported by the EQ-5D, using the algorithm of Shaw and others (2005) mentioned earlier. Although the correlation between the first two measures is relatively high (78 percent), the figure suggests that the way of answering the questions differs between countries. With the second measure, Chile no longer appears as the country with the worst health self-evaluation, and Guatemala and Costa Rica are overtaken by other countries of the region. The correlation between each of these two measures and the EQ-5D-based measure is lower (63 percent and 48 percent, respectively), again suggesting different ways of responding or, more exactly, different forms of correspondence between each of the three ways of evaluating individual health by the populations of the countries.

One possible way of showing these differences is to compare the tolerance of the populations of two countries to their health conditions, considering individual self-evaluation of health state on a scale 0–10. It is expected that the higher the individual evaluation on this scale, the higher the probability that individuals will say they are satisfied with their health. If individuals are very tolerant of their health problems, that probability will be high from low levels of the scale, and vice versa. Consider figure 6-3, which compares Guatemala and Chile. The figure shows the estimated probabilities with a probit regression (for the individuals of each country) of the health satisfaction variable (which only takes values from 0 or 1 for each individual), where the explanatory variable is health state (which takes 8 discrete values from 0–10). In Guatemala tolerance of health problems is

Figure 6-4. *National Measures of Health Intolerance and Dispersion Based on Health Satisfaction and Health State*

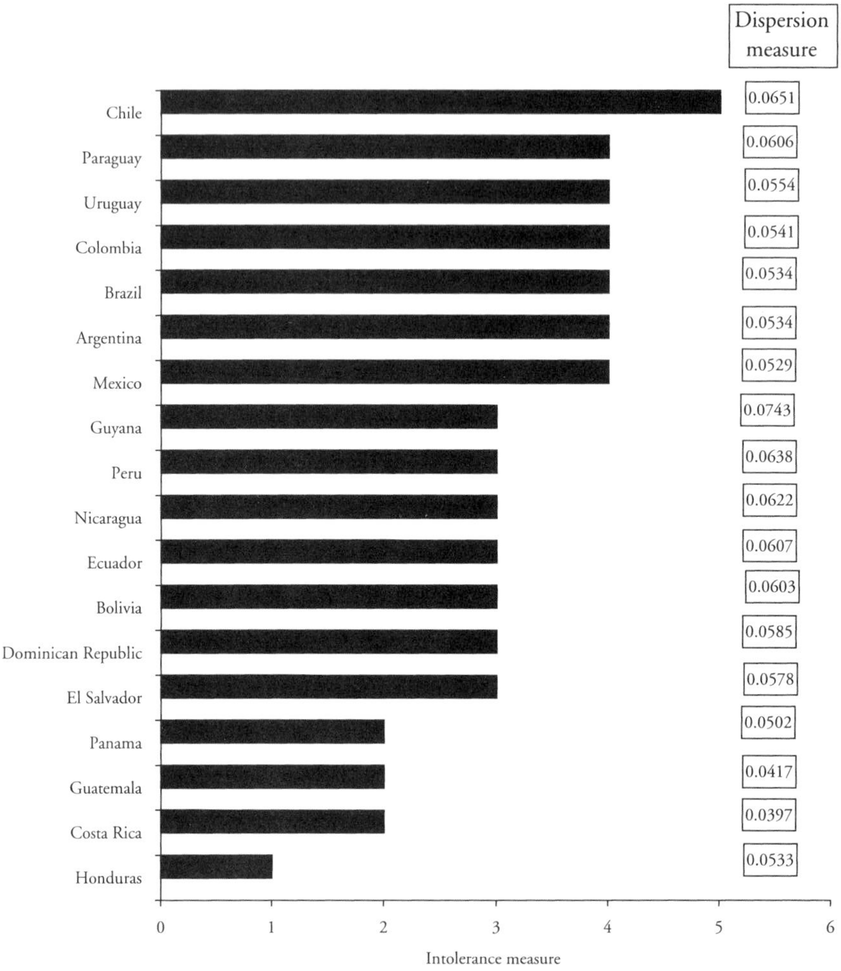

Source: Authors' calculations using Gallup World Poll 2007.

higher than in Chile, so the probabilities of being satisfied with health are sub-stantially higher from low levels of the 0–10 scale.

In order to compare levels of tolerance among all countries with a simple measure, the steepest part of the curve can be taken as "critical tolerance level" because this is the point where an increase (or decrease) of a level on the 0–10 scale has the highest impact on the probability of being satisfied (or dissatisfied) with health. As figure 6-4 shows, Chile appears as the country with the highest intoler-ance followed closely by the other countries of the extreme south of the continent (Argentina, Brazil, Paraguay, and Uruguay). At the other extreme, the most tolerant countries are all Central America (Costa Rica, Guatemala, Honduras, and Panama). These results suggest a regional pattern that could reflect cultural factors and the influence of geographical conditions on health.[9]

These results suggest that cultural response patterns have a strong influence on perceptions of health satisfaction, which limits possibilities of comparison between countries. They also suggest that within the countries, individual perceptions are more comparable in some countries than in others. Since comparability between countries is limited, a cross-section analysis of countries cannot be expected to identify the factors that influence perceptions of health, as discussed below.

Variables Related to Health Satisfaction at the Aggregate Level

A country's income level has a relatively weak and complicated effect on health satisfaction. As might be expected, people in countries with higher income per capita tend to report greater health satisfaction, but the association is rather tenuous, as figure 6-1a above suggests, and the regressions in table 6-1 confirms. Although there is a positive and significant relation between health satisfaction and per capita income, the coefficient is small: doubling average income per capita only increases the percentage of population satisfied with their health by between one to four points. Furthermore, the correlation is weakened when regional dummies are included, and is not robust to the inclusion of some other variables. Surprisingly, health satisfaction is related in a stronger and more robust way with economic growth, and there is an inverse relationship: satisfaction is lower in countries experiencing faster economic growth, as found also by Deaton (2008).[10]

A similar finding has been documented with longitudinal data in the United States, where mortality causes for 8 out of 10 causes studied rise during periods of economic growth compared to periods of recession. Risk factors like tobacco consumption, weight gain, physical inactivity, and unhealthy eating also increase during economic upturns (Ruhm, 2000). This pattern is but one dimension of the "unhappy growth paradox" discussed in chapter 3. As with life satisfaction and several other satisfaction domains, health satisfaction is positively related to income levels and negatively related to income growth. More income allows people to consume goods and services that improve their health, but it can have adverse effects on some aspects of health, and may even raise expectations more rapidly than objective health conditions can improve.[11]

9. This analysis can be adapted to consider the relation between health satisfaction and health state valued by the EQ-5D indicator. In that analysis the most intolerant populations are in Chile, Ecuador, Panama, and Paraguay; the most tolerant are in Costa Rica, Honduras, and Mexico.

10. In our case average growth 2000–05; Deaton (2008) uses the 2000–03 and 1990–2000 periods, but the latter is not significant.

11. Testing these hypotheses is beyond the scope of this work. However, one way of analyzing this is to include in the individual regressions, to be discussed later, a variable that interacts health problems (the question on incapacity of the EQ-5D) with recent economic growth.

Table 6-1. *National Average Health Satisfaction and National Variables*

Dependent variable	National average health satisfaction [0,1]							
	(1)	(2)	(3)	(4)	(5)	(6)	(7)	(8)
Natural logarithm GDP per capita US$ PPP, 2005	0.0191*	0.0157	0.0169*	0.0151	0.0235	0.0138	0.0413***	0.0226
	(2.51)	(1.60)	(2.58)	(1.57)	(1.95)	(1.05)	(3.60)	(1.72)
GDP per capita real average growth rate, 2000–05			−0.0174***	−0.0067*	−0.0180***	−0.0066*	−0.0100***	−0.0043
			(6.58)	(2.24)	(6.89)	(2.12)	(3.75)	(1.44)
Life expectancy at birth, years, 2005					0.0033*	0.0035	0.0018	0.0017
					(2.11)	(1.88)	(1.23)	(0.96)
Infant mortality rate, deaths over 1,000 live births, 2005					0.0012*	0.0004	0.0005	−0.0002
					(2.31)	(0.82)	(1.06)	(0.36)
Absolute distance from the equator line							−0.2282***	−0.1785*
							(4.78)	(2.26)
Share of Christian and Muslim population							0.0009***	0.0010***
							(3.75)	(3.51)
Constant	0.6254***	0.6981***	0.6978***	0.7125***	0.3729*	0.4452*	0.4253	0.6125***
	(9.43)	(6.80)	(12.03)	(7.05)	(2.55)	(2.47)	(3.02)	(3.55)
Number of observations	121	121	121	121	117	117	116	116
R-squared adjusted	0.04	0.43	0.29	0.45	0.33	0.47	0.49	0.54
Regional dummies included	NO	YES	NO	YES	NO	YES	NO	YES

Source: Authors' calculations based on the Gallup World Poll 2006 and 2007.

Notes: *Coefficient is statistically significant at the 10 percent level; **at the 5 percent level; ***at the 1 percent level; no asterisk means the coefficient is not different from zero with statistical significance.

Ordinary Least Square (OLS) models; absolute *t*-values in parentheses; data for 20 Latin American and Caribbean countries.

The regressions in table 6-1 explore the influence of other factors that may affect health satisfaction.[12] Although there is a positive and significant association with life expectancy, as might be expected, the association with infant mortality is also positive and significant, which is contrary to expected. However, these associations lose significance after including regional dummies, again suggesting that cultural or geographical factors could be influencing the result. This is further suggested by the fact that health satisfaction is strongly associated to other variables that may reflect cultural patterns, such as the distance from the center of the country to the equator and the population of each country that says it is Christian (Catholic or Protestant) or Muslim.

Health Perceptions by Gender and Age

Gender and age have a strong influence on health satisfaction and on the frequency of health problems. Based on individual data for the 20 LAC countries from the Gallup Poll 2007 round, figure 6-5 depicts the probability of men and women to declare themselves satisfied with their health throughout their life cycle. More than 90 percent of young men and women are satisfied with their health until their late twenties. Women experience faster reduction of their health satisfaction until approximately age 50–55, and a slower reduction from that age. Until age 75–80 men and women experience similar probabilities of health satisfaction; later, however, while health satisfaction changes little among women reaching a minimum around age 80–85, it falls rapidly among men. The coefficients on which these curves are based show very little change when differences across countries are controlled.

Since men and women have different life cycle patterns of health satisfaction, it is also interesting to ask if they have different standards of tolerance to health. To answer this, we use the same methodology that was applied to the comparison between countries in the previous section. The results do not support the thesis that there are significant differences of tolerance between the genders.[13] This suggests

12. These results must be interpreted with caution due to the potentially endogenous relationship between income and health satisfaction. In particular, causality between health satisfaction and income could run in both directions: people who are more satisfied with their health most likely believe that they will live longer and thus will tend to invest more in human capital and hence have higher incomes. As well, people with higher incomes can invest more in their own health and could therefore be more satisfied with their health. Additionally, people with higher income could have elevated health expectations, which would affect their satisfaction (similar to the aspirations treadmill mentioned in chapter 3 regarding income and life satisfaction). Thus, a causal relationship between income and health satisfaction cannot be established.

13. The curves are very similar and have the same critical tolerance levels (as well as similar heterogeneity measures). While this conclusion is based on analysis of the correlation between health satisfaction on the dichotomous scale with health state on the 0–10 scale, it also holds when the evaluation is based on EQ-5D index. See Graham, Higuera, and Lora (2009).

Figure 6-5. *Relation between Health Satisfaction, Age, and Gender*

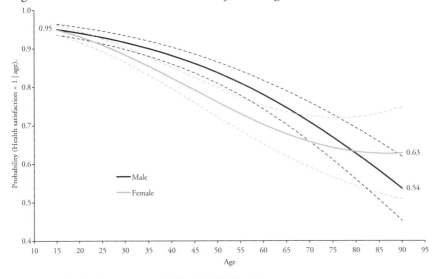

Source: Authors' calculations using Gallup World Poll 2007.

that, unlike what happens between countries, it is admissible to compare health satisfaction by gender.

As noted, gender and age influence satisfaction with health, as well as the frequency of health limitations and problems. Table 6-2a shows the frequency by age group of health conditions reported by EQ-5D. As mentioned, 25 percent of Latin Americans when polled said they suffered pain, 18.5 percent had anxiety, 10 percent mentioned mobility problems, 9.5 percent said they had physical limitations in their daily activities, and 3.8 percent mentioned problems with looking after themselves. The frequency of almost all these conditions is higher in the older age groups, but the increases are far more pronounced at moderate levels of the problems. The only condition where frequency falls with increasing age is moderate anxiety, which is lower in the over-75 age group than in the preceding age group (55–75).[14]

Tables 6-2b and 6-2c show the frequencies by age group for men and women. In general, frequencies are higher for women, with pronounced differences (of at least four percentage points) for moderate mobility problems in the two oldest age groups, daily activities in these two groups, moderate pain and moderate anxiety in all age groups and extreme pain in the oldest age group. Consequently, women suffer more health limitations, especially from age 55.

---

14. Information by country and further econometric results summarized below are in Graham, Higuera, and Lora (2009).

Table 6-2a. *Moderate and Extreme Health Conditions, Men and Women: EQ-5D Components*
Percentage of people

Men and women	Between 15 and 35 years	Between 36 and 55 years	Between 55 and 75 years	More than 75 years	Total
Mobility moderate	3.6	8.5	24.6	37.4	9.6
Mobility extreme	0.2	0.2	0.8	1.3	0.4
Self-care moderate	1.5	2.9	8.7	15.1	3.5
Self-care extreme	0.1	0.2	0.4	1.7	0.3
Usual acts moderate	3.5	8.7	22.0	31.6	9.0
Usual acts extreme	0.3	0.3	1.0	4.1	0.5
Pain moderate	13.6	24.6	39.7	44.2	22.2
Pain extreme	1.3	2.6	6.0	10.4	2.8
Anxiety moderate	12.8	17.2	22.6	19.9	16.0
Anxiety extreme	1.9	2.9	3.6	3.9	2.5

Source: Authors' calculations based on the Gallup World Poll 2006–07.
Note: EQ-5D = European Quality of Life-5 Dimensions.

When these patterns are analyzed more systematically using econometric techniques, it is confirmed that all problems of moderate intensity are significantly less frequent among men, along with problems of extremely intense pain and anxiety. In addition, all problems of moderate intensity and extremely intense pain and anxiety tend to increase significantly with age (although in some cases not linearly). Over the years the differences in frequency between men and women

Table 6-2b. *Moderate and Extreme Health Conditions, Men: EQ-5D Components*
Percentage of people

Men	Between 15 and 35 years	Between 36 and 55 years	Between 55 and 75 years	More than 75 years	Total
Mobility moderate	3.6	8.0	20.4	33.1	8.6
Mobility extreme	0.2	0.2	0.8	0.7	0.3
Self-care moderate	1.6	3.0	6.8	13.7	3.2
Self-care extreme	0.2	0.3	0.4	2.1	0.4
Usual acts moderate	3.3	7.4	19.5	25.2	7.9
Usual acts extreme	0.5	0.4	0.5	4.5	0.6
Pain moderate	11.0	18.2	36.7	42.0	18.3
Pain extreme	1.1	1.9	4.0	5.6	1.9
Anxiety moderate	10.4	12.9	19.7	16.8	12.8
Anxiety extreme	1.6	2.1	2.5	3.2	1.9

Source: Authors' calculations based on the Gallup World Poll 2006–07.
Note: EQ-5D = European Quality of Life-5 Dimensions.

Table 6-2c. *Moderate and Extreme Health Conditions, Women: EQ-5D Components*
Percentage of people

Women	Between 15 and 35 years	Between 36 and 55 years	Between 55 and 75 years	More than 75 years	Total
Mobility moderate	3.6	8.9	27.7	41.2	10.4
Mobility extreme	0.3	0.2	0.9	1.9	0.4
Self-care moderate	1.4	2.8	10.2	16.4	3.7
Self-care extreme	0.1	0.1	0.4	1.3	0.2
Usual acts moderate	3.6	9.7	23.9	37.4	9.9
Usual acts extreme	0.1	0.3	1.3	3.8	0.5
Pain moderate	15.7	29.4	42.0	46.2	25.3
Pain extreme	1.5	3.1	7.5	14.8	3.4
Anxiety moderate	14.8	20.5	24.9	22.6	18.5
Anxiety extreme	2.1	3.5	4.4	4.6	3.0

Source: Authors' calculations based on the Gallup World Poll 2006 and 2007.
Note: EQ-5D = European Quality of Life-5 Dimensions.

increase in moderate pain, extreme problems performing daily activities, and extremely intense anxiety.

Health Perceptions by Income Groups

As discussed above, differences in average income per capita between countries have a significant—although modest—effect on health satisfaction (doubling average income per capita only increases the percentage of population satisfied with its health by one to four points). The differences in income between individuals also seem to have a very modest effect. Table 6-3 presents the percentages of individuals satisfied with their health by per capita household income quintiles in the LAC countries polled by Gallup in 2007. On average for the 20 countries, the health satisfaction gap between the richest and the poorest quintiles within each country is only 7.4 percentage points. These gaps are not uniform from one country to another. In eight countries they exceed 10 percentage points and average 13.3 points. In the other 12 countries the average is only 2.4 points.

Several studies have reported narrow health satisfaction gaps between the rich and the poor, although this is the first that utilizes a uniform source of information for a large number of countries. As mentioned, Suárez-Berenguela (2001) analyzed inequalities in subjective health perceptions in Brazil, Jamaica, and Mexico and found that they were very modest in comparison with the inequalities in income and mortality by income group. Dachs and others (2002) reached the same conclusion when studying responses in polls that asked about health

Table 6-3. *Self-Reported Health Satisfaction by Income Quintiles*
Percentage

	Quintile 1	Quintile 2	Quintile 3	Quintile 4	Quintile 5	Average by country
Costa Rica	90.6	90.2	91.5	98.4	98.0	93.6
Guatemala	92.3	95.2	91.7	95.9	95.1	93.0
Venezuela	87.7	91.9	98.1	91.3	96.3	92.6
Panama	88.4	90.5	89.0	93.5	91.8	89.5
Honduras	91.7	91.0	86.3	90.8	87.4	88.3
Guyana	90.2	78.9	86.4	90.5	84.8	87.3
Mexico	86.3	82.9	85.3	86.5	89.1	86.7
Belize	94.4	95.0	95.0	72.2	92.9	86.4
Argentina	85.1	83.8	82.7	82.8	92.5	86.0
Uruguay	82.0	79.3	85.8	84.6	84.4	84.8
Brazil	81.5	86.6	89.2	81.1	84.7	84.7
Colombia	77.0	82.4	81.2	89.9	89.6	84.2
El Salvador	79.9	83.3	84.4	84.8	92.9	84.1
Dominican Republic	84.8	78.5	82.5	84.3	89.4	83.3
Bolivia	75.6	84.5	87.2	84.9	88.3	82.6
Paraguay	74.4	77.6	80.2	86.7	84.6	80.7
Nicaragua	72.8	77.5	85.1	78.3	86.4	80.5
Ecuador	72.8	82.6	77.3	84.6	82.9	80.0
Peru	71.3	72.2	79.0	83.2	84.0	79.0
Chile	57.8	58.8	65.2	71.6	79.0	68.4
Average by quintile	80.8	82.2	84.0	85.5	88.2	. . .

Notes: Data grouped by country and income quintile.
Source: Authors' calculations based on the Gallup World Poll 2006–07.

problems in 12 LAC countries. According to these authors, the modest inequalities among socioeconomic groups in self-reported health problems could result from cultural and social differences in health perception. Among lower income groups certain deficiencies or common ailments may not be considered health problems.

The EQ-5D question allows us to calculate gradients for health conditions, and to see how they translate into health self-evaluation at the different levels. Table 6-4 presents frequencies of conditions for all LAC countries by per capita household income quintiles (calculated country by country and then averaged for the 20 countries). In general the responses reveal "normal" gradients, with more serious problems expressed in the lowest levels. Some extreme positions do not have a well-defined gradient, which could be due to their low frequency.

Table 6-4. *Moderate and Extreme Health Conditions by Income Quintiles*
Percentage of people

Income quintile	1	2	3	4	5	Total
Mobility moderate	13.0	11.1	9.4	8.0	6.9	9.7
Mobility extreme	0.3	0.4	0.3	0.3	0.7	0.4
Self care moderate	4.7	3.4	3.9	2.1	2.4	3.3
Self care extreme	0.1	0.2	0.3	0.2	0.5	0.2
Usual acts moderate	12.8	10.6	8.7	7.4	5.9	9.1
Usual acts extreme	0.6	0.6	0.5	0.3	0.5	0.5
Pain moderate	26.9	25.6	23.2	21.0	18.2	23.1
Pain extreme	4.6	3.1	2.6	2.8	1.4	2.9
Anxiety moderate	18.8	18.7	16.7	15.2	14.4	16.8
Anxiety extreme	3.5	2.8	2.4	1.9	2.2	2.6

Source: Authors' calculations based on the Gallup World Poll 2007.
Notes: EQ-5D (European Quality of Life-5 Dimensions) components used. Data for 20 Latin American and Caribbean countries.

A more careful econometric analysis confirms the existence of significant (negative) gradients for all moderate conditions and for extreme conditions of pain and anxiety. Some of the gradients are much steeper when calculated after controlling for individual characteristics (gender, age, age squared, and marital status), area of residence and country dummies. This implies that the poor, much more than the rich, suffer from and recognize having a range of deficiencies. Although a few gradients are positive, they are not significant, which would be the case if there were cultural differences that induce individuals at lower levels to ignore their health deficiencies (the only exception, marginally, is the extreme condition of inability to look after oneself where the positive coefficient has a 10 percent statistical significance).[15]

The fact that the socioeconomic gradients of the conditions reported in the EQ-5D are steeper than the health satisfaction gradients suggests that among lower social groups there is a greater tendency to tolerate certain health deficiencies. Although this topic is beyond the focus of this chapter, some preliminary tests indicate that the lowest social groups are more tolerant with moderate pain, while the upper groups are more tolerant with moderate problems of mobility and daily activities. These differences possibly reflect the greater demands of physical work in the low levels and increased access to treatment or help at high levels.

In summary, this analysis suggests that health evaluations are associated with individual socioeconomic levels. The poor declare themselves less satisfied with

15. See Graham, Higuera, and Lora (2009).

their health and suffer most of the conditions with more frequency. However, the rich and the poor seem to have different tolerance thresholds for some of the conditions.

Valuing Health Conditions

A major contribution of the original EQ-5D analysis was to shed light on how individuals value different health states (or, put another way, what the well-being costs of various ailments are). The original EQ-5D studies were conducted in the United Kingdom; they were later implemented in the United States. The U.K. study, led by Dolan (1997), covered 2,997 respondents in England, Scotland, and Wales in 1993.[16] The U.S. study, led by Shaw and others (2005), was conducted in 2002 and was based on a 12,000 respondent, nationally representative sample.[17] A dimension for which there is no problem was assigned a level 1 while a dimension with extreme problems was assigned a level 3. Each health state described by the instrument had a five digit descriptor, ranging from 11111 for perfect health to 33333 for the worst possible state. The resulting descriptive system defined 243 (3 to the power of 5, 3^5) health states.[18]

Health state *preferences,* based on a time trade-off method, were then developed for each context by the same authors. The preference rankings were based on interviews using the time trade-off method for a representative sub-sample of the respondents in each case. Econometric analysis was then used to determine the relative weights to assign to these preferences. In the time trade-off method, individuals were asked to describe their own health using the EQ-5D description system, and then to rate their health state on a 0 to 100 scale, with 0 being the worst imaginable health state and 100 being the best imaginable health state They are then asked to value 13 of the possible health states (rather than 243), using a props method: a set of health state cards and a two-sided time board, one for states considered better than death and one for states considered worse than death. The 13 were 12 EQ-5D states plus unconscious, based on the assumption that respondents could not realistically evaluate a higher number of states; the selection of states was based on the range of responses and interactions among them.[19]

---

16. See Dolan (1997).

17. The study initially over-sampled blacks and Hispanics, to ensure adequate representation of minorities. See Shaw and others (2005).

18. The designers of the EQ-5D emphasize that it is not without flaws. It emphasizes physical conditions over mental ones, for example. People typically imagine that mental health problems are less bad than they actually are, and that physical health problems are worse than they actually are. Despite these imperfections, the EQ-5D is one of the better objective measures that we have.

19. The authors thank Paul Dolan for explaining this selection process.

Respondents were asked time trade-off values for time spent in various states (for example, either losing or gaining time spent in full health; the smallest possible time that an individual could choose to spend in a health state was 0.25 years, and the total time period was 10 years, with 5 years being the middle value offered for full health). Values for worse than death states were transformed and bounded by 0 and −1, with the lowest possible health state being −39, which occurred when 0.25 years in a given state followed by 9.75 years in full health was considered equal to death.[20]

Regression results based on the U.K. responses demonstrated that *any* move away from full health was associated with a substantial loss of utility. The largest decrement for a move from level 1 to level 2 (from no problems to some problems in the particular category) was associated with pain or discomfort, an effect that was four times greater than that for a corresponding move on the usual activities dimension. Pain or discomfort continued to dominate the weighting for level 3, although mobility level 3 (confined to bed) was given a somewhat similar weight. For the mobility, pain or discomfort, and anxiety or depression dimensions, the move from level 2 to level 3 caused a much greater loss in utility than did the move from level 1 to level 2.[21] Thus extreme conditions, as well as pain in general, seemed to have the strongest (negative) effects on well-being.

We conducted an additional analysis of the EQ-5D variable for our sample of Latin American and Caribbean respondents in the Gallup Poll, where we compared the valuations based on the traditional time trade-off valuations with the coefficients on life and health satisfaction, both on the EQ-5D index in general and on its specific components.

We took advantage of having a unique data set combining subjective evaluations of life and health satisfaction on the one hand, and health conditions as measured by the EQ-5D on the other, to study discrepancies between the two measures, and how or if these discrepancies were mediated by socio-demographic factors, such as age, gender, and income, by reference groups, and by cultural and other norms. We also explored the variance across the particular conditions. We then compared our results to those for the United States and the United Kingdom based on the EQ-5D and time trade-off methods.

The EQ-5D is an extremely strong predictor of health satisfaction, as well as a good although less strong predictor of life satisfaction.[22] However, as table 6-5 indicates, aside from the EQ-5D, health satisfaction is strongly associated to

---

20. Shaw and others (2005).

21. For a more detailed discussion of both methodology and results, see Dolan (1997).

22. To some extent, though, the causality between life satisfaction and health satisfaction might run in both directions. Additionally, omitted variables, such as personality traits (which we control for later on), might influence both health satisfaction and life satisfaction—for example, optimistic people are more likely to answer positively to both measures of satisfaction.

Table 6-5. *Health and Life Satisfaction Determinants*

	Health satisfaction (0–10 Scale) (1)	Life satisfaction (0–10 Scale) (2)
1 if male	0.11**	−0.248***
	(2.91)	(5.76)
Age	−0.037***	−0.059***
	(4.71)	(6.07)
Age squared	0**	0.001***
	(2.35)	(4.85)
Logarithm monthly per capita household income, US$ PPP	0.171***	0.302***
	(5.63)	(10.76)
1 if urban	0.131**	0.011
	(2.21)	(0.18)
1 if married	0.043	0.073
	(0.70)	(1.23)
1 if divorced	0.106	−0.035
	(0.99)	(0.43)
1 if widow	0.188*	0.201*
	(1.96)	(1.79)
1 if has one child	0.053	−0.005
	(0.90)	(0.11)
1 if has more than one child	0.093	0.023
	(1.32)	(0.35)
1 if has friends	0.164**	0.444***
	(2.85)	(6.14)
1 if has running water	0.108	0.145
	(1.33)	(1.67)
1 if has electricity	0.128	0.179
	(1.54)	(1.02)
1 if has telephone	−0.026	0.218***
	(0.75)	(3.67)
Assets, PCA 1st component score	0.047***	0.206***
	(3.52)	(6.50)
Psychological traits score	0.112***	0.397***
	(5.46)	(17.73)
EQ-5D index	5.188***	1.436***
	(26.98)	(5.27)
Constant	2.619***	3.974***
	(13.03)	(12.02)
Observations	8,249	8,250
Adjusted R-squared	0.338	0.253
Countries	17	17
Country fixed effects	Yes	Yes

Source: Authors' calculations based on the Gallup World Poll 2006–07.

Notes: *Coefficient is statistically significant at the 10 percent level; **at the 5 percent level; ***at the 1 percent level; no asterisk means the coefficient is not different from zero with statistical significance. Absolute t-statistics in parentheses. EQ-5D index = European Quality of Life-5 Dimensions index. PCA = Principal Components Analysis.

several other socio-demographic variables, indicating not just that the EQ-5D is an incomplete description of health conditions, but also that health perceptions are affected by a host of other factors. The results confirm that health satisfaction is higher for men and falls with age at a declining rate. It also confirms that health satisfaction is higher among people with higher current incomes and more durable assets. The coefficient for current income implies that when the average individual's income doubles his or her probability of moving one step up on the 0–10 health scale increases by 17 percent.[23] Living in an urban area and having friends to rely upon are two other important factors that contribute to health satisfaction. And last, but not least, personality strongly influences health perceptions.[24] The list of factors associated with life satisfaction is very similar (but notice that men are *less* satisfied with their lives, in spite of their higher satisfaction with health).

The analysis of the individual EQ-5D components highlights the importance of any move away from full health, and the relative importance of some conditions. As table 6-6 shows, pain, anxiety and problems with usual activities, in their extreme or moderate levels, have very deleterious effects on health satisfaction and several of them also on life satisfaction. Moderate mobility problems have a somewhat lesser, but still significant effect on health, but not on life satisfaction.[25]

Values based on the overall EQ-5D index, as opposed to its individual components, were typically higher than those on the extreme conditions, perhaps because a small number of respondents report extreme conditions, lowering the coefficients on the individual components, while the composite index includes squared terms for these conditions, accentuating them. The values for life and health satisfaction were much closer for the aggregate index than they were for the components, meanwhile, while the individual components had much higher values for health satisfaction, suggesting that the composite index is better at capturing general effects, while the components attenuate the effects of particular conditions on health satisfaction in particular (tables 6-5 and 6-6).

We used the results of the life satisfaction regressions to calculate the income-equivalent value of each of the health conditions that may affect life satisfaction. Compared to a baseline per capita household income of $93.7 (PPP adjusted), the

23. Notice that this result is not directly comparable with that for the cross country data presented in a previous section, where health satisfaction was measured as a dichotomous variable. When health satisfaction is measured this way, doubling an individual's income increases by 0.9 percent his probability of declaring himself satisfied with his health (compared with 2–4 percent in the cross country data).

24. In order to capture the influence of personality traits on health perceptions we use a simple indicator that reflects the tendency (not explained by objective variables) of the individual to respond in a positive way to the set of subjective questions included in the survey.

25. The regressions in table 6-6 include the same set of additional controls as table 6-5.

Table 6-6. *Effect of EQ-5D Components and Income over Health and Life Satisfaction*

	Health satisfaction 0–10 (1)	Life satisfaction 0–10 (2)
Log, monthly per capita household income, US$ PPP	0.155*** (5.25)	0.302*** (10.67)
Mobility moderate	−0.46*** (6.50)	0.086 (1.03)
Mobility extreme	−0.032 (0.06)	0.091 (0.16)
Self care moderate	−0.142 (0.80)	0.157 (1.25)
Self care extreme	−0.236 (0.51)	0.281 (0.67)
Usual activities moderate	−0.69*** (5.60)	−0.23* (1.92)
Usual activities extreme	−1.136** (1.97)	−0.498 (0.89)
Pain moderate	−1.016*** (15.26)	−0.135 (1.44)
Pain extreme	−2.143*** (12.52)	−0.477** (2.44)
Anxiety moderate	−0.48*** (10.08)	−0.303*** (3.11)
Anxiety extreme	−0.883*** (5.01)	−0.786*** (3.69)
Observations	8,249	8,250
Adjusted R-squared	0.363	0.254
Countries	17	17
Country fixed effects	Yes	Yes

Source: Authors' calculations based on the Gallup World Poll 2006 and 2007.

Notes: *Coefficient is statistically significant at the 10 percent level; **at the 5 percent level; ***at the 1 percent level; no asterisk means the coefficient is not different from zero with statistical significance.

Absolute t-statistics in parentheses. EQ-5D index = European Quality of Life-5 Dimensions index.

Each regression controls for age, age squared, gender, marital status, urban zone, number of children, friendship, access to water, electricity and landline phone, assets, and a psychological traits score.

average respondent in Latin America would need to be compensated 2.1 times the average monthly income for moderate problems with the usual acts, and 2.7 times for moderate anxiety. Extreme pain was more "expensive" in life satisfaction terms: almost 5 times average income, while extreme anxiety was the most "expensive": 13.5 times (figure 6-6).

Both our findings and those based on time trade-off methods highlight the importance of pain and anxiety over those of mobility and self care, albeit with

Figure 6-6. *Income Equivalences of Health Conditions in EQ-5D*
In monthly incomes; comparison income: US$ 93.7 PPP

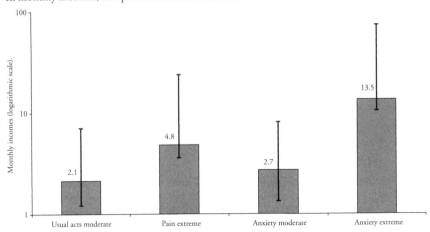

Source: Authors' calculations using Gallup World Poll 2007.

Note: Direct equivalences are based on the effect of each health component on life satisfaction. The EQ-5D equivalences are based on the effect of changes in the EQ-5D index, derived from changes in each health component. Vertical bars represent a 95% confidence interval.

different weights. People's priors tend to be that physical conditions will be worse than they actually are, and that mental conditions are less serious than they actually are. Thus when they actually experience them, they are mediated by these expectations, and the effects of the former are weaker than expected and those of the latter are stronger.

The less framed health and life satisfaction questions (as opposed to the time trade-off methods, TTO) may be more effective at picking up the psychological effects of these conditions than are questions that are more framed by the particulars of the conditions, as are the TTO questions. At the same time, those same psychological conditions can influence life and health satisfaction responses, biasing them toward more negative assessments. While TTO methods could be influenced by similar biases, it is hard to tell in what direction. While less happy (more anxious) people answer both life and health satisfaction questions more negatively, it is not clear that less happy, more anxious people value healthy life years versus ill life years differently than happier ones do.

While most people's priors are to value physical conditions more negatively, our findings highlight the importance of mental illness and of conditions that create uncertainty (pain, anxiety, and difficulties with usual activities).

We also feel that the method of combining different kinds of assessments, while far from perfect, contributes to our understanding of the welfare effects of health. In addition to the usual effects of income levels on both life and health satisfaction, we found some modest differences in age, gender, and income cohorts. The elderly, for example, seem to cope better than average with mobility/self care problems, but worse than average with anxiety.

Our methodological contributions can also inform health policy. Individuals seem to be better at adapting to health shocks that lead to a one-time change— such as a loss in mobility—than they are to conditions that are associated with constant uncertainty, such as pain and anxiety. The appropriate balance of investments in physical versus mental health is a question that must be resolved taking into account culture and society traits. Yet our findings suggest that a better understanding of the causes of anxiety, and how anxiety varies across cohorts, countries, and cultures, might go a long way toward improving health and well-being in general. The strong negative effects of uncertainty in conditions rather than one-time shocks might also affect how we think about and/or calculate policy-relevant measures such as quality adjusted life years (QALYs).

Our findings also highlight the role of comparison effects on health evaluations. The effect of a reference group mean EQ-5D score, where reference groups are defined by gender, age, area of residence, and education level, was positive (though weakly significant) on health satisfaction (controlling for own and reference group income). (See table 6-7.) This is an important contrast with the usual reference group effects of income on other life dimensions: as discussed in chapter 3, comparison effects of income in the material domains of life tend to be negative (due to greed and envy?). In contrast, it is possible that comparisons in the health arena provide more positive signals.

This suggests that most people do not react to changes in their health conditions the same way that they do to changes in income. While rapid income growth, for example, is often associated with unhappiness and lower satisfaction with many life aspects among some cohorts, better health seems more likely to produce positive signals. For example, it is more enjoyable to be surrounded by healthy people, while being surrounded by people with ill health often risks contagion, among other negative externalities. Meanwhile, a number of health improvements are related to technological innovations rather than to income gains. This suggests an important role for norms of health in explaining cross country differences in health policies and outcomes.

In sum, our work based on the EQ-5D and life and health satisfaction indices suggests that standard valuations of health conditions may overestimate the effects of physical conditions, and under-estimate those of conditions that are associated with uncertainty and unpredictability, as well as mental illnesses such as extreme anxiety. The findings suggest that individuals are better able to adapt to a one-time health shock than they are to less extreme but constantly changing conditions. In addition, our research suggests that there are reference group effects in the health arena—being surrounded by neighbors with better health seems to have positive effects on life and health satisfaction. This suggests that broader

Table 6-7. *Reference Groups Results*

	Health satisfaction (0–10 scale)			
	(1)	*(2)*	*(3)*	*(4)*
1 if has friends			0.158**	0.156**
Logarithm, monthly per capita household income, US$ PPP	0.169***	0.147***	0.164***	0.143***
EQ-5D index	5.277***	5.335***	5.259***	5.317***
Education reference group				
Mean EQ-5D	0.630*	0.654*	0.59	0.198
Mean income		0.175***		0.166***
Observations	7,725	7,572	7,684	7,532
Reference groups	992	1,600	992	1,600
Countries	17	17	17	17

	Life satisfaction (0–10 scale)			
	(5)	*(6)*	*(7)*	*(8)*
1 if has friends			0.447***	0.438***
Log, monthly per capita household income, US$ PPP	0.308***	0.288***	0.297***	0.280***
EQ-5D index	1.575***	1.556***	1.488***	1.469***
Education reference group				
Mean EQ-5D	0.309	0.37	0.323	−0.207
Mean income		0.179***		0.158**
Observations	7,725	7,572	7,684	7,532
Reference groups	993	1,601	993	1,601
Countries	17	17	17	17

Source: Authors' calculations based on the Gallup World Poll 2006 and 2007.

Notes: *Coefficient is statistically significant at the 10 percent level; **at the 5 percent level; ***at the 1 percent level; no asterisk means the coefficient is not different from zero with statistical significance. Each regression controls for age, age squared, gender, marital status, urban zone, number of children, friendship, access to water, electricity and landline phone, assets, and a psychological traits score.

investments in public health could have unpredicted and not easily observable positive externalities.

Happiness and Health More Generally

Our empirical findings need to be considered in the context of the broader relationship between happiness and health. As noted in several places in the book, health is one of the most important correlates of well-being. Of all the variables in the standard happiness equations for Latin America,[26] health status—as gauged

26. For an explanation of the standard happiness equations for Latin America, see chapter 4 of this book titled "Satisfaction beyond Income."

by an index of a number of questions on self-reported health—has the strongest coefficient. This is consistent with studies in other countries and regions. Higher levels of happiness are also associated with better health outcomes.[27] For example, a recent study in the OECD countries finds that hypertension prevalence and average country-level happiness rankings are negatively correlated (a finding that is not driven by doctor availability).[28]

There is also evidence of adaptation as income levels go up. Analogous to the Easterlin paradox, where country-level income matters to happiness more at lower levels of income than at higher ones, the Preston curve shows that income matters much more to health and longevity at lower levels of income than at higher ones (see figure 6-7). Income gains in poor countries are associated with rapid improvements in basic health and in defeating preventable diseases and lowering infant mortality rates. The availability of clean water and electricity can make a huge difference in the diarrheal diseases that claim so many infant deaths in poor countries.[29] At higher levels of per capita income, technology and scientific innovation play more of a role than income in generating cures for the types of diseases that are more typical of developed economies, such as cancer. Gains in longevity at higher levels of life expectancy, meanwhile, are much harder to achieve. At the same time, due to technological advances, poor countries are able to enjoy much higher levels of life expectancy at lower income levels than they could in the past.[30]

The health and happiness relationship may well reflect these trends, if not exactly mirroring the Easterlin paradox. People no doubt adapt to better health conditions, and in turn expect them. As noted earlier, satisfaction with health (which is highly correlated with happiness) and income per capita are surprisingly very weakly correlated across countries worldwide or within Latin America. For happiness and health, meanwhile, once a certain level of health standards and longevity are achieved, there is no consistent cross country relationship. What that threshold level is remains an open question (as it does for income in the Easterlin paradox). Within countries, however, healthier people are happier—similar to difference in the across and within country relation between income and happiness.

A recent study, based on a sub-sample of wealthy European countries, finds that happiness and longevity are *negatively* correlated.[31] Health expenditures and happiness are also negatively correlated for this sample. All of the countries in the sample have widely available care. At these socioeconomic levels, where people have come to expect good health, factors other than longevity may mediate

27. Dolan (2006). For the effects of happiness on income and health in Russia, see Graham, Eggers, and Sukhtankar (2004).

28. Blanchflower and Oswald (2004).

29. Adrianzen and Graham (1974).

30. Deaton (2008); Preston (1975).

31. See Blanchflower and Oswald (2004).

Figure 6-7. *Life Expectancy and GDP, by Country Size*

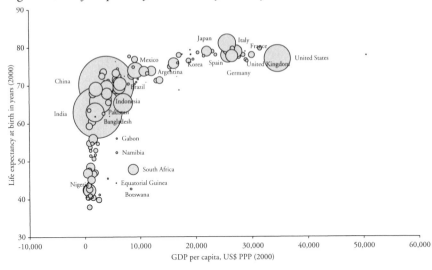

Source: Authors' calculations using Gallup World Poll 2006 and 2007, and World Bank (2007).

the happiness and health relationship, such as norms about health standards. In addition, longevity is only one measure of health, and slightly shorter but healthier life years may matter more to happiness than extending already long life expectancies. Similar to income, after a certain point more health may not buy more happiness, and other factors related to quality of life matter more. Meanwhile, it is also possible that, given an overall high standard and widely available health care, less healthy (and less happy) people demand more health expenditures. At the bottom end of the income scale, meanwhile, some countries with extremely poor health standards, such as Nigeria, Pakistan, Honduras, and Guatemala, have relatively high average happiness scores. Yet *within* each set of these same countries, healthier people are happier, again echoing the Easterlin paradox.

The positive relationship between happiness and health tends to be stronger for psychological health than it is for physical health.[32] While serious psychological illness or disability have significant and negative effects on happiness, individuals with these conditions often adapt their expectations for health status downward over time and return—at least partly—to their initial happiness levels. Their reference norms often change to others with the same disease or disability rather than to other healthy individuals. Individuals suffering from depression, in contrast, are much less likely to experience this kind of adaptation.[33]

32. Dolan (2006).
33. Dolan (2006).

We have limited understanding of the health-happiness relationship among the very poor, meanwhile. The results on health satisfaction reported above highlight the higher tolerance for illness among the poor. One possibility is that health shocks have less of a negative effect on their reported happiness because their expectations for good health are lower. Alternatively, health problems—either for individuals or for members of their household—increase the income insecurity of the poor, who rarely have insurance or access to good medical care. Insecurity is associated with lower happiness levels.[34] Banerjee and Duflo (2007) and Deaton (2008), based on surveys from India, find that the poor report to being under a great deal of financial and psychological stress. Case and Deaton (2005) have similar findings for South Africa, India, and the United States. The most frequently cited reason for stress is health problems (29 percent of respondents). At the same time, their reported happiness is not particularly low. The authors, like others, find that the poor do not in general complain about their health or about life in general.[35]

An obvious challenge for this line of research is understanding if poor health is not fully reflected in the poor's responses to happiness surveys because they have low expectations or are unaware that better standards are possible, or whether the health-happiness relationship is truly different (for example, has a different slope) when health standards are materially lower. We do not have sufficient data at present to explore how or if the health and happiness relationship differs among the poor, and if the difference is driven by levels (for example, differences in basic health levels and expectations about them) or by the slope (for example, do improvements in basic health generate more results in terms of happiness at higher levels of income than at lower ones?).

Conclusions and Policy Implications

This is the first study of health perceptions across Latin America and the Caribbean with identical polls of representative samples of the populations. The national averages of health satisfaction of LAC countries do not differ significantly from the averages in other regions of the world, where the differences in satisfaction across countries have a robust association with variables that reflect cultural differences (such as religion or the geographical location of the country), rather than with aggregate economic variables or with traditional health indicators. Satisfaction with health *tends* to be higher in countries with higher income levels and lower in countries with higher economic growth, but these statistical associations are not very robust. Neither life expectancy nor infant mortality has a significant association with health satisfaction.

---

34. Bannerjee and Duflo (2007).
35. Bannerjee and Duflo (2007) and Case and Deaton (2005).

The influence of cultural factors is evident in the case of Latin America. In some countries, such as Guatemala, where the population is very tolerant of health problems, individuals who rate their health relatively low on a 0 to 10 scale are much more likely to say they are satisfied with their individual health than individuals in countries such as Chile, where the population is much less tolerant of health problems (and at the same time objective health indicators are much better). Demographic factors also play a role. Health satisfaction declines with age, but more continuously in men than in women. Women experience a more rapid reduction of their health satisfaction until approximately age 50–55, and a slower reduction from then on.

Not surprisingly, health satisfaction is associated with the health conditions reported in EQ-5D. The conditions that most affect the evaluation that persons make of their own health (on 0–10 scale) are extreme pain, moderate pain, extreme anxiety and extreme limitations on performing daily activities. These are followed in importance by moderate limitations on performing daily activities, moderate anxiety problems and moderate mobility problems. Other conditions do not have a statistically significant effect (possibly because of their lower frequency).

Health evaluations are also associated with individual socioeconomic levels, although the channels by which this takes place are not clear. The poorest levels (by income quintile) suffer most of the conditions and, especially pain and anxiety, with more frequency. Even after isolating the influence of individual socio-demographic characteristics, and even personality traits, socioeconomic level (measured either by income quintile or by individual income) directly influences health self-evaluation, likely through a number of unobservable channels that we were unable to identify precisely.

The findings do suggest that tolerance for certain health conditions—particularly pain and anxiety—is lower among lower income groups, and thus that there is more of a relationship between health tolerance and income within countries than across countries. The latter shows little, if any, correlation with per capita incomes. This is a puzzle that is analogous to the happiness and income relationship, and one that merits further study and will likely be the subject of some debate.

Our closer analysis of the relation between the EQ-5D reported conditions and life and health satisfaction rankings aimed to further our understanding of the variance in health valuation across specific conditions and cohorts. Our findings highlight the importance of mental illness and of conditions that create uncertainty (pain, anxiety, and difficulties with usual activities), while standard priors are to value physical conditions more negatively. We also found some modest differences across age, gender, and income cohorts.[36]

---

36. The regression results and more detail on these interactions are in Graham, Higuera, and Lora (2009).

EQ-5D score was positive and significant on health satisfaction (controlling for own and reference group income). This is an important contrast with the usual effects of reference group income on other life dimensions, which tend to be negative (due to greed and envy?). It is possible that comparisons in the health arena provide more positive signals. While rapid income growth, for example, is often associated with unhappiness and lower satisfaction with several life dimensions among some cohorts, better health seems more likely to produce positive signals, as being surrounded by healthier people likely has positive externalities.

The more general relationship between health and happiness yields some insights. The positive relationship between happiness and health tends to be stronger for psychological health than it is for physical health.[37] While serious illness or disability have significant and negative effects on happiness, individuals with these conditions often adapt their expectations for health status downward over time and return, at least partly, to their initial happiness levels. Their reference norms change to others with the same disease or disability rather than to other healthy individuals. Individuals suffering from depression, in contrast, are much less likely to experience this kind of adaptation.[38]

Better understanding the effects that aspirations and awareness have on responses to surveys remains a challenge, meanwhile. We do not have sufficient data to explore how or if the health and happiness relationship differs among the poor, and if the difference is driven by levels (for example, differences in basic health levels and expectations about them) or by the slope (for example, do health improvements generate more results in terms of happiness or health satisfaction at higher levels of income than at lower ones?).

Perhaps the most prevalent theme of this chapter is the extent to which norms and expectations of health vary a great deal across countries and cohorts within them. This helps explain the lack of a linear relationship between happiness and health across countries. Understanding this variance is critical to the design and implementation of effective health policy. Low expectations among the poor, for example, are likely to result in insufficient levels of demand for health care precisely from the cohorts that most lack it. At the same time, different levels of tolerance for ill health across countries can help explain why health systems are less well advanced in some countries than in others.

Perceptions data also help us better understand the value that individuals place on different health conditions and how that varies across cohorts. Our analysis suggests that the variance across physical and mental conditions is more important than that across cohorts. Conditions that are associated with anxiety and uncertainty produce the most unhappiness and suffering, while individuals adapt better to physical problems, particularly as they age. Given the novel and at times

37. Dolan (2006).
38. Dolan (2006).

anachronistic nature of these data, however, they should be seen as useful inputs into policy discussions, rather than the basis for making decisions about particular public health investments.

References

Adrianzen, B., and G. Graham. 1974. "The High Costs of Being Poor." *Archives of Environmental Health* 28: 312–15.

Bannerjee, A., and E. Duflo. 2007. "The Economic Lives of the Poor." *Journal of Economic Perspectives* 21 (1): 141–61.

Blanchflower, D., and A. Oswald. 2004. "Well-Being over Time in Britain and the USA." *Journal of Public Economics* 88: 1359–86.

Case, A., and A. Deaton. 2005. "Health and Wealth among the Poor: India and South Africa Compared." *American Economic Review Papers and Proceedings* 95 (2): 229–33.

Clifton, J., and N. Gingrich. 2007. "Are the Citizens of the World Satisfied with their Health?" *Health Affairs* 26(5): 545–51.

Dachs, J. N., M. Ferrer, C. Florez, A. Barros, R. Narváez, and M. Valdivia. 2002. "Inequalities in Health in Latin America and the Caribbean: Descriptive and Exploratory Results for Self-Reported Health Problems and Health Care in Twelve Countries." *Pan American Journal of Public Health* 11 (5–6): 335–55.

Deaton, A. 2008. "Income, Health, and Well Being around the World: Evidence from the Gallup World Poll." *Journal of Economic Perspectives* 22 (2).

Dolan, P. 1997. "Modeling valuations for health states," *Medical Care* 11: 1095–108.

Dolan, P. 2006. "Happiness and Policy: A Review of the Literature." DEFRA Report, Whitehall, U.K.

Dolan, P., and D. Kahneman. 2008. "Interpretations of Utility and Their Implications for the Valuation of Health." *Economic Journal* 118 (525): 215–34.

EFILWC (European Foundation for the Improvement of Living and Working Conditions). 2004. *Quality of Life in Europe: First European Quality of Life Survey 2003.* Luxembourg: Office for Official Publications of the European Communities.

Gallup Poll. 2006. Gallup World Poll. Available at www.gallup.com/consulting/worldpoll/24046/about.aspx.

———. 2007. Gallup World Poll. Available at www.gallup.com/consulting/worldpoll/24046/about.aspx.

Graham, C. 2008. "Happiness and Health: Lessons—and Questions—for Public Policy." *Health Affairs* 27 (1): 72–87.

Graham, C., L. Higuera, and E. Lora. 2009. "Valuing Health States across Cohorts, Countries, and Cultures: Insights from a New Method Based on Happiness Surveys." Mimeo, Brookings.

Graham, C., A. Eggers, and S. Sukhtankar. 2004. "Does Happiness Pay? An Initial Exploration Based on Panel Data from Russia." *Journal of Economic Behavior and Organization* 55 (3): 319–42.

Groot, W. 2000. "Adaptation and Scale of Reference Bias in Self-Assessment of Quality of Life." *Journal of Health Economics* 19: 403–20.

Idler, E. L., and R. J. Angel. 1990. "Self-rated Health and Mortality in the NHANES-I Epidemiologic Follow-up Study." *American Journal of Public Health* 80 (4): 446–52.

Idler, E. L., and Y. Benyamini. 1997. "Self-rated health and mortality: a review of twenty-seven community studies." *Journal of Health and Social Behavior* 38 (1): 21–37.

Jürges, H. 2007. "True health vs response styles: exploring cross-country differences in self-reported health" (http://ideas.repec.org/a/wly/hlthec/v16y2007i2p163-178.html).

Kahneman, D. 2000. "Evaluation by Moments: Past and Future." In D. Kahneman and A. Tversky, eds., *Choices, Values, and Frames.* Cambridge University Press and Russell Sage Foundation.

Mossey, J. M., and E. Shapiro. 1982. "Self-rated health: a predictor of mortality among the elderly." *American Journal of Public Health* 72 (8): 800–08.

Murray, C. J. L., and L. C. Chen. 1992. "Understanding Morbidity Change." *Population and Development Review* 18 (3): 481–503.

NIMH (National Institute of Mental Health). 2009. "The Numbers Count: Mental Disorders in America" (www.nimh.nih.gov/health/publications/the-numbers-count-mental-disorders-in-america.shtml).

Preston, S. 1975. "The Changing Relation between Mortality and Level of Development." *Population Studies* 29 (2): 239–48.

Robine, J. M., C. Jagger, C. D. Mathers, E. M. Crimmins, and R. M. Suzman. 2003. *Determining Health Expectancies.* Boston: John Wiley & Sons.

Ruhm, C. J. 2000. "Are Recessions Good for Your Health?" *Quarterly Journal of Economics* 115 (2): 617–50.

Sen, A. 2002. "Health: Perception versus Observation." *British Medical Journal* 324: 860–61.

Shaw, J. W., J. A. Johnson, and S. A. Coons. 2005. "U.S. Valuation of the EQ-5D Health States: Development and Testing of the D1 Valuation Model." *Medical Care* 43 (3).

Suárez-Berenguela, R. 2001. "Health System Inequalities and Inequities in Latin America and the Caribbean: Findings and Policy Implications." In Pan American Health Organization, *Investment in Health. Social and Economic Returns.* Washington D.C.: Pan American Health Organization.

World Bank. 2007. World Development Indicators Online (http://publications.worldbank.org/ecommerce/catalog/product-detail?product_id=631625&).

7

Education and Life Satisfaction: Perception or Reality?

MAURICIO CÁRDENAS, CAROLINA MEJÍA,
AND VINCENZO DI MARO

This chapter focuses on education, and more precisely on perceptions about the quality of the educational system, as one of life's many dimensions that may be associated with well-being, understood as self-reported satisfaction.

Education is one of the pillars of development, being both an end in itself and a mean toward the attainment of higher income, equity, and personal self fulfill-ment. Development studies have long emphasized that the quality of education provided is as important, or even more, as the quantity of education received by the population (that is, years of schooling and enrollment rates), particularly among the poor.

This is particularly relevant for Latin America where, as Navarro (2007) men-tions, significant increases in educational expenditures, as well as in enrollment rates, have neither resulted in proportionate progress in economic growth nor in declines in income inequality. Consequently, much of the debate now focuses on improving the quality of education and providing better access to the poor. How-ever, little or no attention has been placed on people's perceptions of education quality, their relationship with well-being, and the way in which these variables can influence policy.

There are two main motivations for this chapter. First, perceptions of educational quality are important on their own, as a crucial component of individual welfare. Second, they might play an important role in shaping public opinion and the for-mulation of public actions, including the allocation of government expenditures.

More concretely, this chapter addresses two main research questions: 1) Are objective measures (for example, test scores and individual educational attainment) important in the formation of perceptions about educational quality? 2) Are educational quality perceptions and educational outcomes relevant for well-being? To explore this set of questions, a multi-country approach based on the Gallup World Poll (2006 and 2007) is used. Three dimensions of well being are used: (i) overall life satisfaction, (ii) satisfaction with living standards, and (iii) satisfaction to choose freely over one's life.

The analysis of the relation between education and happiness is not new. Earlier work by Wilson (1967) shows a positive, strong correlation between education attainment and life satisfaction. Di Tella and others (2003), for the United States and Europe, and Frey and Stutzer (2002) also obtain a positive correlation, after explicitly controlling for income and health, which are possible channels through which education may influence well-being. Recent work by Blanchflower (2008) also shows that life satisfaction is higher for the more educated. Helliwell (2002) analyses measures of subjective well-being from three successive waves of the World Values Survey and finds no effect of increasing levels of educational attainment, both at the individual and national level. The author argues that the mentioned effect may be already captured through higher income, better health and higher trust levels as well as higher political participation rates among the most educated. Similar results are obtained by Schwarze and Winkelmann (2005), using data from the German Socio-Economic Panel, which provides the advantage of allowing to include individual fixed effects that may capture unobservable characteristics that could bias statistical results.

The main conclusion of this chapter is that educational outcomes explain a great deal of the perceptions about the quality of the educational system, so that in a sense perceptions are aligned with reality. In particular, people (individuals and business managers) in countries with higher scores on standardized tests report to be more satisfied with the quality of education in their city and country.

In addition, educational quality perceptions affect self-reported well-being at the individual level, once we control for other variables (that is, age, sex, marital status, income, employment status, etc.). People satisfied with the educational system of the city or area where they live report higher life satisfaction in general. An interesting result is that the positive relationship between educational quality perceptions and well-being indicators is independent of the level of education of the respondent.

Although the results are robust to different specifications, and remain unchanged when estimations use country averages instead of individual data, a word of caution is necessary. Solving a potential endogeneity problem—overall life satisfaction may affect educational quality perceptions—is a challenge. Therefore, results should be interpreted carefully.

This chapter starts with a description of the datasets used in the empirical analysis and then presents some descriptive statistics of the educational quality perceptions, educational outputs and well-being measurements focusing on Latin America and the Caribbean.[1] The rest of the chapter answers the research questions using several econometric models.

The Data

To study the link between educational quality perceptions and well-being, the Gallup World Poll (or Gallup Survey), in a multi-country approach, is mainly used. The analysis is complemented with the use of two international standardized tests measuring quality of education (PIRLS and PISA) and the 2006 Global Competitiveness Report (GCR). This section provides a brief description of the data used.

• *The Gallup World Poll:* It is an extensive database on quality of life from household surveys in over 130 countries, many of them from Latin America. As explained in detail in the following sections, the survey enquires on self-reported perceptions on educational quality, educational attainment and socioeconomic background. The 2006 and 2007 waves are used, noting that the latter only covers Latin American and North American countries.

• *International standardized tests measuring quality of education:* PIRLS (Progress in International Reading Literacy Study) and PISA (Programme for International Student Assessment).[2] The 2001 PIRLS database contains reading scores for 4th grade students, while the 2003/2006 PISA dataset contains math literacy, problem solving, reading and scientific literacy scores for 15-year-old students. In all cases, the scores are comparable among countries, and thus can be used as objective measure of educational quality.

• *Global Competitiveness Report (GCR)—World Economic Forum:* covering 125 economies, the report assesses the ability of countries to provide high levels of prosperity to their citizens. It provides information on institutions, infrastructure, macroeconomic variables, health and primary education, markets' efficiency, technology and innovation and business development. Of particular interest is the respondents' (mostly from businesses) assessment on whether the educational system of their country meets the needs of a competitive economy.[3]

---

1. The term *Latin America* will refer to Latin America and the Caribbean for the rest of this chapter.

2. For more information on PISA, see OECD (2003 and 2006). For more information on PIRLS, see TIMSS & PIRLS International Study Center (2001).

3. For more information on the *Global Competitiveness Report,* see World Economic Forum (2006).

Educational Quality Perceptions, Educational Outputs and Well-being in Latin America

Throughout the analysis, the following indicators of educational quality perceptions (*EQP*) based on the Gallup World Poll questions, waves 2006 and 2007, are used:

In the city or area where you live, are you satisfied (1) or dissatisfied (0) with the educational system or the schools?[4]

Is education [in the country] accessible to anybody who wants to study, regardless of his or her economic situation, or not?

Generally speaking, would you say the education that college students receive in this country is of superior or inferior quality than that of most countries?[5]

Figure 7-1 depicts the first two indicators of EQP for a set of twenty Latin American countries in the year 2007. In both cases, average perceptions vary significantly from one country to another. While in Peru only 45 percent of the respondents are satisfied with the educational system, in Venezuela and Costa Rica this percentage rises to more than 80 percent. In a similar fashion, while in Venezuela 84 percent of the respondents consider that education is accessible regardless of socioeconomic considerations, in Paraguay only 17 percent share this opinion. Figure 7-2 shows that educational quality perceptions (at the individual level) do not vary considerably with income level. If anything, individuals in the highest income quintile are slightly less satisfied with the educational system and consider that education is accessible in a lesser proportion. Interestingly, more individuals are satisfied with the educational system than with education accessibility.

As can be expected, perceptions may differ from the objective indicator of what is being measured. For example, in Chile—a reform leader in education—only 63 percent of the population is satisfied with the education system. Similarly, less than 20 percent of the respondents in Paraguay consider education to be accessible irrespective of income, even though enrollment rates for youngsters of 6 to 7, 8 to 13 and 14 to 18 years are, respectively, 94 percent, 98.1 percent and 75 percent.[6]

Another indicator comes from the Global Competitiveness Report and captures the managers' average perception on the education quality of the labor force in a particular country, measured in a 1 to 7 scale. More precisely,

---

4. Only observations from individuals reporting having children under 16 are used (to capture the opinion of those closer to the educational system).

5. In the 2007 wave, this question is only available for two out of twenty countries, so it is considered neither in the descriptive statistics of this year nor in the econometric exercises of that year.

6. CAF (2007).

Figure 7-1. *Educational Quality Perceptions in Gallup Survey*

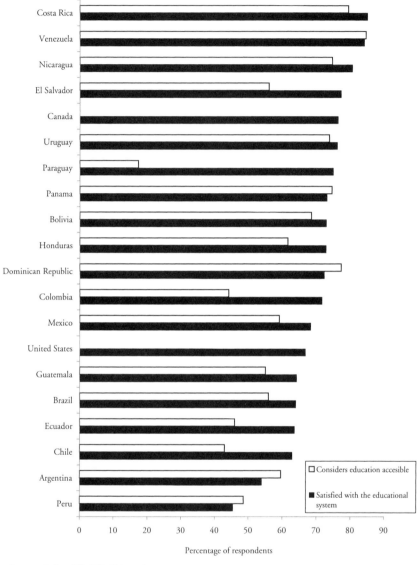

Percentage of respondents

Source: Gallup World Poll (2007).

The educational system in your country: 1=does not meet the needs of a competitive economy, 7=meets the need of a competitive economy.

Again, as shown in figure 7-3, educational quality perceptions are heterogeneous throughout the region. In this case, the two highest income countries (United States and Canada) score 5 points, followed by Costa Rica (4.1). These perceptions are very low for Bolivia, Peru, and Paraguay.

Figure 7-2. *Educational Quality Perceptions in Gallup World Poll by Income Quintiles for Latin America*

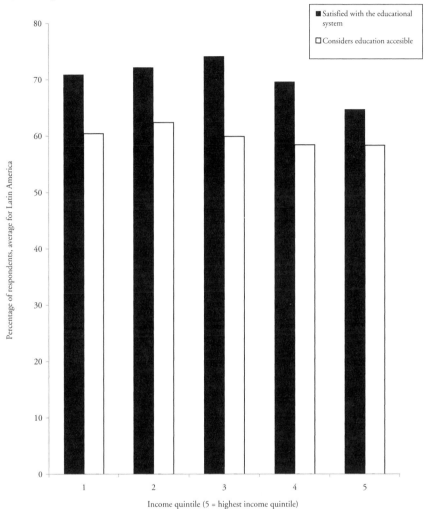

Source: Gallup World Poll (2007).

A central aspect of the analysis is the reference group to which respondents compare when asked for the quality of education. The first of the indicators refers to the education quality of the city (area) compared to other cities (areas), while the others refer to the education system of the country compared to other countries.

Regarding the measurements of educational output (EO), we consider scores in reading, math, science, and problem solving tests from PISA 2003 and 2006 as

Figure 7-3. *Educational Quality Perceptions in the Global Competitiveness Report, 2006*

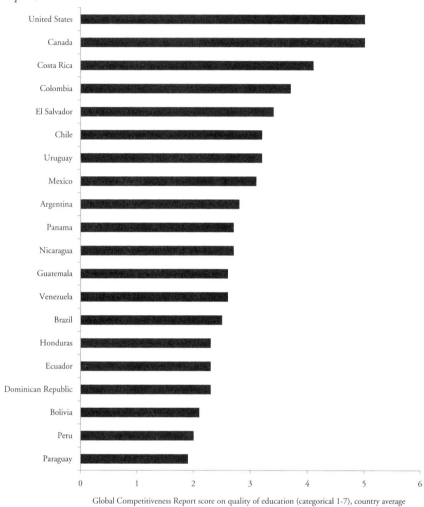

Global Competitiveness Report score on quality of education (categorical 1-7), country average

Source: World Economic Forum (2006).

well as the reading scores from PIRLS 2001, at the national level.[7] Unfortunately, PISA 2003 scores are only available for five countries (United States, Canada, Uruguay, Brazil, and Mexico) and the PISA 2006 for eight (the same five plus Chile, Argentina, and Colombia), as shown in figure 7-4. On average, and as with the GCR 2006 data, the United States and Canada score better in all test areas.

7. The problem solving scores are not available in the PISA 2006 data.

Figure 7-4. *Program for International Student Assessment (PISA) Scores, 2006*

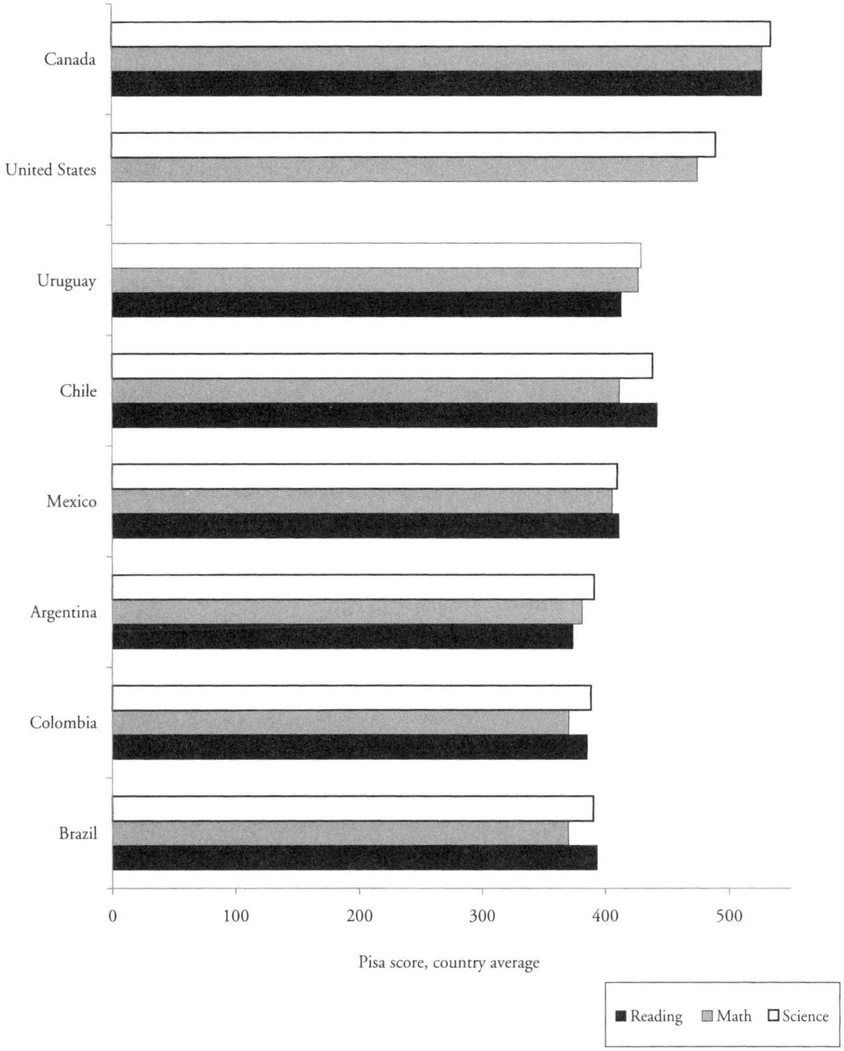

Pisa score, country average

■ Reading   ▥ Math   □ Science

Source: OECD (2006).

The rest of the countries in the sample report similar average scores, and, almost in every case, math scores are lower than the scores in other areas.

The 2007 wave of the Gallup World Poll contains information on individual educational attainment (albeit only for Latin American countries). The fact that it is possible to trace the respondent's highest educational level completed is crucial for this chapter. However, a note of caution is relevant because education categories vary from country to country, so the broadest category definitions were used and all the observations in the surveys were recoded. More concretely, categorical variables ranging from 1 (no level of education completed) to 10 (postgraduate studies) were used. The complete set of categories is as follows: 1—None, 2—Incomplete primary, 3—Complete primary, 4—Incomplete secondary, 5—Complete secondary, 6—Incomplete technological, 7—Complete technological, 8—Incomplete college, 9—Complete college and 10—Postgraduate studies.

Figure 7-5 presents the average educational level completed in each country. As expected, the United States and Canada present the highest levels of attainment. The average respondent in the United States has completed technological studies (and completed high school and begun some technical studies in Canada). There is significant variance across Latin American countries. While in Peru, Panama, Brazil, and Colombia complete secondary is the average level attained, in most Central American countries, average respondents rarely reach that stage (with the exception of Panama). As anticipated, income and educational attainment are positively correlated (see figure 7-6). In quintiles 1 and 2, the average individual from our sample of countries completed primary, while in quintiles 4 and 5 the average education levels are complete secondary and incomplete technological studies, respectively.

Importantly, there is significant variation of the educational level *within* each country. The largest differences in educational attainment within the population are presented in countries like Peru, Nicaragua, Guatemala, and Bolivia.

Regarding the indicators of well-being, the (0–10) "ladder" question of the Gallup World Poll (2006 and 2007 waves) is used in addition to:

• Are you satisfied (1) or dissatisfied (0) with your standard of living, all the things you can buy and do?

• (In your country) Are you satisfied (1) with the freedom to choose what you do with your life?

The value of these indicators presents significant dispersion across the region, as shown in chapter 5.

As with the ladder question, satisfaction with living standards is higher for individuals with higher income (figure 7-7). The average percentage of respondents satisfied with all the things that they can buy and do (as the questions asks) in quintile 5 is around 80 percent, while in the case of quintiles 1 and 2 it is 57 percent and 63 percent, respectively. This is not that evident in the case of positive answers to the question related to freedom to choose upon one's life. A plausible explanation is that this is a non-monetary dimension of well-being, more dependent on factors such as the political regime of the country and repressive actions from various groups, than on personal income. This pattern holds as well at the country level.

Figure 7-5. *Average Educational Level Completed*

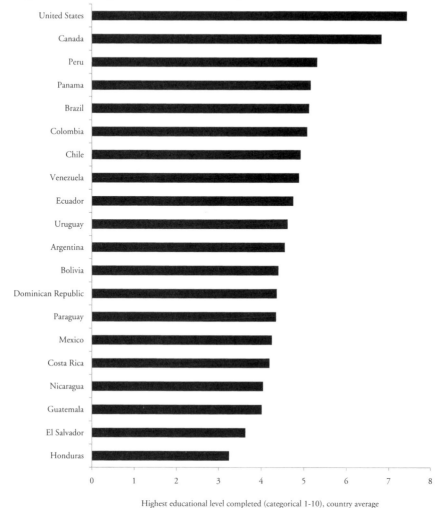

Highest educational level completed (categorical 1-10), country average

Source: Authors' calculations based on Gallup World Poll (2007).

Understanding Educational Quality Perceptions and their Effect on Well-being

Breen and Goldthorpe (1997) developed a model of educational decision making, where families make rational choices on their children's quality of education based on the concordance of the quality of education they observe their children are obtaining and the expected results of that education in terms of social mobility.[8] Among many other factors, such as socioeconomic level and the education

Figure 7-6. *Highest Educational Levels Completed in Latin America by Income Quintiles*

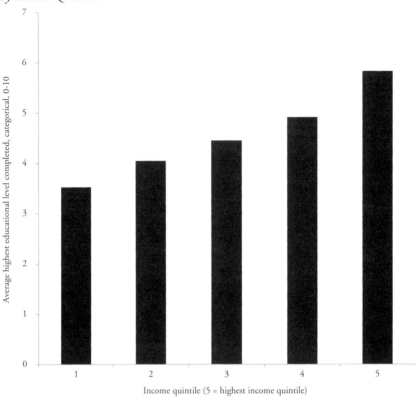

Income quintile (5 = highest income quintile)

Source: Authors' calculations based on Gallup World Poll (2007).

attainment of the parents, an important element that may affect these subjective opinions of both actual educational quality and future expected returns is the country's performance in international standardized tests, such as the ones described in the previous section.

Similarly, as mentioned above, perceptions are an important component of well-being along with other circumstances such as income, unemployment, inequality and family status. In particular, we expect that better perceptions on the quality of the educational system of their country, city or area, should increase people's overall satisfaction with life. High-quality education represents social

8. The authors of this chapter would like to thank Carolina Florez and Maria Soledad Herrera for introducing them to this literature.

Figure 7-7. *Well-Being Indicators in Gallup World Poll by Income Quintiles for Latin America*

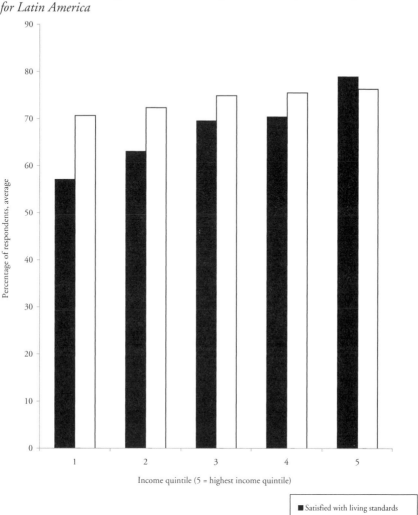

Income quintile (5 = highest income quintile)

■ Satisfied with living standards

□ Satisfied with freedom to choose

Source: Authors' calculations based on Gallup World Poll (2007).

mobility and opportunities, which can be interpreted as higher future income, social status, or simply satisfaction with new knowledge.

Determinants of Educational Quality Perceptions

The first task to be addressed is to understand how educational quality perceptions (EQP) are formed. In particular, it is relevant to establish if people's EQP are based on education outputs or if they are independent of objective measurements, such as aptitude tests and individual educational attainment.

It must be noted that educational quality is a broad concept, including other dimensions different from standardized tests. This is particularly true within the context of a household, where factors such as location, facilities, and reputation may also be important. Aware that educational quality might not be entirely captured by standardized tests, this information is used since it is comparable across countries. Also, there is wide recognition of standardized test scores as accurate proxies of educational quality.[9]

The econometric analysis is based on the estimation of the following model, with individual-level data:

$$EQP_{(i),j} = \alpha_0 + \alpha_1 EO_{(i),j} + \alpha_2 S_{i,j} + \alpha_3 SC_{i,j} + \alpha_4 C_{i,j} + \alpha_5 OP_{i,j}$$
$$+ \alpha_6 W_{i,j}^t + \alpha_7 CC_j + \varepsilon_{i,j}, \tag{1}$$

where i indexes individuals and j denotes countries.

- $EQP_{(i),j}$ is the satisfaction with the school system (1,0) [Source: Gallup World Poll]. Alternatively, the managers' average perception on the educational system in country j measured in a scale from 1 to 7 is used (in this case the subscript i is dropped[10]).[11]

- $EO_{(i),j}$ represents country j average scores for the PISA 2003/2006 and PIRLS 2001 tests (reading, math, science and problem solving) or the highest level of education of individual i in country j (measured as a categorical variable ranging from 1 to 10 or by 9 dummy variables for each educational category, excluding the category *no education*).[12]

- $S_{i,j}$ (*socioeconomic controls set*) are socioeconomic characteristics: zone (urban or rural, 1,0), male (1,0), age, age squared, married (1,0), employed (1,0), monthly household income (PPP dollars), number of adults in the household, and access to electricity (1,0), clean water (1,0) and telephone (1,0).[13]

- $SC_{i,j}$ (*social capital controls set*) measures social capital with dummy variables from the Gallup World Poll. Specifically, if the respondent trusts family and friends in difficult times, if one can progress in life with hard work, if the individual trusts the national government and the police, and if the individual thinks corruption is widespread in business and the government.

---

9. See Navarro (2007).
10. Naturally, in this case all the individuals of country j are assigned the same value of the variable.
11. Global Competitiveness Report (2006) from the World Economic Forum.
12. PISA, PIRLS, and Gallup World Poll.
13. Gallup World Poll.

- $C_{i,j}$ (*city and country perceptions controls set*) contains variables capturing the individual's satisfaction with other dimension of life. These are binary variables indicating whether or not the person is satisfied with the city where he/she lives and whether or not the person considers that the country's current economic conditions are good. A categorical variable (in a 0 to 10 scale) that captures the individual's perception on the country's current situation is also used.

- $OP_{i,j}$ (*other perceptions controls set*) includes binary variables relating to other perceptions of the respondent, in concrete, if the respondent is satisfied with his or her current housing and with his or her personal health status.[14]

- $W^t_{i,j}$ (*emotional status controls set*) represents well-being perceptions by the individual referring to other time periods (past and future). In particular, overall satisfaction with life five years before the survey as perceived by the respondent at the moment of the survey (categorical variable ranging from 0 to 10) is used as well as overall satisfaction with life in the future (five years ahead) as perceived by the respondent at the moment of the survey (categorical variable ranging from 0 to 10). These variables are critical since they allow to control for the emotional state of the respondent at the moment of the survey and, partially, for the respondent's inherent psychological traits (that is, structural optimism or pessimism).[15]

- CC_j (*country controls set*) includes log of 2005 GDP per capita (in PPP dollars, lngdp05), 2006 inflation rate (inf), GINI coefficient (more recent available, gini), education gini[16] (egini) and dummies for world income group—low, middle, upper middle, developing, high OECD, high non-OECD.[17]

- Finally, $\varepsilon_{i,j}$ is an error term, which is assumed to be clustered at the country level.

Equation 1 is estimated using a probit model on the EQP variable that takes the value of 1 if the respondent is satisfied with the educational system of the area/city of residence. A standard OLS is used when EQP is measured as the country average of the managers' perception on the competitiveness of the educational system. In both cases (and in all empirical exercises from now on), the sample is restricted to individuals reporting having children younger than 16 years old, and thus being closer to the actual quality of the education system, and robust standard errors are used to correct for any heteroskedasticity.

Before focusing on the interplay between educational output and perceptions, it is relevant to discuss the relationship between various socioeconomic variables and educational quality perceptions. Satisfaction with the educational system decreases with age and with the number of household members. Additionally,

14. Gallup World Poll.
15. Gallup World Poll.
16. As calculated by Thomas, Wang, and Fan (2001).
17. IDB Research Department Database and Thomas, Wang and Fan (2001).

Table 7-1. *Satisfaction with Educational System*
1 is satisfied, 0 if not

	Probit	
	2006[a]	*2007*[b]
PISA 2003 mean reading scores	0.0033	0.0047
	(5.83)***	(3.47)***
Urban[c]	0.0636	−0.0146
	(0.95)	(0.3)
Male[c]	−0.0052	
	(0.32)	
Age	−0.0049	−0.0079
	(1.26)	(7.10)***
Age squared	0.0001	0.0001
	(1.14)	(3.38)***
Married[c]	0.0568	0.0282
	(5.53)***	(3.98)***
Employed[c]	−0.0157	−0.0169
	(0.38)	(1.85)*
Number of household members over 15	−0.0189	
	(6.20)***	
Household income US$ PPP (monthly)	0.01	0.01
	(2.57)**	(1.52)
Running water[c]	0.1447	
	(6.83)***	
Electricity[c]	0.1118	
	(2.04)**	
Telephone[c]	−0.0102	
	(0.25)	
Number of observations	1,981	1,119
Pseudo R-squared	0.142	0.082

Source: Authors' calculations based on Gallup World Polls (2006 and 2007).

*Coefficient is statistically significant at the 10 percent level; **at the 5 percent level; ***at the 1 percent level; no asterisk means the coefficient is not different from zero with statistical significance.

Notes: Robust Z-statistics in parenthesis. Errors clustered by country. PISA = Program for International Student Assessment.

a. Controls: Socioeconomic characteristics, social capital, city and country perceptions, other perceptions, welfare, and country controls.

b. Controls: Zone, age, age^2, married, employed, income, social capital, city and country perceptions, other perceptions, welfare, 2005 GDP (natural logarithm, US$), gini and egini.

c. Dummy variable that takes the value of 1 if condition holds, 0 otherwise.

employed individuals seem to be less satisfied with the educational system. On the other hand, married individuals, as well as those in households with higher income and better household characteristics (such as having access to running water and electricity), report better educational perceptions. As can be seen in table 7-1, results vary slightly depending on the data used and also, although not shown, on the indicators of educational quality perceptions and educational output included in the exercise.

Table 7-2 presents the marginal coefficients of the probit estimation of α_1 throughout the different specifications, using the information from the 2006 and 2007 waves of the Gallup World Poll. Although the number of observations is significantly reduced due to limited availability of the standardized test scores and some country controls, the estimation shows that educational output at the national level positively affects individual educational quality perceptions. This is true for the scores of all the fields of the PISA 2003 and 2006 tests (except for the latter using the 2007 Gallup data), but not for the reading scores of the PIRLS 2001 test. In short, an additional point in the country average reading score of PISA (ranging from 200 to 600) increases the probability that a person living in that country be satisfied with the local educational system by 0.3 percent (range goes from 0.2 percent to 0.5 percent).

As mentioned in the previous section, a major concern when assessing subjective satisfaction responses is the presence of unobserved characteristics, such as optimism and pessimism (trait factors), that may bias the results, constraining generalizations from the empirical exercises. In order to overcome this obstacle, as mentioned in chapter 5, van Praag and Ferrer-i-Carbonell (2008) suggest a methodology to control for this element.[18] It basically consists of extracting the individual personality trait factor from different questions related to distinct satisfaction domains posed to the same respondent. The intuition is that the individual personality factor would bias the answers to these questions in the same direction; say for example an optimist will overrate both his/her satisfaction with life and his/her perception of the country's situation.

In brief, the procedure is to individually regress each satisfaction dimension or question against the same set of explanatory variables, estimate the predicted residual of each regression, and obtain the common factor of these residuals using the principal component method. The underlying assumption is that the most important omitted variable in the regression is the personality trait element and that it should be the common factor of the residuals.

As the different satisfaction dimensions, the following six variables are used: current, past and future life satisfaction ladder question and current, past and future perception of country situation (also categorical variables ranging from 0 to 10). As regressors, we use the same set of socioeconomic, social capital and country controls, variables described previously.

As shown in table 7-3, the effect of educational output on satisfaction remains unchanged when controlling for personality traits using the 2006 Gallup data, but is lost when the Latin American data (2007 data) are used.

---

18. Ideally, one would like to account for it, via individual fixed effects using panel data. Unfortunately, the World Gallup Poll is not a panel survey.

Table 7-2. *Satisfaction with Educational System*
1 is satisfied, 0 if not

| | *Probit estimation of α_1 (marginal effects)* | | | | | |
| | 2006[a] | | | 2007[b] | | |
	Coefficient	*Number of observations*	*Pseudo R-squared*	*Coefficient*	*Number of observations*	*Pseudo R-squared*
PISA 2003						
Reading scores	0.0033	1,981	0.142	0.0047	1,119	0.082
(mean)	(5.83)***			(3.47)***		
Math scores	0.003	1,981	0.141	0.0034	1,119	0.081
(mean)	(5.83)***			(3.47)***		
Science scores	0.0028	1,981	0.143	0.0041	1,119	0.080
(mean)	(5.83)***			(3.47)***		
Problem solving scores	0.0025	1,981	0.142	0.0052	1,119	0.081
(mean)	(5.83)***			(3.47)***		
PISA 2006						
Reading scores	0.003	5,652	0.071	-0.00002	2,109	0.076
(mean)	(2.49)**			(0.04)		
Math scores	0.0033	5,951	0.073	-0.0003	2,109	0.077
(mean)	(3.29)***			(0.42)		
Science scores	0.002	5,951	0.067	0.0007	2,109	0.078
(mean)	(1.83)*			(0.89)		
PIRLS 2001						
Reading scores	0.0029	1,123	0.110	0.0673	639	0.093
(mean)	-0.39			(3.19)***		

Source: Authors' calculations based on Gallup World Polls (2006 and 2007).

*Coefficient is statistically significant at the 10 percent level; **at the 5 percent level; ***at the 1 percent level; no asterisk means the coefficient is not different from zero with statistical significance.

Notes: Robust Z-statistics in parentheses. Errors clustered by country. PISA = Program for International Student Assessment. PIRLS = Program in International Reading Literacy Study.

a. Controls for PISA 2003 and PIRLS 2001: socioeconomic characteristics, social capital, city and country perceptions, other perceptions, welfare, and country controls. Controls for PISA 2006: socioeconomic characteristics, hardwork, other perceptions, welfare, 2005 GDP (natural logarithm, US$), gini, egini, and income dummies.

b. Controls for PISA 2003 and 2006: Zone, age, age squared, married, employed, income, social capital, city and country perceptions, other perceptions, welfare, 2005 GDP (natural logarithm, US$), gini, and egini. Controls for PIRLS 2001: socioeconomic characteristics, social capital, city and country perceptions, other perceptions, welfare, 2005 GDP (natural logarithm, US$), gini, and egini.

Table 7-3. *Satisfaction with Educational System*
1 is satisfied, 0 if not

| | Probit estimation of α_1 (marginal effects) controlling for personality | | | | | |
| | 2006[a] | | | 2007[b] | | |
	Coefficient	Number of observations	Pseudo R-squared	Coefficient	Number of observations	Pseudo R-squared
PISA 2003						
Reading scores	0.0029	4,294	0.095	-0.0191	1,005	0.046
(mean)	(2.53)**			-1.28		
Math scores	0.0031	4,294	0.100	0.0017	1,005	0.046
(mean)	(5.09)***			-1.28		
Science scores	0.0023	4,294	0.095	0.0033	1,005	0.046
(mean)	(3.37)***			-1.28		
Problem solving scores	0.0026	4,294	0.098	0.0037	1,005	0.046
(mean)	(4.02)***			-1.28		
PISA 2006						
Reading scores	0.0022	4,442	0.058	0.00020	1,991	0.053
(mean)	-1.46			-0.98		
Math scores	0.0032	4,724	0.062	0.0003	1,991	0.053
(mean)	(3.04)***			-0.98		
Science scores	0.0016	4,724	0.056	0.0004	1,991	0.053
(mean)	-1.45			-0.98		
PIRLS 2001						
Reading scores	0.0003	3,084	0.089	0.0559	639	0.072
(mean)	-0.1			(3.57)***		

Source: Authors' calculations based on Gallup World Polls (2006 and 2007).

*Coefficient is statistically significant at the 10 percent level; **at the 5 percent level; ***at the 1 percent level; no asterisk means the coefficient is not different from zero with statistical significance.

Notes: Robust Z-statistics in parenthesis. Errors clustered by country. PISA = Program for International Student Assessment. PIRLS = Program in International Reading Literacy Study.

a. Controls for PISA 2003 and PIRLS 2001: Socioeconomic characteristics, social capital, personality and country controls. Controls for PISA 2006: Socioeconomic characteristics, hardwork, personality, 2005 GDP (natural logarithm, US$), gini, egini, and income dummies, among others.

b. Controls for PISA 2003 and 2006: Zone, age, age, married, employed, income, social capital, personality, 2005 GDP (natural logarithm, US$), gini, and egini. Controls for PIRLS 2001: socioeconomic characteristics, social capital, personality, 2005 GDP (natural logarithm, US$), gini, and egini.

In the case of individual educational outcomes, that is, the highest level of education attained in its categorical version, the marginal effect is negative and significant, as shown in the first column of table 7-4. The result suggests that as individuals become more educated, their standards to evaluate the quality of education are raised and, therefore, their assessment is less favorable. This finding is confirmed by the result shown in the second column, where it is clear that the higher the educational level attained, the larger the negative impact over educational quality perceptions. For example, having completed postgraduate studies diminishes the probability of satisfaction by 32 percent, while having completed technical studies by 10 percent. The general idea is that higher education creates more awareness about the limitations of the schooling system. Interestingly, the effect is nonlinear as it tends to increase more than proportionally with educational attainment. Columns three and four show that results are robust when controlling for estimated personality traits.

The findings remain unchanged if the educational quality perceptions indicator from the 2006 Global Competiveness Report is used as the dependent variable (see table 7-5). A 1 percent increase in the mean score of the PISA standardized tests, regardless of the field and year of the test, is associated with about a 2.5 percent increase in the businessmen's perception of educational quality (ranging from 1 to 7). As before, it seems that individual perceptions reflect the PISA tests but not the PIRLS 2001 tests, although this does not imply that the latter are not an accurate proxy of the quality of education across the world. Once more, the right-hand panel shows that results remain unchanged using van Praag and Ferrer-i-Carbonell (2008) methodology to control for unobservable personality traits.

To test for robustness, the model is also estimated using country averages instead of individual values (considering that the units of observation for the standardized test scores are countries). The results are unchanged except for the effect of the math and science PISA 2003 test scores on educational quality perceptions, which lose significance. In another set of exercises, the assessment of college education in the country, compared to other countries, and the accessibility of education are used as indicators of educational quality. However, the results are neither significant nor robust. Finally, it was not found that the relationship between educational output and educational quality perceptions changes with gender, age and income. That is, the interaction between the educational output variables and the individual's key characteristics did not come out significant.[19]

Effect of Educational Quality Perceptions on Reported Well-being

The next question to be addressed is if educational quality perceptions affect well-being once it is controlled for the standard determinants of life satisfaction

---

19. These robustness tests are not included for the sake of brevity.

Table 7-4. *Determinants of Satisfaction with Educational System*
1 is satisfied, 0 if not

| | Probit estimation of α_1 (marginal effects) | | | |
| | 2007[a] | | 2007[b] | |
	1	2	3	4
Highest level of education completed[a] (categorical)	−0.0248 (7.22)***		−0.0246 (6.04)***	
Incomplete primary[c]		0.027 −0.71		0.0385 −1.02
Complete primary[c]		0.04 −0.93		0.0488 −1.22
Incomplete secondary[c]		0.0476 −1.12		0.0575 −1.43
Complete secondary[c]		−0.0267 −0.54		−0.0111 −0.24
Incomplete technical school[c]		−0.069 −1.32		−0.0679 −1.17
Complete technical school[c]		−0.0962 (1.65)*		−0.0923 (1.79)*
Incomplete university studies[c]		−0.0909 (1.75)*		−0.0743 −1.51
Complete university studies[c]		−0.1109 (2.31)**		−0.0958 (1.91)*
Postgraduate studies[c]		−0.3281 (3.38)***		−0.3249 (3.64)***
Number of observations	4,945	4,956	4,961	4,972
Pseudo R-squared	0.101	0.104	0.088	0.091

Source: Authors' calculations based on Gallup World Polls (2006 and 2007).

*Coefficient is statistically significant at the 10 percent level; **at the 5 percent level; ***at the 1 percent level; no asterisk means the coefficient is not different from zero with statistical significance.

Notes: Robust Z-statistics in parentheses. Errors clustered by country.

a. Controls: Socioeconomic characteristics, social capital, city and country perceptions, other perceptions, welfare, and country controls.

b. Controls: Socioeconomic characteristics, social capital, personality, and country controls.

c. Dummy variable that takes the value of 1 if condition holds, 0 otherwise.

mentioned in a previous section. For the econometric analysis, the three indicators of well-being described previously are used (ladder question, satisfaction with living standards and satisfaction with freedom to decide upon one's life) in addition to three measures of EQP (satisfaction with educational system, college education relative to other countries, and accessibility of education). The question from the Global Competitiveness Report on the quality of the educational system as perceived by the business community is used as well.

Table 7-5. *Perception on the Quality of the Educational System (Global Competitiveness Report, 2006)*

	Ordinary least squares estimation of α_1					
	2006[a]			2007[b]		
	Coefficient	Number of observations	R-squared	Coefficient	Number of observations	R-squared
PISA 2003						
Reading scores	2.3546	2,190	0.778	2.082	4,427	0.521
(log of mean)	(2.19)*			(2.71)**		
Math scores	2.5064	2,190	0.906	2.0337	4,427	0.672
(log of mean)	(4.06)***			(3.22)***		
Science scores	2.4638	2,190	0.900	1.7944	4,427	0.560
(log of mean)	(3.82)**			(2.34)**		
Problem solving scores	2.2496	2,190	0.879	1.7288	4,427	0.594
(log of mean)	(3.18)**			(2.63)**		
PISA 2006						
Reading scores	2.989	2,410	0.667	2.0383	4,592	0.536
(log of mean)	(2.51)**			(2.20)**		
Math scores	3.2927	2,410	0.807	1.9972	4,876	0.637
(log of mean)	(3.89)***			(2.88)***		
Science scores	3.0493	2,410	0.741	1.8266	4,876	0.538
(log of mean)	(3.70)**			(2.29)**		
PIRLS 2001						
Reading scores	−1.6274	1,171	0.545	−1.1592	3,206	0.479
(log of mean)	(1.16)			(1.95)*		

Source: Authors' calculations based on Gallup World Polls (2006 and 2007).

*Coefficient is statistically significant at the 10 percent level; **at the 5 percent level; ***at the 1 percent level; no asterisk means the coefficient is not different from zero with statistical significance.

Notes: Robust *t*-statistics in parentheses. Errors clustered by country. Perception on the quality of the educational system is in logs. PISA = Program for International Student Assessment. PIRLS = Program in International Reading Literacy Study.

a. Controls: Socioeconomic characteristics, social capital, city and country perceptions, other perceptions, welfare, 2005 GDP (natural logarithm, US$), and egini.

b. Controls: Socioeconomic characteristics, social capital, personality, 2005 GDP (natural logarithm, US$), and egini.

The reduced model for the econometric analysis capturing the effect of EQP on well-being is described by equation 2:

$$W_{i,j} = \beta_0 + \beta_1 EQP_{i,j} + \beta_2 S_{i,j} + \beta_3 SC_{i,j} + \beta_4 C_{i,j} + \beta_5 OP_{i,j} + \beta_6 W_{i,j}^t$$
$$+ \beta_7 CC_j + \varepsilon_{i,j}, \tag{2}$$

where, as before, i indexes individuals and j denotes countries. All variables are as defined in equation 1 and errors are clustered by countries.

As before, this section starts by discussing some of the results related to the set of socioeconomic controls, before it engages in a more detailed analysis of the effects of EQP on well-being, which is its main focus. The results reported in table 7-6 confirm the findings of previous studies. For example, well-being decreases with age and with the number of household members, but increases with marriage and employment. The coefficient on monthly household income is positive and significant (although very small). Similarly, men report to be less satisfied with life. (These results hold when the other well-being and educational quality perception measurements are used.) Once again, these results would also be consistent with a reverse causality: Individuals who are intrinsically less satisfied with life might be less likely to feel satisfied with the educational system, naturally biasing our estimates. The fact that the results vanish when we control for personality traits suggests that there is possibly endogeneity between the variables at hand.

Another point raised by van Praag and Ferrer-i-Carbonell (2008) is that questions like the ladder question may neglect the cardinal information of the responses. For instance, even if the possible answers to this question are only integers, a response of 7 can refer to any number between 6.55 and 7.45. To overcome this limitation, they propose the COLS procedure, which basically consists in the cardinalization of the original ladder question before running an OLS. More specifically, it first assumes that any of the responses can correspond to an interval of range 1 (for example, a 5 corresponds to the interval (4.5,5.5); extreme values are treated as follows: 1 correspond to (0,0.5) and 10 to (9.5,10). Then it is possible to construct a variable ZCOLS $= E[Z|u_i{-}1{<}Z{<}u_i]$, where Z is $N(0,1)$ distributed and the u_i term comes from the interval values as defined above.

Instead of the original values, the regressions were estimated using the transformed variable as dependent variable. In practice, ZCOLS is the original life satisfaction variable standardized (mean and standard deviation by country), with this to be kept in mind when interpreting the coefficients of the COLS estimation. Table 7-7 shows the results.

The probit estimations for the other two indicators of well-being (satisfaction with living standards and with freedom to choose over life) are presented

Table 7-6. *Overall Satisfaction with Life*
1–10, ladder question

	Ordinary least squares	
	2006[a]	2007[b]
Satisfaction with educational system in area/city	0.1491	0.1326
(1 if satisfied)	(2.55)**	(1.82)*
Urban[c]	−0.0914	−0.0926
	(1.17)	(1.1)
Male[c]	−0.1443	−0.0138
	(1.88)*	(0.28)
Age	−0.0305	−0.0216
	(2.69)**	(1.93)*
Age squared	0.0004	0.0002
	(2.49)**	(1.64)
Married[c]	0.198	0.0873
	(3.27)**	−1.39
Employed[c]	0.1244	0.0904
	(1.95)*	(1.44)
Number of household members over 15	−0.0254	−0.0566
	(1.67)	(1.45)
Household income US$ PPP (monthly)	0	0.0001
	(2.83)**	(4.58)***
Running water[c]	−0.0479	0.2878
	(0.29)	(2.82)**
Electricity[c]	0.0696	0.4931
	(0.87)	(3.36)***
Telephone[c]	0.2613	0.2274
	(1.82)	(2.97)***
Number of observations	3,633	5,678
R-squared	0.569	0.428

Source: Authors' calculations based on Gallup World Polls (2006 and 2007).

*Coefficient is statistically significant at the 10 percent level; **at the 5 percent level; ***at the 1 percent level; no asterisk means the coefficient is not different from zero with statistical significance.

Notes: Robust *t*-statistics in parenthesis. Errors clustered by country.

a. Controls: Socioeconomic characteristics, social capital, other perceptions, welfare, and country controls, among others.

b. Controls: Socioeconomic characteristics, hardwork, police, other perceptions, welfare, and country controls, among others.

c. Dummy variable, which takes the value of 1 if condition holds, 0 otherwise.

Table 7-7. *Overall Satisfaction with Life*
1–10, ladder question COLS

	COLS estimation of β_1					
	2006[a]			2007[b]		
	Coefficient	*Number of observations*	*R-squared*	*Coefficient*	*Number of observations*	*R-squared*
Satisfaction with educational systems in area/city (1 if satisfied)	0.0606 (2.48)**	3,633	0.572	0.0532 (1.80)*	5,678	0.432
College education is superior (1 if satisfied)	−0.0674 −1.45	1,173	0.35			
Education is accessible (1 if yes)	0.0943 −1.22	1,200	0.35	0.0822 (3.65)***	5,707	0.431
Quality of educational system, 2006 (Competitiveness report, 1–7, logs)	−0.0521 −0.2	3,693	0.569	0.2045 −1.63	5,797	0.433

Source: Authors' calculations based on Gallup World Polls (2006 and 2007).

*Coefficient is statistically significant at the 10 percent level; **at the 5 percent level; ***at the 1 percent level; no asterisk means the coefficient is not different from zero with statistical significance.

Notes: Robust Z-statistics in parentheses. Errors clustered by country. COLS = cardinalized ordinary least squares.

a. Controls: Socioeconomic characteristics, social capital, other perceptions, welfare, and country controls.

b. Controls: Socioeconomic characteristics, hardwork, police, other perceptions, welfare and country controls, among others.

in table 7-8 and table 7-9, respectively.[20] The key results remain unchanged: satisfaction with the local educational system raises the probability of reporting satisfaction in both dimensions in a range from 3.2 percent to 8.2 percent. As before, college education does not come out significant, while the Global Competitiveness Report variable presents contradictory results, suggesting that the opinion of business leaders does not coincide with the opinion of individuals surveyed by Gallup.

Additionally, the model is also estimated using country average variables, to check for the robustness of the results. The signs, magnitudes and significances of the coefficients remain unchanged. Moreover, contrary to the exercise pursued at the individual level, the coefficient on the variable that measures educational accessibility comes out positive and significant.[21]

With the purpose of analyzing possible non-linearities in the relation between well-being and educational quality perceptions, dummy variables that aggregate the EQP indicators (only for the 2006 data, given data availability) were constructed. In this way $EQP1$ takes the value of 1, if at least one of the three EQP indicators[22] takes the value of 1 (0 otherwise), $EQP2$ takes the value of 1 if any two EQP indicators take the value of 1 (0 otherwise), and $EQP3$ takes the value of 1 if all three of them take the value of 1.

Of the 2006 sample, 17.3 percent of the respondents were satisfied with the educational system according to all three dimensions ($EQP3$=1) and only 12.4 percent were not satisfied at all. Most of the respondents, 39.2 percent, were satisfied in two dimensions and 31.1 percent with at least one.

The specification when the EQP index dummies are used is the same as equation 2:

$$W_{i,j} = \delta_0 + \delta_1 EQP1_{i,j} + \delta_2 EQP2_{i,j} + \delta_3 EQP3_{i,j} + \delta_4 S_{i,j} + \delta_5 SC_{i,j}$$
$$+ \delta_6 C_{i,j} + \delta_7 OP_{i,j} + \delta_7 W_{i,j}^t + \delta_9 CC_j + \varepsilon_{i,j}. \tag{3}$$

As before, i indexes individuals and j denotes countries. All control variables are as defined in equation 1 and errors are clustered by countries.

Table 7-10 presents the results for each of the three well-being indicators considered throughout the paper. In the specification using the ladder question,

---

20. Results remain unaffected when using the personality traits estimated using van Praag and Ferrer-i-Carbonell (2008) methodology as controls, except for the relationship between the GCR 2006 indicator of educational quality and satisfaction with freedom to choose.

21. Results available upon request.

22. Satisfaction with the educational system of the area/city where you live considers college education in the country superior and considers that the educational system is accessible regardless of socioeconomic extraction.

Table 7-8. *Satisfaction with Living Standards*
1 if satisfied

| | Probit estimation of β_1 | | | | | |
| | 2006[a] | | | 2007[b] | | |
	Coefficient	Number of observations	Pseudo R-squared	Coefficient	Number of observations	Pseudo R-squared
Satisfaction with educational systems in area/city (1 if satisfied)	0.0472 (1.68)*	3,963	0.168	0.0633 (3.58)***	4,920	0.226
College education is superior (1 if satisfied)	−0.0152 −0.37	1,175	0.164			
Education is accessible (1 if yes)	0.0002 0	1,200	0.165	0.0315 (1.95)*	4,956	0.224
Quality of educational system, 2006 (Competitiveness report, 1–7)	0.259 (12.82)***	4,021	0.231	0.0203 −0.93	5,010	0.220

Source: Authors' calculations based on Gallup World Polls (2006 and 2007).

*Coefficient is statistically significant at the 10 percent level; **at the 5 percent level; ***at the 1 percent level; no asterisk means the coefficient is not different from zero with statistical significance.

Notes: Robust Z-statistics in parenthesis. Errors clustered by country.

a. Controls Gallup variables: Socioeconomic characteristics, social capital, city and country perceptions, health, welfare, and country controls. Controls Global Competitiveness Report: Socioeconomic characteristics, social capital, city and country perceptions, other perceptions, welfare, and country controls.

b. Controls: Socioeconomic characteristics, social capital, city and country perceptions, other perceptions, welfare and country controls.

Table 7-9. *Satisfaction with Freedom to Choose over Life*
1 if satisfied

	Probit estimation of β_1					
	2006[a]			2007[a]		
	Coefficient	Number of observations	Pseudo R-squared	Coefficient	Number of observations	Pseudo R-squared
Satisfaction with educational systems in area/city	0.0323	3,936	0.141	0.082	4,914	0.104
(1 if satisfied)	(1.79)*			(5.10)***		
College education is superior	0.0181	1,173	0.145			
(1 if satisfied)	(0.72)					
Education is accessible	0.0695	1,197	0.156	0.1015	4,944	0.106
(1 if yes)	(2.26)**			(6.01)***		
Quality of educational system, 2006	−0.1663	4,003	0.141	−0.0321	4,997	0.096
(Competitiveness report, 1–7)	(10.13)***			(0.96)		

Source: Authors' calculations based on Gallup World Polls (2006 and 2007).

*Coefficient is statistically significant at the 10 percent level; **at the 5 percent level; ***at the 1 percent level; no asterisk means the coefficient is not different from zero with statistical significance.

Notes: Robust Z-statistics in parenthesis. Errors clustered by country.

a. Controls: Socioeconomic characteristics, social capital, city and country perceptions, other perceptions, welfare, and country controls.

Table 7-10. *Non-Linearities in the Relationship between Well-Being and Educational Quality Perception*

	Estimation of δ_1		
	2006		
	Overall satisfaction with life (1–10, ladder question)	*Satisfaction with living standards (1 if satisfied)*	*Satisfaction with freedom to choose over life (1 if satisfied)*
	OLS[a]	*Probit*[b]	*Probit*[c]
Satisfied with	0.1869	0.0882	0.0248
education[d]	(8.87)**	(3.02)***	−0.65
Education is	0.3708	0.1252	0.0824
accessible[d]	(3.23)*	(3.25)***	(1.74)*
College education	0.2553	0.069	0.0891
is superior[d]	(5.66)**	−1.19	(1.81)*
Number of	1,140	1,143	1,141
observations			
R-squared /	0.349	0.172	0.159
pseudo R-squared			

Source: Authors' calculations based on Gallup World Polls (2006 and 2007).

*Coefficient is statistically significant at the 10 percent level; **at the 5 percent level; ***at the 1 percent level; no asterisk means the coefficient is not different from zero with statistical significance.

Notes: Robust Z-statistics in parentheses. Errors clustered by country.

a. Ordinary Least Squares. Controls: Socioeconomic characteristics, social capital, other perceptions, welfare, and country controls, among others.

b. Controls: Socioeconomic characteristics, social capital, city and country perceptions, health, welfare, and country controls.

c. Controls: Socioeconomic characteristics, social capital, city and country perceptions, other perceptions, welfare, and country controls.

d. Dummy variable, which takes the value of 1 if condition holds, 0 otherwise.

there is no increasing effect of the educational quality indicators on overall well-being, meaning that being satisfied with the educational system in three dimensions does not necessarily increase well-being more that being satisfied in two of them. In other words, when two of the three dimensions in which individuals express their perception about educational quality are favorable, the effect on well-being is larger relative to what occurs when individuals consider as favorable only one dimension. A third dimension of positive perceptions does not add much in terms of satisfaction with living standards, raising the point that there might be limits to the effect of education perceptions on life satisfaction. However, satisfaction with the educational system, along with a positive view about college education in the country and accessibility, renders higher freedom to choose type of welfare than when only two of these dimensions of EQP are met.

Interestingly, satisfaction in just one dimension of EQP is not associated with perceived freedom.[23]

Including Educational Output in the Analysis of Determining Well-Being

As mentioned beforehand, more education is a synonym for higher income and social status, and, therefore, it should be associated with higher overall life satisfaction. More educated individuals may also obtain jobs that suit their preferences better and other factors that may enhance well-being, such as refined culture. In order to contribute to the debate, this study uses the 2007 Gallup World Poll, which allows to explore the relationship between life satisfaction and education at the individual-level data, using the highest level of education completed variable.

The reduced model used in the analysis resembles equation 2, except for the fact that EQP indicators are replaced by individual education output in its two versions: categorical variable and the set of dummies. The specification follows equation 4.

$$W_{i,j} = \phi_0 + \phi_1 EO_{i,j} + \phi_2 S_{i,j} + \phi_3 SC_{i,j} + \phi_4 C_{i,j} + \phi_5 OP_{i,j} + \phi_6 W^t_{i,j}$$
$$+ \phi_7 CC_j + \varepsilon_{i,j}, \tag{4}$$

where, as before, i indexes individuals and j denotes countries. All variables are as defined in equation 1 and errors are clustered by countries.

As table 7-11 shows, results on the relationship of educational attainment and well-being are contradictory. In the first two columns, when the ladder question is used as dependent variable, a higher educational level increases overall satisfaction with life. In fact, having completed postgraduate studies increases well-being by almost 0.7 (in a 0 to 10 range), while having completed secondary, by 0.4. On the contrary, when the well-being indicator employed is satisfaction with living standards, the relationship is negative and of lower magnitude, even though the dummy variables specifications do not confirm this result. The exercises using satisfaction with freedom to choose did not turn out significant.

The main message here is that the educational outcomes at the individual level (actual educational attainment) do not have a clear relationship with well-being, in line with previous mixed findings. This contrasts with the relationship between EQP and well-being, where much stronger results were found. It is possible, although speculative, that higher education outcomes are associated with higher aspirations

---

23. For the most part, results remain robust when using the COLS transformation and estimates of non-observable individual personality traits are included as controls.

Table 7-11. *Relationship between Well-Being and Individual Educational Attainment*

	Estimation of Φ_1					
			2007			
	Overall satisfaction with life (1–10, ladder question)		Satisfaction with living standards (1 if satisfied)		Satisfaction with freedom to choose over life (1 if satisfied)	
	OLS[a]		Probit[b]		Probit[b]	
	1	2	1	2	1	2
Highest level of education completed (categorical)	0.074} (4.57)***		−0.0057 (2.56)**		−0.0007 −0.25	
Incomplete primary[c]		0.071 −0.54		−0.0032 −0.1		0.0417 −1.22
Complete primary[c]		0.1874 −1.37		0.0169 −0.6		0.0397 −1.07
Incomplete secondary[c]		0.3023 (2.15)**		−0.0142 −0.47		0.0531 −1.34
Complete secondary[c]		0.3844 (3.76)***		−0.0079 −0.31		0.0279 −0.73
Incomplete technical school[c]		0.5118 (1.90)*		−0.0901 (2.73)***		−0.0667 −1.17
Complete technical school[c]		0.6182 (3.87)***		−0.0511 −0.98		0.0425 −0.79

(continued)

Table 7-11. *Relationship between Well-Being and Individual Educational Attainment (Continued)*

	Estimation of Φ_1					
	2007					
	Overall satisfaction with life (1–10, ladder question)		Satisfaction with living standards (1 if satisfied)		Satisfaction with freedom to choose over life (1 if satisfied)	
	OLS[a]		Probit[b]		Probit[b]	
	1	2	1	2	1	2
Incomplete university studies[c]		0.5028		−0.0302		0.057
		(3.28)***		(1.12)		(1.97)**
Complete university studies[c]		0.6053		−0.0317		0.0239
		(3.51)***		(0.89)		(0.55)
Postgraduate studies[c]		0.6914		0.0208		0.0466
		(2.56)**		(0.3)		(0.73)
Number of observations	8,640	8,659	7,875	7,891	7,842	7,860
Pseudo R-squared	0.254	0.254	0.211	0.211	0.103	0.101

Source: Authors' calculations based on Gallup World Poll (2007).

*Coefficient is statistically significant at the 10 percent level; **at the 5 percent level; ***at the 1 percent level; no asterisk means the coefficient is not different from zero with statistical significance.

a. Ordinary Least Squares. Controls: Socioeconomic characteristics, social capital, city and country perceptions, other perceptions, and country controls. Robust Z-statistics in parentheses.

b. Controls: Socioeconomic characteristics, social capital, city and country perceptions, other perceptions, welfare, and country controls. Robust Z-statistics in parentheses.

c. Dummy variable, which takes the value of 1 if condition holds, 0 otherwise. Robust Z-statistics in parentheses.

and, therefore, less satisfaction with living standards, in contrast with life satisfaction reported by the ladder question.

When we estimate the relationship controlling for individual personality traits obtained through the procedure suggested by van Praag and Ferrer-i-Carbonell (2008), differentials in the education level attained do not longer translate into higher overall life satisfaction (ladder question), but higher levels still present a negative correlation with material satisfaction or satisfaction with living standards.

Naturally, it is also relevant to enquire if educational quality perceptions still influence well-being after controlling for educational outputs. This would suggest that educational quality perceptions matter in their own right, regardless of educational outputs. In order to explore if this is the case, individual educational attainment is included as an additional covariate in the original well-being equation (equation 2), to obtain equation 5:

$$W_{i,j} = \phi_0 + \phi_1 EO_{i,j} + \phi_2 EQP_{i,j} + \phi_3 S_{i,j} + \phi_4 SC_{i,j} + \phi_5 C_{i,j} + \phi_6 OP_{i,j}$$
$$+ \phi_7 W_{i,j}^t + \phi_8 CC_j + \varepsilon_{i,j}. \tag{5}$$

The same three well-being indicators (overall satisfaction with life, satisfaction with living standards and satisfaction with freedom to choose over life) and the EQP measures that turned out significant in the empirical exercises using the 2007 Gallup World Poll data (that is, satisfaction with educational system and considering education accessible) are used.

Table 7-12 presents the estimation results for the ladder question (overall satisfaction with life). In three out of four cases, the effect of educational quality perceptions on welfare holds, in sign and significance, after controlling for educational output. Moreover, the magnitude of the effect is slightly larger when using accessibility of education. Consequently, the relationship of educational quality perceptions and well-being is independent of educational output at the individual level. An interesting result is that educational output, in both its versions, no longer explains overall well-being. Perceptions are what matter for well-being. Reality may matter as well, but only inasmuch as it affects perceptions.

This is also true when satisfaction with living standards and freedom to choose are used as dependent variables (results available upon request). As before, when controlling for individual personality traits, the relationship between educational quality perceptions and life satisfaction measured through the ladder question is no longer significant. However, for the other two well-being indicators, the positive effect of education quality perceptions and the negative effect of educational attainment on well-being are unaffected.

Table 7-12. *Overall Satisfaction with Life*
1–10, ladder question

	Ordinary least squares estimation of Φ_1 and Φ_2			
	2007[a]			
	1	2	3	4
Satisfaction with educational systems in area/city (1 if satisfied)	0.1256	0.1272		
	−1.75	(1.79)*		
Education is accessible (1 if yes)			0.2123	0.2105
			(3.12)***	(3.16)***
Quality of educational system, 2006 (Competitiveness report, 1–7)				
Highest level of education completed (categorical)	−0.0175		−0.0145	
	−1.21		−0.87	
Incomplete primary[b]		−0.1117		−0.1158
		−1.04		−0.84
Complete primary[b]		0.0144		0.0695
		−0.15		−0.57
Incomplete secondary[b]		−0.1711		−0.1007
		(1.76)*		−1.05
Complete secondary[b]		−0.1521		−0.0782
		−1.4		−0.64
Incomplete technical school[b]		−0.2156		−0.2557
		−0.86		−1.14
Complete technical school[b]		−0.1552		0.014
		−0.79		−0.06
Incomplete university studies[b]		−0.226		−0.1976
		−1.15		−0.85
Complete university studies[b]		−0.1355		−0.0842
		−1.05		−0.58
Postgraduate studies[b]		−0.048		−0.0668
		−0.17		−0.21
Number of observations	5,665	5,678	5,739	5,754
Pseudo R-squared	0.428	0.429	0.423	0.424

Source: Authors' calculations based on Gallup World Poll (2007).

*Coefficient is statistically significant at the 10 percent level; **at the 5 percent level; ***at the 1 percent level; no asterisk means the coefficient is not different from zero with statistical significance.

Notes: Robust Z-statistics in parentheses. Errors clustered by country.

a. Controls: socioeconomic characteristics, hardwork, police, other perceptions, welfare, and country controls, among others.

b. Dummy variable, which takes the value of 1 if condition holds, 0 otherwise.

Conclusions

This paper analyzes the determinants of educational quality perceptions and their effect on self-reported well-being, an unexplored dimension in the welfare literature. Using a multi-country approach (based on the Gallup World Poll for 2006 and 2007), the study finds that educational quality perceptions are based on objective measures of educational quality, such as scores from international standardized tests. Therefore, individuals in countries whose students perform better are more satisfied with the existing educational system.

An interesting result is that individuals with higher levels of education are less satisfied with the quality of the education provided, suggesting that higher educational attainment raises a person's expectations on the quality of education to be provided. Interestingly, higher educational outcomes could result in lower satisfaction with the educational system and, possibly, in more political pressure to raise standards in the sector. This is a non-obvious mechanism that results in better educational outcomes.

Similarly, the study finds robust evidence indicating that educational quality perceptions are one of the determinants of self-reported well-being, measured by overall satisfaction with life, satisfaction with current living standards, and freedom to choose what to do with one's life. Even after controlling for educational output at the individual level, perceptions remain a significant factor at explaining well-being indicators, notwithstanding causality issues. These results suggest that mere perceptions are an important factor for reported well-being. Finally, a puzzling result obtained in the study is that the relation between individual educational attainment and well-being is ambiguous, depending on the indicator of well-being used.

In the exercises performed with the data base constructed, actual educational outcomes matter for well-being, but mostly because they affect perceptions. Moreover, there is no robust evidence of a direct and positive effect of educational attainment on well-being. However, we consider that further research is needed to test the robustness of these results.

In sum, this study shows that educational quality perceptions matter for the well-being of individuals. In this case, perceptions are aligned with objective indicators of education quality, such as standardized test scores. Latin American policymakers should then focus on measuring the quality of education at all levels. Poor results trigger dissatisfaction, which ultimately motivates policy changes.

References

Blanchflower, D. 2008. "International Evidence on Well-being." IZA Discussion Paper No. 3354. Bonn: Institute for the Study of Labor.

Breen, R., and J. Goldthorpe. 1997. "Explaining Educational Differentials: Towards a Formal Rational Action Theory." *Rationality and Society* 9 (3): 275–305.

Corporación Andina de Fomento (CAF). 2007. "Oportunidades en América Latina: Hacía una mejor política social." Reporte de Economía y Desarrollo.

Di Tella, R., R. MacCulloch, and A. Oswald. 2003. "The Macroeconomics of Happiness." *The Review of Economics and Statistics* 85 (4): 809–27.

Frey, B., and A. Stutzer. 2002. "Beyond Outcomes: Measuring Procedural Utility." Paper 63. Working Paper Series. Berkeley Program in Law and Economics.

Gallup World Poll. 2006. Gallup World Poll (www.gallup.com/consulting/worldpoll/24046/about.aspx).

———. 2007. Gallup World Poll (www.gallup.com/consulting/worldpoll/24046/about.aspx).

Helliwell, J. F. 2002. "How's Life? Combining Individual and National Variables to Explain Subjective Well-Being." Working Paper No. 11988. Cambridge, MA: National Bureau of Economic Research.

Navarro, J. C. 2007. "Education Reform as Reform of the State: Latin America since 1980." In E. Lora, ed., *The State of Reform in Latin America.* Washington D.C.: Inter-American Development Bank and Stanford University Press.

OECD (Organization for Economic Cooperation and Development). 2003. The PISA International Database (http://pisa2003.acer.edu.au/index.php).

———. 2006. The PISA International Database (http://pisa2006.acer.edu.au/).

Schwarze, J., and R. Winkelmann. 2005. "What Can Happiness Research Tell Us about Altruism? Evidence from the German Socio-Economic Panel." IZA Discussion Paper No. 1487. Bonn: Institute for the Study of Labor.

Thomas, V., Y. Wang, and X. Fan. 2001. "Measuring Education Inequality: Gini Coefficients of Education for 140 Countries, 1960–2000." Policy Research Working Paper 2525. Washington, D.C.: World Bank (later published in *Journal of Education Planning and Administration* 17).

TIMSS & PIRLS International Study Center. 2001. PIRLS 2001 International Database and User Guide (http://timss.bc.edu/pirls2001.html).

van Praag, B. M. S., and A. Ferrer-i-Carbonell. 2008. *Happiness Quantified: A Satisfaction Calculus Approach.* Oxford University Press.

Wilson, W. 1967 "Correlates of Avowed Happiness." *Psychological Bulletin* 67: 294–306.

World Economic Forum. 2006. *The Global Competitiveness Report 2006–2007: Creating an Improved Business Environment.* Geneva: World Economic Forum.

8

Job Insecurity and Life Satisfaction

NAERCIO AQUINO MENEZES-FILHO, RAPHAEL BOTURA CORBI,
AND ANDREA ZAITUNE CURI

High job turnover rates are a fact of life in any market economy, either developed or developing. Data compiled by the IDB for 12 countries show that gross rates of job creation and destruction range between 8 and 20 percent, adding up to total job turnover rates that range between 16 and 35 percent.[1] A total job turnover rate of 35 percent implies that about one in every three jobs is created or destroyed in a given year. In comparison, changes in net employment, that is, the difference between job creation and destruction, are substantially smaller. For instance, Brazil in the 1990s had an annual rate of job creation of 1.1 percent a year, as 16.1 percent of all jobs were created and 15 percent were lost per year. The two Latin American economies for which comparable data on turnover for the whole economy are available—Brazil and Mexico—show turnover rates that are within the ranges observed in developed countries. Job turnover is central to the process of resource reallocation, as existing firms expand or contract, and as new firms enter the market while others shut down.

If job turnover rates are high, *worker* turnover rates are frantic, both in developed and in developing countries. As firms close positions, workers are forced to relocate to new jobs. However, workers also move across jobs and between employment, unemployment, and inactivity as a result of their own personal decisions. Therefore worker turnover rates are higher than job turnover rates,

---

1. IDB (2004).

typically by a margin of three. That is, for each job created or destroyed in a year, approximately three workers either change from one job to another or move from or to unemployment (or leave the work force).

While developing countries are no different in these respects to developed countries, two other interrelated features make job insecurity a much more serious problem in developing countries. One is that, due to the extent of informality, large numbers of workers are not entitled to severance payments, unemployment benefits and other provisions to help them transit between jobs. The other is that, due to the lower income levels and lack of access to credit, workers are very seldom prepared to face spells of unemployment without facing severe economic hardship, including food insecurity. However, contrary to dualistic labor market theories, informality is not mainly the result of exclusion from the formal segments of the economy. Transitions between formality and informality are intense in both directions and, more often than not, workers opt out of the formal sector on their own will, attracted by the flexibility and the better economic prospects that independent employment offers them. Consistent with this, job satisfaction is not necessarily higher among workers with formal jobs.[2]

The main aim of this chapter is to examine the determinants of job insecurity and its consequences in terms of life satisfaction in Latin America.[3] There is now an extensive literature examining the determinants of job insecurity and its effects on job and life satisfaction.[4] The results tend to show that job security is very important for job satisfaction and that satisfaction at work is also very important for life satisfaction as a whole. A particular branch of this literature looks at the impact of employment protection and flexibility on job satisfaction and uncovers a positive relationship between the relaxation of the employment protection legislation that took place in many European countries and job satisfaction in these countries.[5] Other research also finds a positive relationship between work flexibility and job satisfaction in a sample of countries of the Organization for Economic Cooperation and Development (OECD).[6] In terms of social security, Auerbach, Genoni, and Pagés (2007) find that individual and household variables are important determinants of social security contributions, so that the demand for insurance may explain part of its variation within countries. In the next sections of this chapter we contribute to this line of research by using the results of the Gallup World Poll to shed some light on the relationship between job insecurity, formality and life satisfaction in Latin America.

---

2. IDB (2008, chapter 7).
3. In this chapter, the term *Latin America* includes the Caribbean.
4. See, for example, Blanchflower and Oswald (2004).
5. Salvatori (2006).
6. Origo and Pagani (2006).

Econometric Methodology

In order to explore how job insecurity affects life satisfaction, an econometric model that relates life satisfaction to perceived job insecurity and social security is estimated, after controlling for other potential determinants of life satisfaction. Job insecurity here basically means the perceived risk of losing the job, while social security is measured by the affiliation to a retirement plan for income mainte-nance. With a sample of individuals (i) living in Latin American countries (j), the equation to estimate is:

$$LIFESAT_{ij} = \alpha_j + \beta JOBINSEC_{ij} + \gamma SOCIALSEC_{ij} + \lambda X_{ij} + \lambda W_{ij} + \varepsilon_{ij}, \quad (1)$$

with α_j being the country-specific fixed effects; X_{ij} the demographic character-istics (such as age, education, gender, marital status); and W_{ij} the measures of household assets. In some specifications the country fixed-effects is replaced with country-specific indicators of labor market rigidity, such as the ones collected by Botero and others (2004). Since it is only possible to examine the impact of job insecurity on life satisfaction for those individuals who actually have a job, who are not a random selection of the country samples, it was necessary to use the Heckman's two-step estimator to fix the selection problem.[7]

Regression (1) (and the regressions below) may suffer from endogeneity prob-lems. Omitted variables, such as personality traits toward optimism, will bias the estimates if they are correlated with the regressors (as more optimistic people may have a psychological tendency to declare themselves more satisfied with their lives and to see their jobs as more secure).[8] This difficulty could be overcome by allow-ing individual fixed-effects in the equation or by instrumental variable estima-tion. Since panel data are not available in the Gallup Surveys, it is not possible to control for individual fixed-effects in the regressions. As recognized in the lit-erature on life satisfaction, it is difficult to find convincing instruments to solve the endogeneity problem.[9] This chapter tries to obtain some reassurance in this respect, however, by controlling for individual perceptions of past or future life satisfaction in order to capture whether the individual is optimistic or pessimistic at the time of interview. Since the life satisfaction measure is ordinal, equation (1) is estimated with a Multinomial Ordered Probit model.[10]

7. Heckman (1979).

8. In other words, if $Corr(c_i, JOBQUALITY) \neq 0$, where c_i is the unobserved individual fixed effect, then $E[u_i/JOBQUALITY] \neq 0$ and our estimators of β will be inconsistent.

9. Di Tella and others (2003).

10. This is an efficient model to be applied in cases where the dependent variable is discrete and whose values establish some sort of non-linear ranking of the possible outcomes. An ordinary least squares (OLS) regression in this case would not be efficient due to the ordinal nature of the data. However, as suggested by van Praag and Ferrer-i-Carbonell (2007), in practice the OLS and the ordered Probit methods render almost identical coefficients, except for a scale factor. OLS is used in some regressions below as a robustness exercise and as a step previous to the use of the Heckman esti-mator, which uses OLS.

This chapter also investigates the determinants of job insecurity and social security. In order to do that, these measures are regressed on a series of individual-level (i) and country-level (j) objective indicators of working conditions, controlling for individual specific demographic characteristics:

$$JOBINSEC_{ij} = \alpha_j + \beta Z_{ij} + \theta X_{ij} + \lambda W_{ij} + SOCSEC + \varepsilon_{ij} \qquad (2a)$$

$$SOCSEC_{ij} = \alpha_j + \beta Z_{ij} + \theta X_{ij} + \lambda W_{ij} + \varepsilon_{ij}, \qquad (2b)$$

where Z_{ij} represents objective indicators of the labor market, such as occupation and sector of activity, including the Botero and others[11] national level index that measures labor market regulations.[12] $JOBINSEC_{ij}$ is a dummy variable that equals 1 if individual i reports joblessness as a likely event in the following six months, and $SOCSEC_{ij}$ is a variable indicating whether there is contribution to any form of social security.

Data

The main source of data is the 2007 wave of the Gallup World Poll, which has extensive information on the quality of life of individuals from 23 countries in Latin America and the Caribbean (for a more detailed description see chapter 2). Table 8-1 describes the main variables used in this chapter. Life satisfaction is measured through the ladder question (wp16) discussed in other chapters. Variables of interest from the Gallup World Poll that are specific to this chapter's topic include whether or not the individual is satisfied with her job, whether or not perceives a risk of losing her job in the next six months and whether or not is affiliated to a retirement plan (an indicator of being in the formal segment of the labour market).

Figure 8-1 shows the share of respondents in each country that feared they could lose their jobs in the next six months. There is a great deal of variation in this proportion across countries, ranging from more than 25 percent of the respondents in Mexico to about 10 percent in Paraguay. The figure shows also the share of respondents that contributed to a retirement plan in each country. This percentage exhibits a lot of variation across the Latin American countries, from 66 percent in Chile and Uruguay to about 20 percent in Bolivia, Honduras Guatemala and Paraguay. Figure 8-2 compares the rates of life satisfaction (on a 0–10 scale) with those of job satisfaction (percentages satisfied). The correlation between both at the country level for the Latin American countries is positive, as expected, while the correlation between job satisfaction and job insecurity is negative, but rather moderate.

11. Botero and others (2004).
12. This index captures the legal protection of workers in 85 countries in 1997 by gathering data on the three components of the national legal framework for worker protection: (i) employment laws; (ii) industrial (collective) relations laws, and (iii) social security laws.

Table 8-1. *Description of Regressions Variables*

Variable	Description	Mean
Individual-Level Subjective		
Life satisfaction	Self-reported life satisfaction, from 0 to 10	6.2
Job satisfaction	1, if satisfied with job	0.9
Perceived health	1, is satisfied with health	0.7
Living standards	1, if satisfied with standard of living	0.7
Future life satisfaction	Self-reported life satisfaction 5 years from now, from 0 to 10	7.1
Past life satisfaction	Self-reported life satisfaction 5 years ago, from 0 to 10	5.7
Job insecurity	1, if one thinks he/she could lose the job in six months	0.2
Individual-Level Objective		
Female	1, if female	0.6
Job	1, if employed	0.4
Income	Monthly household per capita income in US$ adjusted for PPP	162.9
Age	Age in years	40.2
Phone	1, if landline telephone at home	0.6
Electricity	1, if electricity at home	1.0
Television	1, if television set at home	0.9
Computer	1, is computer at home	0.3
Free hospital	1, if health care is paid by the social security system	0.4
Retirement plan	1, if affiliated to a retirement plan	0.4
Education secondary	1, if access to secondary education	0.4
Education high school	1, if access to high school education	0.1
Education college	1, if access to college education	0.2
Country-Level Indicators[a]		
Botero index	Botero and others (2004) index that measures labor market regulations	1.6
Employment index	(i) employment laws	1.7
Industrial relations	(ii) industrial (collective) relations laws	1.3
Social security	(iii) social security laws	1.9
Unemployment	National unemployment rate	0.1
LGDP	GDP per capita (logarithm), 2005	9.6
Inflation	Inflation rate 2006, CPI	0.1
Doing Business Variables, 2006[a]		
Difficulty hiring	Difficulty of hiring index	43.6
Rigidity hours	Rigidity of hours index	42.5
Difficulty firing	Difficulty of firing index	27.7
Rigidity employment	Rigidity of employment index	37.9
Labor costs	Nonwage labor cost (% of salary)	15.8
Firing costs	Firing costs (weeks of wages)	60.2

Source: Authors' calculations based on Gallup World Poll (2007).

a. Country-Level Indicators' scores range between 0 and 3. Doing Business Variables' scores range between 0 and 100.

Figure 8-1. *Job Insecurity and Retirement Plan*

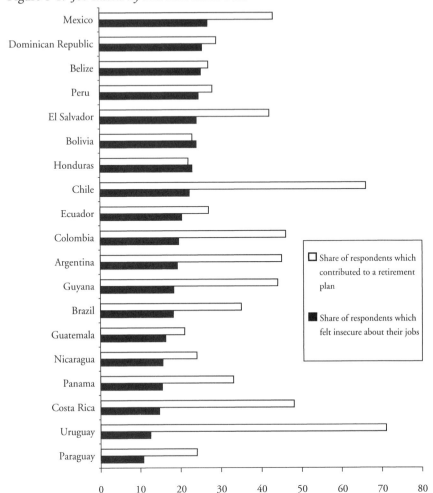

Source: Authors' calculations based on Gallup World Poll (2007).

How Job Conditions Affect Life Satisfaction

To see how job conditions may influence life satisfaction, it is convenient to explore first how having a job relates to job satisfaction. If we start with a simple (ordered probit) regression between both variables, we find that there is a positive and very significant correlation (column 1 of table 8-2). Since life satisfaction may be influenced by a host of other individual variables, column 2 includes other socio-economic and demographic characteristics. Although that reduces the magnitude of the effect of having a job, the coefficient remains statistically significant.

Figure 8-2. *Life and Job Satisfaction*

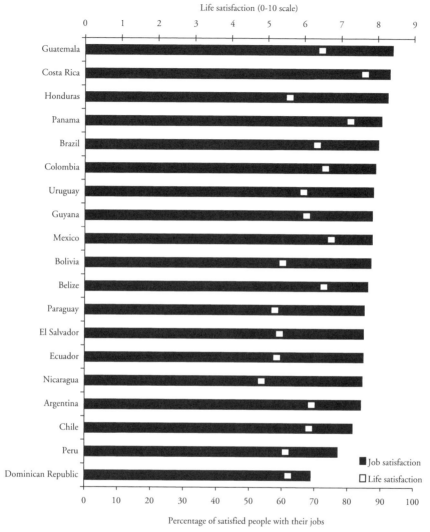

Source: Authors' calculations based on Gallup World Poll (2007).

Column 3 includes the individual assessment of past and future life satisfaction to control for the personality traits (and the mind frame of the respondents when answering the questionnaire). As it turns out, these variables are highly correlated with present life satisfaction, but they hardly alter the job status effect. Finally, column 4 includes the country dummies, which have only a minor impact on the job status effect, which means that the cross-sectional relationship also holds within countries.

Table 8-2. *Having a Job and Its Influence on Life Satisfaction*

	1	2	3	4
Employed	0.14 ***	0.05 **	0.05 **	0.07 ***
	(6.81)	(2.45)	(2.37)	(3.02)
Female		0.06 ***	0.05 **	0.07 ***
		(2.95)	(2.17)	(3.15)
Age		−1.97 ***	−0.73 **	−1.03 ***
		(−5.900)	(−2.168)	(−3.017)
Age squared		−1.63 ***	0.79 **	1.19 ***
		(4.46)	(2.15)	(3.21)
Phone		0.22 ***	0.10 ***	0.10 ***
		(9.95)	(4.62)	(4.05)
Electricity		0.27 ***	0.14 **	0.17 **
		(4.18)	(2.21)	(2.55)
Television		0.29 ***	0.20 ***	0.18 ***
		(6.46)	(4.34)	(3.85)
Computer		0.12 ***	0.09 ***	0.09 ***
		(4.66)	(3.48)	(3.21)
Satisfied with health		0.31 ***	0.20 ***	0.17 ***
		(10.46)	(6.84)	(5.63)
Satisfied with living standard		0.57 ***	0.41 ***	0.39 ***
		(25.40)	(17.76)	(17.00)
Past life satisfaction			0.16 ***	0.15 ***
			(37.14)	(33.93)
Expected future life satisfaction			0.24 ***	0.24 ***
			(56.26)	(54.78)
Number of observations	10,804	10,804	10,804	10,804
Dummies				
Country	. . .	. . .	. . .	Yes
Education	. . .	Yes	Yes	Yes
Marital status	. . .	Yes	Yes	Yes

Source: Authors' calculations based on Gallup World Poll (2007).

*Coefficient is statistically significant at the 10 percent level; **at the 5 percent level; ***at the 1 percent level; no asterisk means the coefficient is not statistically different from zero.

. . . Not applicable.

Notes: Estimates are the ordered probit coefficients. Dependent variable is life satisfaction. The values in parentheses are *t*-statistics.

The fact that having a job systematically improves subjective wellbeing, even when holding personal real income constant (and many other individual characteristics), corroborates the idea that unemployment imposes non-pecuniary costs on individuals. These extra costs can be thought of as a consequence of the fact that jobs are not only sources of income, but they also provide feelings of self-esteem, social identity and responsibility. Similar results have been found by other authors (see Clark and Oswald, 1994). It may be argued that the causality runs in the

Figure 8-3. *Marginal Effect of Being Employed across Levels of Life Satisfaction, 0–10 Scale*

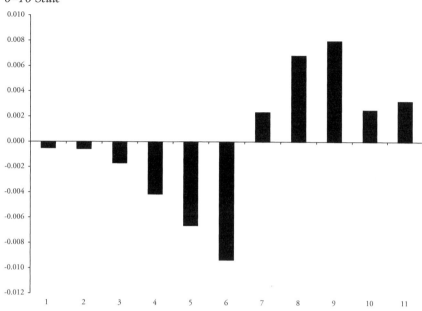

Source: Authors' calculations based on Gallup World Poll (2007).

opposite direction, that is, unhappy people are not good employees and, therefore, are unemployed more frequently. Using panel data, Winkelmann and Winkelmann (1998) find evidence that joblessness indeed has a negative impact on well-being.

With respect to the other variables, females report higher life satisfaction than males, the number of children has a negative impact on wellbeing, life satisfaction has a convex relationship with age, good health is very important for life satisfaction, as is household income, living standards and household assets.

Figure 8-3 shows the marginal effect of being employed on the probability of reporting each level of life satisfaction. The pattern is very revealing: being employed reduces the probability that a person positions herself on step six or lower, and increases the probability of steps seven or higher. But, interestingly, the largest negative effect occurs, not at the lowest steps, but at the middle ones, and especially at step six. Therefore, being unemployed does not seem to make a big difference for people severely unsatisfied with their lives, but it does for people beyond a certain level of life satisfaction. Notice also that the largest positive effects occur at steps eight and nine, suggesting that having employment makes an important difference to reach relatively high levels of life satisfaction, but not to get to the best possible life (where other things may be needed). This echoes the well-known "hierarchy of needs" approach used in psychology, originally proposed by Maslow (1943). However, employment (or more precisely, security of employment), is placed by Maslow in one of the lowest levels of needs (as part of the safety and security needs), only ahead of the physiological needs, but below love and belonging, and esteem.

Table 8-3 explores the relationship between job satisfaction and life satisfaction (estimated only for those individuals with a job at the time of the survey). As expected, those that are satisfied with their jobs also tend to be satisfied with their life. The direct relationship between both variables (column 1) weakens somewhat when socio-economic and demographic characteristics are controlled for (column 2), but it remains statistically significant. The relationship remains after controlling for past and expected future life satisfaction, in an attempt to isolate personality traits (column 3) and also if country dummies are included (column 4). Therefore, job satisfaction seems to influence life satisfaction in a significant way. In contrast, having a retirement plan, which is often considered an essential component of a good job, does not seem very important for life satisfaction (columns 2 to 4).[13]

In column 5 we report the results of OLS regressions, which treat the reported life satisfaction answers as cardinal values. The results do not display any qualitative change, despite their change in magnitude. In column 6 we again use the OLS model to control for selectivity bias, using Heckman's traditional two-step approach. Again the results do not change qualitatively (with the coefficient on the Mill's ratio being statistically not significant).

Table 8-4 reports estimates of the relationship between job insecurity, affiliation to a retirement plan and life satisfaction, only for those individuals that currently have a job. Estimates of column 1 reveal that those that feel threatened of losing their jobs in the next six months tend to have a lower probability of reporting high levels of life satisfaction. This relationships weakens somewhat but remains statistically significant when we control for socio-economic and demographic characteristics. Respondents affiliated to a retirement plan tend to report higher levels of life satisfaction, but this effect turns not significant when socio-economic and demographic characteristics are included in the regression. Controlling for past and expected future life satisfaction and for country dummies (column 3) does not qualitatively alter these estimated effects. Figure 8-4 presents the estimated marginal effects of job insecurity on life satisfaction by steps (on the basis of the results in column 4). Job insecurity increases the probability of reporting intermediate levels of satisfaction and decreases the probability of high satisfaction levels, the mirror pattern found for employment in figure 8-3.

Column 4 of table 8-4 includes an interaction between retirement plans and job insecurity to check whether those in the formal sector are more likely to be

---

13. The retirement plan variable was omitted from table 8-3 for this reason.

Table 8-3. *Job Satisfaction and Its Relationship with Life Satisfaction*

	1	2	3	4	5 OLS	6 Heckman
Job satisfaction	0.54***	0.24***	0.22***	0.20***	0.31***	0.36***
	(12.24)	(5.05)	(4.51)	(4.04)	(4.15)	(4.78)
Income (logarithm)		0.13***	0.08***	0.09***	0.14***	−0.10
		(7.28)	(4.31)	(4.63)	(4.56)	(−0.38)
Female		0.00	0.03	0.06	0.08	2.74
		(0.11)	(0.87)	(1.63)	(1.50)	(0.63)
Age		−1.11	0.09	−0.52	−0.73	−3.21
		(−1.64)	(0.13)	(−0.75)	(−0.68)	(−0.61)
Age squared		0.78	0.05	0.77	1.08	0.03
		(0.98)	(0.06)	(0.94)	(0.86)	(0.59)
Phone		0.14***	0.02	0.02	0.02	0.33*
		(3.86)	(0.66)	(0.41)	(0.32)	(1.81)
Electricity		0.30***	0.20*	0.18	0.31*	0.27**
		(2.63)	(1.71)	(1.59)	(1.72)	(2.00)
Television		0.18**	0.15*	0.13	0.18	0.19***
		(2.25)	(1.88)	(1.55)	(1.42)	(3.01)
Computer		0.13***	0.12***	0.10**	0.15**	0.31***
		(3.35)	(2.99)	(2.49)	(2.34)	(3.40)
Satisfied with health		0.25***	0.18***	0.16***	0.24***	0.59***
		(4.94)	(3.47)	(3.02)	(3.00)	(9.35)
Satisfied with living standard		0.51***	0.38***	0.36***	0.54***	0.26***
		(13.63)	(9.90)	(9.24)	(9.09)	(22.40)
Past life satisfaction			0.17***	0.16***	0.24***	0.40***
			(24.54)	(22.47)	(22.71)	(36.63)
Expected future life satisfaction			0.25***	0.25***	0.39***	0.36***
			(35.93)	(34.51)	(37.26)	(4.78)
Inverted Mills ratio						0.28
						(0.56)
Number of observations	4,350	4,350	4,350	4,350	4,350	4,350
Dummies						
Country	. . .	. . .	. . .	Yes	Yes	Yes
Occupation	. . .	Yes	Yes	Yes	. . .	. . .
Marital status	. . .	Yes	Yes	Yes	Yes	Yes
Education	. . .	Yes	Yes	Yes	Yes	Yes

Source: Authors' calculations based on Gallup World Poll (2007).

. . . Not applicable.

*Coefficient is statistically significant at the 10 percent level; **at the 5 percent level; ***at the 1 percent level; no asterisk means the coefficient is not statistically different from zero

Notes: Unless otherwise mentioned, estimates are ordered probit coefficients. Life satisfaction is the dependent variable. The values in parentheses are t-statistics. OLS = Ordinary Least Squares.

Table 8-4. *Relationship between Job Insecurity, Retirement Plan, and Life Satisfaction*

	1	2	3	4	5
Job insecurity	−0.28***	−0.18***	−0.11***	−0.07	−0.10
	(−7.11)	(−4.33)	(−2.71)	(−1.37)	(−1.23)
Has retirement plan	0.25***	0.02	0.02	0.04	0.07
	(7.49)	(0.60)	(0.47)	(1.04)	(1.14)
Job insecurity * retirement				−0.13	−0.21*
				(−1.45)	(−1.59)
Female		−0.01	0.04	0.04	0.00
		(−0.277)	(1.23)	(1.23)	(0.01)
Age		−1.22*	−0.31	−0.32	0.79
		(−1.75)	(−0.44)	(−0.44)	(0.25)
Age squared		0.60	0.30	0.30	−1.01
		(0.74)	(0.36)	(0.37)	(−0.26)
Log Income		0.15***	0.09***	0.09***	0.16***
		(7.09)	(3.80)	(3.82)	(3.27)
Satisfied with living standard		0.54***	0.39***	0.39***	0.63***
		(14.51)	(10.30)	(10.31)	(10.14)
Past life satisfaction			0.17***	0.17***	0.24***
			(22.63)	(22.63)	(22.54)
Expected future life satisfaction			0.26***	0.26***	0.39***
			(33.91)	(33.91)	(33.91)
Number of observations	4,098	4,098	4,098	4,098	4,098
Dummies					
Country	. . .	. . .	Yes	Yes	Yes
Household	. . .	Yes	Yes	Yes	Yes
Marital	. . .	Yes	Yes	Yes	Yes
Occupation	. . .	Yes	Yes	Yes	Yes
Education	. . .	Yes	Yes	Yes	Yes

Source: Authors' calculations based on Gallup World Poll (2007).

. . . Not applicable.

*Coefficient is statistically significant at the 10 percent level; **at the 5 percent level; ***at the 1 percent level; no asterisk means the coefficient is not statistically different from zero.

Notes: Estimates are the ordered probit coefficients. Life satisfaction is the dependent variable. The values in parentheses are *t*-statistics.

affected by job insecurity. The coefficient of the interaction term is marginally statistically significant (at the 10 percent level) with a negative sign, which suggests that formal sector workers tend to experience a stronger loss of life satisfaction when they fear that they might lose their jobs (this does not imply that they consider more likely to lose their jobs than informal workers).

The reason for this cannot be discerned with our dataset, but it may be due to the fact that informal sector workers are more able to withstand higher doses of economic stability, or that they are more used to move from one job to another.

Figure 8-4. *Marginal Effects of Perceived Job Insecurity across Levels of Life Satisfaction*

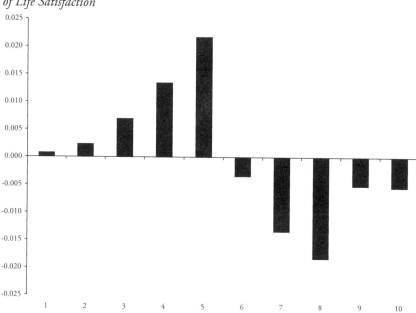

Source: Authors' calculations based on Gallup World Poll (2007).

It may also be that they are more confident of their own capabilities as income earners. Controlling for selection (column 5) does not alter these main results.

Since the impact of job insecurity on life satisfaction might be stronger in more vulnerable groups of individuals, in a set of additional regressions (not presented) we included interaction variables combining job insecurity with the respondent's age, gender, household income, number of kids and household condition. In none of these cases did we find significant coefficients, which implies that the effect of job insecurity does not seem to vary substantially across groups.

The influence of job insecurity on life satisfaction does not seem to be an artifact of the database used for these estimations. Using the Latinobarómetro database we have confirmed the same results, and that it is robust to the inclusion of all available demographic and socio-economic characteristics of the respondents, as well as to the inclusion of country dummies.

Determinants of Job Insecurity

Since job insecurity clearly has deleterious effects on life satisfaction, it is relevant to explore what lies behind people's fears of job insecurity. Do those fears mainly reflect personality traits or personal characteristics, such as gender, age, family size

Table 8-5. *Determinants of Job Insecurity*

	1	2	3	4 Heckman
Female	−0.03**	−0.02*	−0.02*	−0.08
	(−1.99)	(−1.92)	(−1.92)	(−1.56)
Age	−0.21	−0.30	−0.30	0.43
	(−0.78)	(−1.11)	(−1.12)	(0.46)
Age squared	−0.04	0.04	0.04	−0.84
	(−0.13)	−0.12	−0.13	(−0.74)
Income (logarithm)	−0.01*	−0.01	−0.01	−0.01
	(−1.67)	(−1.12)	(−1.15)	(−0.34)
Has retirement plan	0.00	0.00		
	(0.18)	(−0.15)		
Satisfied with health	−0.03	−0.03	−0.03	−0.01
	(−1.51)	(−1.37)	(−1.37)	(−0.45)
Satisfied with living standards	−0.10***	−0.10***	−0.10***	−0.10***
	(−6.76)	(−6.79)	(−6.80)	(−6.94)
Past life satisfaction	0.00	0.00	0.00	0.00
	(−0.36)	(−0.12)	(−0.12)	(−0.52)
Expected future life satisfaction	−0.01***	−0.01***	−0.01***	−0.01***
	(−3.14)	(−4.58)	(−4.58)	(−4.11)
Number of observations	4,335	4,335	4,335	4,335
Dummies				
Country	. . .	Yes	Yes	Yes
Occupation	. . .	Yes	Yes	Yes
Marital status	. . .	Yes	Yes	Yes
Household assets	. . .	Yes	Yes	Yes

Source: Authors' calculations based on Gallup World Poll (2007).

. . . Not applicable.

*Coefficient is statistically significant at the 10 percent level; **at the 5 percent level; ***at the 1 percent level; no asterisk means the coefficient is not statistically different from zero.

Notes: Estimates are probit coefficients. Job insecurity is the dependent variable. The values in parentheses are *t*-statistics.

or marital status, that leave little room for policy intervention? Are those fears stronger in people more economically and socially vulnerable, such as the poor or the less educated? Is job insecurity lessened by the adoption of more stringent labor codes that make job dismissals more difficult for firms? Is job insecurity related to the macroeconomic situation of the country?

Table 8-5 offers responses to the first two questions. Column 1 includes the basic demographic and socio-economic variables and shows that women tend to be less insecure about their jobs than males and those satisfied with their health and with their living standards also tend to have less job insecurity. As expected, individuals with more optimistic expectations about the future are less likely to feel insecure about their jobs. These results suggest that either there is a matching process between certain types of jobs and certain types of individuals—something highly unlikely—or that the feeling of insecurity varies systematically along with these characteristics. In order to test that these results are not merely the result of differences across countries, column 2 includes country dummies to the basic specification, and the results remain basically unchanged. Interestingly, being enrolled in a retirement plan, which is equivalent to having a formal job, does not affect the feelings of job insecurity. Column 3 shows that the previous results are not altered when this explanatory variable in excluded from the regressions. Finally, in order to verify that a selection bias is not at play in the results, column 4 implements Heckman's correction with no substantive changes in the results.

The regressions included in table 8-6 are aimed at answering the two remaining questions from the list above. Since the purpose of these regressions is to assess the influence of country-level variables on individual-level job insecurity, estimates are substantially less precise than those presented so far because the variance of these (additional) explanatory variables is very limited (in all the regressions, individual characteristics are also included as regressors). The results of column 1 indicate that workers tend to feel more insecure in larger countries, but the unemployment rate does not seem to matter much, but these effects may be due to other country-specific omitted variables. In order to test the possible association of job insecurity with different aspects of the labor code, column 2 includes a measure of labor market rigidity (from Botero and others, 2004, as described in table 8-1), and column 3 disaggregates this overall measure into its three main sub-components: employment security, industrial relations protection, and social security protection. Only the last of these three sub-components seems to have some effect on perceived job insecurity: in countries with a more 'protective' social security legislation, job insecurity is somewhat lower.

The remaining columns of the table make use of an alternative set of employment rigidity indicators, compiled by the World Bank's *Doing Business* publication.[14] A summary indicator of employment rigidity from this source is *positively* related to job insecurity, although again the estimates are not statistically significant. When the summary indicator is separated by components, rigidity of hours seems to decrease job insecurity, and firing costs (in terms of weeks of wages) seem to *increase* job insecurity. Therefore, if anything, these results suggest that some aspects of the protection offered by the labor codes have the unintended consequence of creating a stronger feeling of insecurity. This would be consistent with the finding that higher employment rigidity reduces job creation. However, these results have to be taken with a pinch of salt due to the limited variability of the explanatory variables, as mentioned, and because the labor market legislation indexes could be correlated with other unobserved country-specific variables

14. World Bank (2008).

Table 8-6. *Labor Legislation and Job Insecurity*

	1	2	3	4	5
GDP (logarithm)	0.03*	0.00	0.01	0.03**	0.05***
	(1.94)	(0.12)	(0.51)	(2.17)	(2.74)
Unemployment	−0.05	0.26	0.37	−0.09	0.02
	(−0.25)	(0.76)	(1.02)	(−0.42)	(0.11)
Employment security index			−0.01		
			(−0.25)		
Industrial relations protection			−0.01		
			(−0.25)		
Social security protection			−0.04		
			(−1.43)		
Botero index		−0.04			
		(−1.17)			
Employment rigidity index				0.00	
				(0.99)	
Difficulty hiring					−0.03
					(−0.764)
Rigidity hours					−0.14**
					(−2.226)
Difficulty firing					0.00
					(0.17)
Labor costs					0.02
					(0.23)
Firing costs					0.03
					(1.56)
Number of observations	3,989	2,734	2,734	3,989	3,706
Occupation dummies	Yes	Yes	Yes	Yes	Yes
Household assets dummies	Yes	Yes	Yes	Yes	Yes
Marital status dummies	Yes	Yes	Yes	Yes	Yes

Source: Authors' calculations based on Gallup World Poll (2007).

*Coefficient is statistically significant at the 10 percent level; **at the 5 percent level; ***at the 1 percent level; no asterisk means the coefficient is not statistically different from zero.

Notes: Estimates are probit coefficients. Job insecurity is the dependent variable. The values in parentheses are *t*-statistics. The scores on the following indexes range from 0 to 3: employment security index, industrial relations protection, social security protection, and the Botero index. Meanwhile, the scores on the following indexes range from 0 to 100: employment rigidity index, difficulty hiring, rigidity hours, difficulty firing, labor costs, and firing costs.

(which we cannot test directly, since country dummies cannot be included in regressions that have country-level explanatory variables).

To try to solve this problem, the regressions in table 8-7 do include country dummies and, instead of using the labor code indices as separate explanatory variables, interact them with demographic variables. With this trick we are still unable to know what is the effect of the labor code on job insecurity on the whole sample of individuals, but we can check if some groups of individuals are more affected

Table 8-7. *Labor Legislation and Job Insecurity: Interactions*

	1	2	3	4	5
Firing costs*age	−0.0155**				
	(−2.34)				
Firing costs*age squared	0.0006***				
	(2.59)				
Firing costs*female		0.0116			
		(0.34)			
Firing costs* income			−0.0303**		
			(−2.09)		
Firing costs*unemployment				−1.6600***	
				(−3.79)	
Firing costs*retirement plan					−0.0080
					(−0.45)
Number of observations	3,792	3,792	3,792	3,706	3,792
Household assets dummies	Yes	Yes	Yes	Yes	Yes
Marital status dummies	Yes	Yes	Yes	Yes	Yes
Occupation dummies	Yes	Yes	Yes	Yes	Yes

Source: Authors' calculations based on Gallup World Poll (2007).

*Coefficient is statistically significant at the 10 percent level; **at the 5 percent level; ***at the 1 percent level; no asterisk means the coefficient is not statistically different from zero.

Notes: Estimates are probit coefficients. Job insecurity is the dependent variable. The values in parentheses are *t*-statistics.

than others. Interestingly, it seems that firing costs lead to *less* job insecurity for prime age workers but to more insecurity for older workers. Moreover, they tend to lead to *less* job insecurity when household income and unemployment rates are higher. Another way of interpreting this result is to say that the effect of the country's unemployment rate on job insecurity is lower when firing costs are high. This makes sense because those already employed have lower risk of losing their jobs, but since higher hiring costs lower job creation, unemployment rates are higher. Consistent with this interpretation, we also find that for those affiliated to a retirement plan (that is, belonging to the formal sector), higher firing costs lead to lower job insecurity. However, the effect is statistically insignificant.

Who Affiliates to a Retirement Plan?

Contrary to expectations, being affiliated to a retirement plan does little to dispel job insecurity fears. Since affiliation to such plans is required in formal jobs, we interpret that result as evidence that job insecurity is unrelated to being part of the informal or the informal sector. Even worse, some of the evidence presented suggests that some of the legal provisions aimed at improving job security and stability may produce exactly the opposite effect, at least for some groups. We now

Table 8-8. *Determinants of Retirement Plan Affiliation*

	1	2	3 Heckman
Secondary education	0.10***	0.14***	0.11***
	(4.61)	(6.45)	(5.76)
High school education	0.18***	0.30***	0.25***
	(4.47)	(7.92)	(6.18)
College education	0.10***	0.30***	0.26***
	(3.21)	(10.95)	(8.20)
Female	−0.06***	−0.04**	−0.03
	(−3.33)	(−2.17)	(−0.56)
Age	1.90***	2.02***	1.48*
	(5.30)	(5.64)	(1.68)
Age squared	−1.92***	−2.22***	−1.60
	(−4.53)	(−5.27)	(−1.51)
Satisfied with health	−0.03	−0.02	−0.03
	(−1.32)	(−0.89)	(−1.33)
Income (logarithm)	0.09***	0.07***	0.06***
	(9.17)	(6.78)	(4.58)
Past life satisfaction	0.00	0.00	0.00
	(−0.39)	(−0.340)	(−0.66)
Expected future life satisfaction	0.00	0.00	0.00
	(0.69)	(1.18)	(1.07)
Job Insecurity	−0.01	—	—
	(−0.69)		
Satisfied with living standard	0.04**	0.04**	0.03**
	(2.21)	(2.45)	(2.05)
Number of observations	4,226	4,335	4,335
Dummies			
Country	. . .	Yes	Yes
Occupation	Yes	Yes	. . .
Household assets	Yes	Yes	Yes
Marital status	Yes	Yes	Yes

Source: Authors' calculations based on Gallup World Poll (2007).
*Coefficient is statistically significant at the 10 percent level; **at the 5 percent level; ***at the 1 percent level; no asterisk means the coefficient is not statistically different from zero.
Notes: Estimates are the probit coefficients. Affiliation with a retirement plan is the dependent variable. The values in parentheses are *t*-statistics.

examine how a series of household and country-level indicators influence the probability that an individual will contribute to a retirement plan, which indicates that he/she is working in the formal sector.

The results in table 8-8 indicate that the probability of having a retirement plan increases strongly with education and age, as found by other authors.[15] Males,

15. See Auerbach, Genoni and Pagés (2007).

Table 8-9. *Legislation and Retirement Plan Affiliation*

	1	2	3	4	5
GDP (logarithm)	0.49***	0.57***	0.36***	0.42***	0.54***
	(9.44)	(8.71)	(4.56)	(7.62)	(8.53)
Unemployment rate	−1.86**	−3.41***	−5.36***	−1.45*	−0.51
	(−2.53)	(−2.89)	(−4.30)	(−1.94)	(−0.63)
Employment security index			−0.48***		
			(−5.11)		
Industrial relations protection			−0.32***		
			(−4.51)		
Social security protection			0.22**		
			(2.43)		
Botero index		−0.69***			
		(−5.30)			
Employment rigidity index				−0.55***	
				(−3.51)	
Difficulty hiring					−0.42***
					(−3.11)
Rigidity hours					0.01
					(0.06)
Difficulty firing					−0.21**
					(−2.19)
Labor costs					−1.28***
					(−4.20)
Firing costs					−0.10
					(−1.53)
Number of observations	4,015	2,754	2,754	4,015	3,729
Household assets dummies	Yes	Yes	Yes	Yes	Yes
Marital status dummies	Yes	Yes	Yes	Yes	Yes
Occupation dummies	Yes	Yes	Yes	Yes	Yes

Source: Authors' calculations based on Gallup World Poll (2007).

*Coefficient is statistically significant at the 10 percent level; **at the 5 percent level; ***at the 1 percent level; no asterisk means the coefficient is not statistically different from zero.

Notes: Estimates are probit coefficients. The scores on the following indexes range from 0 to 3: employment security index, industrial relations protection, social security protection, and the Botero index. Meanwhile. the scores on the following indexes range from 0 to 100: employment rigidity index, difficulty hiring, rigidity hours, difficulty firing, labor costs, and firing costs. Affiliation with a retirement plan is the dependent variable. The values in parentheses are *t*-statistics.

individuals with higher income, those more satisfied with their living standards and those with more household assets are also more likely to contribute to a retirement plan. Since the inclusion of country dummies does not affect these conclusions, it can be said that they are not the result of differences in the legislation, or other macro-level variables across countries. However, as explored in the regressions of table 8-9, national-level differences do affect the average rates of affiliation, and by extension of formality, by country.

Results of column 1 of table 8-9 show that contribution to a retirement plan is higher in richer countries and where unemployment is lower. Column 2 indicates that countries with a more restrictive legislation (as measured by the Botero Index) tend to have a lower share of its population contributing toward a retirement plan. Moreover, the effect is stronger when the employment regulation and the laws regulating industrial relations are more protective. The same conclusions are obtained when the "Doing Business" indicators are used: the summary index (employment rigidity index) is also negatively related to the probability of having a retirement plan, as are two of its sub-components: the difficulty of hiring and, especially, the level of non-wage labor costs (represented by the *Labor Cost* variable in table 8-9). In additional regressions we also tested if different socioeconomic groups are affected more severely by the labor legislation. We found that the relationship between income and affiliation to the retirement plans is stronger in the countries with more rigid labor codes. Therefore, more protective labor codes produce the unintended effect of protecting more the high-income workers while discouraging lower-income workers from taking formal jobs.

Conclusions

In this chapter we have used the 2007 wave of the Gallup World Poll to examine the subjective implications and the possible reasons of the fears of job insecurity in the region. On average 20 percent of Latin American workers feel insecure about their jobs, with the numbers varying from about 10 percent in Paraguay to 27 percent in Mexico.

Having a regular job has a positive and significant impact on life satisfaction, even conditional on health, wealth and other subjective measures that capture the respondent's psychological traits and frame of mind at the time of the interview. Job satisfaction is also strongly related to life satisfaction. But those workers that fear losing their job suffer a severe decline in life satisfaction.

Formal employment, as measured by affiliation to a retirement plan, represents a bare 40 percent of total employment, with the lowest rates occurring in Bolivia, Guatemala, Honduras and Paraguay (about 20 percent) and the highest reaching 66 percent in Chile and 71 percent in Uruguay.

Surprisingly for those who associate good quality jobs with formal employment, workers in formal employments are no more satisfied with their lives than those in informal occupations. And contrary to expectations, in spite of all the regulations aimed at protecting formal jobs, formal workers feel more strongly the negative effects of job insecurity on their lives.

Individuals working in countries with more regulated social security systems seem to feel more confident about their jobs, while the opposite occurs in countries where firing costs are high. Finally, informality tends to be much higher in countries with more regulated labor markets, especially in the cases where hiring new workers is costly and non-wage costs are high.

References

Auerbach, P., E. Genoni, and C. Pagés. 2007. "Social Security Coverage and the Labor Market in Developing Countries." RES Working Paper 4421. Washington, D.C.: Inter-American Development Bank.

Blanchflower, D., and A. Oswald. 2004. "Well-Being over Time in Britain and the USA." *Journal of Public Economics* 88: 1359–86.

Botero, J., S. Djankov, R. Porta, and F. Lopez-De-Silanes. 2004. "The Regulation of Labor." *Quarterly Journal of Economics* 119 (4): 1339–82.

Clark, A., and A. Oswald. 1994. "Unhappiness and Unemployment." *Economic Journal* 104: 648–59.

Di Tella, R., R. MacCulloch, and A. Oswald. 2003. "The Macroeconomics of Happiness" *Review of Economics and Statistics* 85 (4): 809–27, 09.

Gallup World Poll. 2007. Gallup World Poll (www.gallup.com/consulting/worldpoll/24046/about.aspx).

Heckman, J. J. 1979. "Sample Selection Bias as a Specification Error." *Econometrica* 47: 153–61.

Inter-American Development Bank (IDB). 2004. *Good Jobs Wanted: Labor Markets in Latin America.* Washington, D.C.: Inter-American Development Bank.

———. 2008. *Beyond Facts: Understanding Quality of Life.* Washington D.C.: Inter-American Development Bank.

Maslow, A. 1943. "A Theory of Human Motivation." *Psychological Review* 50: 370–96.

Origo, F., and F. Pagani. 2006. "Flexicurity and Workers Well-Being in Europe: Is Temporary Employment Always Bad?" Working Paper 141. University of Milano-Bicocca.

Salvatori, A. 2006. "Labour Contract Regulations and Workers' Wellbeing: International Longitudinal Evidence." Unpublished manuscript, University of Warwick.

van Praag, B. M. S., and A. Ferrer-i-Carbonell. 2007. "Inequality and Happiness." In W. Salverda, B. Nolan, and T. Smeeding, eds., *Oxford Handbook of Economic Inequality.* Oxford University Press

Winkelmann, L., and R. Winkelmann. 1998. "Why are the Unemployed so Unhappy?" *Economica* 65 (257): 1–15.

World Bank. 2008. *Doing Business 2009.* Washington, D.C.: Palgrave Macmillan.

Contributors

JERE R. BEHRMAN
W. R. Kenan Jr. Professor of Economics, Department of Economics, University of Pennsylvania

MAURICIO CÁRDENAS
Senior Fellow and Director, Latin American Initiative, Brookings Institution. Cárdenas is also former minister of economic development and transportation and director of national planning of Colombia and president of the Latin American and Caribbean Economic Association (LACEA).

JUAN CAMILO CHAPARRO
Ph.D. student in economics at the University of Toronto. At the time of this writing, Chaparro was research assistant with the Research Department, Inter-American Development Bank.

RAPHAEL BOTURA CORBI
Master's degree from the Universidade de São Paulo

ANDREA ZAITUNE CURI
Master's degree from the Universidade de São Paulo

WALTER SOSA ESCUDERO
Associate Professor and Director, Department of Economics, Universidad de San Andrés, Argentina

LEONARDO GASPARINI
Director, CEDLAS (Center for the Study of Distribution, Labor and Social Affairs), Facultad de Ciencias Económicas (School of Economic Sciences), Universidad Nacional de La Plata, Argentina

CAROL GRAHAM
Senior Fellow and Charles Robinson Chair, Brookings Institution, and College Park Professor, University of Maryland

EDUARDO LORA
General Manager, Research Department, and Chief Economist, Inter-American Development Bank

MARIANA MARCHIONNI
Researcher, CEDLAS (Center for the Study of Distribution, Labor and Social Affairs), Facultad de Ciencias Económicas (School of Economic Sciences), Universidad Nacional de La Plata, Argentina

VINCENZO DI MARO
University College London (UCL), University of Parthenope in Naples, and Inter-American Development Bank

CAROLINA MEJÍA
Researcher, Fedesarrollo (Fundación para la Educación Superior y el Desarrollo), Colombia.

NAERCIO AQUINO MENEZES-FILHO
Professor of Economics, Insper Institute of Education and Research and the Universidade de São Paulo

SERGIO OLIVIERI
Researcher, CEDLAS (Center for the Study of Distribution, Labor and Social Affairs), Facultad de Ciencias Económicas (School of Economic Sciences), Universidad Nacional de La Plata, Argentina

MARÍA VICTORIA RODRÍGUEZ-POMBO
Master's student in public policy at Harvard University. At the time of this writing, Rodríguez-Pombo was research assistant with the Research Department, Inter-American Development Bank.

Index